UNCOVERING HEIAN JAPAN

ASIA-PACIFIC

Culture, Politics, and Society

Editors: Rey Chow, H. D. Harootunian,

and Masao Miyoshi

Uncovering Heian Japan

An Archaeology of Sensation and Inscription

Thomas LaMarre

Duke University Press   Durham and London 2000

© 2000 Duke University Press
All rights reserved
Printed in the United States of America on acid-free paper ∞
Typeset in Quadraat by Tseng Information Systems, Inc.
Library of Congress Cataloging-in-Publication Data
appear on the last printed page of this book.

CONTENTS

ACKNOWLEDGMENTS

Over the past ten years, the chapters of this book have proliferated as insistently as Heian waka and their commentaries, threatening to unfurl across continents and eras with countless leaves of words. I wish to express my heartfelt thanks to those who have helped me hack back the ranker growth.

The research itself seemed to occupy the larger part of my graduate years at the University of Chicago, where Norma Field in particular guided and encouraged my efforts at every step along the way, from teaching classical Japanese to introducing me to Japanese scholars, and patiently and generously reading various drafts. Moreover, Norma and the other members of my committee, Harry Harootunian, Mellie Ivy, and Bill Sibley, did a great deal to establish the critical trajectory of this study, advising me to consider seriously the question of the mediation of tradition with respect to Heian Japan and directing my attention to the formation of modernity in Japan. I am deeply indebted to them for their intellectual commitment and encouragement over the years.

Because of the complexity of the project, however, it was only after I had completed a dissertation dealing with Meiji and Taishō Japan that I was able to devote a full year (1991–92) in Japan to further research, under the guidance of Mitani Kuniaki, without whose expertise and enthusiasm I would have been unable to steer my way through the labyrinth of classical scholarship. Narita Makoto and especially Tsuzura Junji also contributed to the project in various ways.

The bulk of this book was composed during a year (1994–95) at the Society for the Humanities at Cornell University, where conversations with other fellows and with members of the Cornell East Asia program had a profound impact on its arguments and presentation. I wish particularly to express my thanks to Brett de Bary for her invaluable comments on this and other projects, to Naoki Sakai for continually taking time from his own work to read and comment on the manuscript in progress, and to Tim Murray, David Rodowick, and other members of the Deleuze study group.

At McGill University, Ken Dean has unstintingly offered emotional support, intellectual encouragement and administrative assistance, and Brian Massumi a range of insights and suggestions. Moreover, I could not have completed the manuscript without grants, time releases, and services provided by the Fulbright-Hayes Foundation, the Social Science and Humanities Research Council of Canada, and Fonds pour la Formation de Chercheurs et l'Aide à la Recherche.

Finally, special thanks to Christine LaMarre for her superhuman efforts to hold Zéro and Maline in check, together with Ethan Nasreddin-Longo and Stuart Sumida.

A NOTE ON TRANSLITERATION
AND ILLUSTRATIONS

Although pinyin is the preferred system of romanization for Chinese, because all the English-language sources for this study employ the Wade-Gilles system, I have used the latter throughout. For the romanization of modern Japanese, I use the Hepburn system, with certain standard modifications. For Heian Japanese, in order to indicate its differences from modern Japanese, I use *ti*, *tu*, and *si* instead of *chi*, *tsu*, and *shi*. In addition, following standard practice, I adhere to the syllables of classical Japanese rather than transforming them into modern pronunciations: for example, *seu* rather than *shō*, and so on. While some scholars also mark the h of *ha*, *hi*, *hu*, and so on with an F in order to indicate the different pronunciation of the Heian h, I simply employ h. For the most part, in the text I use the Heian transliteration for Heian terms such as *omohu* or *wominahesi*. In some other instances the modern term is so familiar that I use modern transcription, notably with *awase* (rather than the Heian *ahase*).

Transliteration of the poems of *Man'yōshū* is quite complex. In the very few instances in which I transliterate words from *Man'yō* poems, I use Heian transliteration to avoid introducing yet another system of transliteration. Since, in nearly all these cases, I give some version of the original in Chinese characters, those who are concerned with phonetic transliteration can refer to the original. In a couple poems it was impossible to provide all the characters of the original (because of the paucity of characters in my Japanese software); these rare substitutions or omissions are described in the notes.

As regards illustrations, there are nine examples of calligraphy appended to the text, to which I refer repeatedly. This is a strategy intended to encourage the reader to return to the same figure at various junctures, in the discussion of papers, of characters, of styles, of histories, and so forth. In this way, with repeated consultation of the same figures, the reader may get a better sense of the choreography of Heian text, its coordination and differentiation of different layers and registers of expression.

INTRODUCTION. *Unstating Heian Japan*

Between the National and the Classical

One of the paradoxes of the modern nation, writes Benedict Anderson, concerns "the objective modernity of nations to the historian's eye versus their subjective antiquity in the eyes of nationalists." Those who have a sense of the nation—nationality or "nationness"—find its sources not in the historical processes of the last two hundred or so years but in the far distant past. "If nation-states are widely conceded to be 'new' and 'historical,'" Anderson explains, "the nations to which they give political expression always loom out of an immemorial past, and, still more important, glide into a limitless future."[1]

Part of the historian's job then is to break down the sense of nationness that locates the modern nation in antiquity. Anderson turns to the "great sacral cultures" and "great classical communities"—Christendom, Ummah Islam, the Middle Kingdom, Buddhism, and so forth—to show that these cultural systems operated in ways entirely different from those of modern nations. He sketches a number of general differences implicit in the "classical" imagination of community, at least four of which are relevant to an account of the imperial courts of ancient Japan and their relations to dynastic China.

—All the great classical communities conceived of themselves as cosmically central, through the medium of a sacred language linked to a superterrestrial order of power.

. . .

—And, as truth-languages, imbued with an impulse largely foreign to nationalism, the impulse [was] toward conversion. By conversion, I mean not so much the acceptance of particular religious tenets, but alchemical absorption. . . . The whole nature of man's being is sacrally malleable.

. . .

—In the modern conception, state sovereignty is fully, flatly, and evenly operative over each square centimetre of a legally demarcated territory. But in the older imagining, where states were defined by centres, borders were porous and indistinct, and sovereignties faded imperceptibly into one another.

. . .

—One must also remember that these antique monarchical states expanded not only by warfare but by sexual politics. . . . In realms where polygyny was religiously sanctioned, complex systems of tiered concubinage were essential to the integration of the realm. In fact, royal lineages often derived their prestige, aside from any aura of divinity, from, shall we say, miscegenation?[2]

Anderson's description challenges the three cornerstones of the modern notion of the nation: (1) linguistic homogeneity (in a spoken vernacular); (2) ethnic, racial, or cultural purity, with its strategies of exclusion and inclusion; and (3) territoriality. These three assumptions are built into the Wilsonian model of nationalism, a model that continues to exert its influence over our imagination of classical communities. None of these national unities, however, were major modes in classical communities. Anderson tells us that the latter were indifferent to linguistic differences, ethnically diffuse, territorially porous, and culturally absorptive.

Early Japan, for the most part, has been imagined in terms of this national model. Scholars look for territorial consolidation, linguistic purification, and ethnic or racial unification—in short, for Japan as nation. Naturally this view, which I term following Anderson the *national imagination*, attaches itself to different moments of early Japan, in accordance with shifts in what is desired as well as what is empirically sustainable. Moreover, different disciplines pursue somewhat different trajectories. Nonetheless, two distinct scenarios are common.

In the first scenario, the earliest texts of Japan—the stories, myths, and songs compiled in the *Kojiki* (ca. 702) and *Man'yōshū* (ca. 759)—come to the fore. These are unusual texts that bring together diverse materials in a rather diffuse fashion. To locate Japan in such texts, scholars must posit the existence of an already-unified Japan before the advent of Chinese practices; the scholarly emphasis therefore falls on whatever seems to come before, or lie outside, continental customs, scripts, institutions, and so on. This involves a tendentious search for anything that does not seem marked as "foreign"; these (by default) "native" elements are then drawn into the imagination of a Japan before and beyond China. The boundaries of a Japanese community are established linguistically and ethnically in opposition to dynastic China.

This scenario would seem fairly easy to problematize. In the eighth century on the Japanese archipelago, the Yamato clan gradually assumed the preeminent position in a coalition of clans; it did so through force and alliances under a sovereign who modeled his rule after Chinese emperorship. With the removal of the capital to Heijō-kyō (present-day Nara) in 710, the court attempted to realize fully the continental imperial model. For a variety of reasons, the court subsequently moved, from Heijō-kyō or Nara to Heian-kyō, which saw a flourishing of the styles and practices of T'ang China. (These two capitals today provide the names for two eras of early Japan, the Nara period (710–794) and the Heian period (794–1185).) With respect to religions, institutions, scripts, edifices, and so forth, Nara and Heian Japan are impossible to separate from the larger classical community—the Middle Kingdom, as it were. Yet the major object of a great deal of scholarship on early Japan has been the search for Japanese particularity and the effort to isolate and define it. With the texts that date roughly from Nara Japan, the strategy is to search for signs of an earlier world that reigned before Chinese influence—an unadulterated Japan often called Yamato Japan.

With texts from Heian Japan, a second strategy usually comes into play: a search for transformation of the Chinese model. The emphasis is on reception, absorption, and domestication; in a number of instances, scholars have construed all historical transformations as acts of Japanese resistance to Chinese influence, or even as a resurgence or revival of Japaneseness amid Chineseness. In postwar Japan, the scholarly emphasis shifted generally toward this Heian scenario, partly in response to the legacy of the Allied Occupation. Yet that shift has many other facets. Narratives of Japanese resistance to Chinese influence in Heian Japan can be construed in any number of ways: as, for instance, a simple effort to promote one national particular over another; or, as an attempt to free the local from the universal. Throughout this study I will return to the complex agendas that accompany accounts of early Japan, particularly the Heian period. At the outset, however, I wish to underscore the workings of the national imagination in the construction of our knowledge of early Japan.

Although, on one level, it might seem easy to debunk the national imagination, the national scenario is not merely an empty illusion or spurious fantasy that can be readily discredited and dispelled. The object of study itself—"early or ancient Japan"—emerged along with the modern nation.[3] The national imagination gives early Japan its status as an object, its objectivity. It imparts linguistic homogeneity, ethnic purity, and territorial unity, establishing these as the grid of intelligibility for early Japanese history, culture, and language. Recently, a number of scholars have begun to explore the construction of Japan as an object of knowledge, particularly in early modern Japan. To some extent, it has become easier to speak of the historical emergence of a modern discourse that combines language and ethnicity and arises with nationness.

For instance, scholars like Naoki Sakai have looked at how "nativist" scholars of early modern, or Tokugawa, Japan (1603–1868) invented a new sense of language that forges links between identity and speech. From the texts of early Japan, these scholars summoned forth and homogenized an ancient language—one that was as much contemporary dialect as historical language.[4] The nativists began to systematize what we refer to as *kogo,* or "classical Japanese." Subsequently, with the rise of what Anderson calls "print capitalism," all obstacles to reading ancient texts in a vernacular-style language were gradually removed. Thus the modern nation built upon the early modern construct of a timeless and ancient Japanese speech and consolidated it with modern modes of production and discipline. The result is the mass production of a systematic grammar that constitutes ancient or classical Japanese. It should not be forgotten that, for all their layers and ambiguities, modern standard editions of early Japanese texts are contemporary to the newspaper and the novel. They are similar not only in their principles of organization, production, and dissemination but also in the ways in which the reader relates to the text, enters into it, and is interpolated, embodied, or "subjectified" in the act of reading or writing. Needless to say, I imply with such comments that the texts of early Japan originally involved a very different sense of boundary, subject, and language manifested in different processes of reading, writing, interpellation, embodiment, and subjectification. Yet, if early Japan was, first and foremost, imagined or invented in the modern era, how are we to get at those differences?

To assert that early Japan is always imagined through the modern nation is not to claim that early Japan is nothing but an arbitrary fabrication without any empirical or material nexus. The choice is not between arbitrary fabrication and empirical reality. One might say that early Japan and the modern nation are mutually contingent. Yet they are not equal partners, for Heian texts—especially the poetic and literary texts discussed in this study—do not have the discursive or conceptual consistency of modern academic disciplines. As a result, Heian texts are able to confound and undermine the scholarly apparatus as it strives for unity; and yet, they are dependent upon that apparatus to be read at all. For this reason, any account of early Japan must deal critically with the modern agendas that form the field. Because it is not possible to sweep away the constructedness of knowledge, this study turns time and again to contemporary theory and modern aesthetics in an effort to work through the national imagination.

With its fragmentary and heterogeneous texts, early Japan remains an important site of alterity for the modern nation, one that can disrupt and shift the national imagination. If, on the one hand, it is clear that the national imagination constructs early Japan, there are, on the other hand, all manner of incompatible bits and pieces—exotica, as it were—that do not fit. To get at the "otherness" of early Japan (not only Japan without the West, but also Japan without Japan, and even China without China), this study peruses these exotica or heteroglossia in order to disrupt the sense of national familiarity. It is possible to turn to ancient artifacts and use them to confront the national imagination—with its forgotten contingencies and suppressed materials—though there are no guarantees or predictable results. It is a vexed enterprise, for it could always be argued that familiarity and nationality are so entrenched in early Japan that its differences can only emerge as curios, as exotic commodities or reified phantasmagoria that serve, ultimately, only to reenchant the domain of the national imagination.

For these reasons, I evoke Anderson's framework at the outset; it prepares some critical trajectories for an exploration of the otherness of early Japan. This study highlights many of the elements Anderson attributes to classical communities: (1) emphasis on cosmological language, written script, and nonarbitrary signs (along with indifference to vernacular language); (2) ethnic hybridity; (3) diffuse and porous territoriality; and (4) a malleable and heterogeneous subjectivity. All these aspects are usually overlooked, omitted, or suppressed in studies of Heian Japan. Their omission and suppression is, in fact, part of the constitution of the field itself, part of the national imagination.

Critical Matters

The essential problem of nationness for the study of early Japan has three moments. In the first, ancient texts are read as encoded (vernacular) speech. In the second, speech is taken as a marker of ethnicity. Finally, in the third, ethnicity comes to stand for national community and imposes a modern logic of territoriality in which sovereignty appears flatly, evenly distributed. There are, of course, a variety of ways to deal with the threefold problem of nationness as it informs our knowledge of early Japan. In the fields of anthropology and archaeology, one could question the notion of an isolated Japanese folk who are racially or ethnically distinct from the other peoples of East Asia.[5] In the realm of institutional history and sociology, one could question the varied modern claims for an ancient Japaneseness in terms of social institutions such as the emperor, the clan (uji), the regency, and so forth. My preference in this study, however, is to use poetics as a point of departure for getting at some of the trickier intersections of language, ethnicity, and territory.

It would be an overstatement to say that language is the central problematic of Heian studies; yet it is true that the problem of vernacular speech, by grounding the ethnolinguistic community, overdetermines the modern imagination of early Japan. Nowhere so much as in ancient poetry does the notion of vernacular speech seem so naturalized; nowhere does speech seem to translate so readily into national community as in modern accounts of ancient poetry.

In addition, disciplinary divisions for the study of early Japan have served to protect poetry's role as the aesthetic kernel of the national imagination. By and large, only in literary studies does the question of the political effects of poetry receive detailed treatment. Yet there is still only one thesis about how poetry brings order to Heian society: namely, that it enables the formation of an ethnic speech community. Naturally, a number of analyses of the rhetorical ways in which poetry imparts unity or consistency center on this thesis. In the final analysis, however, literary studies insist on vernacular speech as a marker of ethnic community, and other disciplines seem to accept this interpretation. Even though institutional historians often see Heian Japan in direct relation to T'ang China, they do not challenge the notion of a vernacular speech community; nor do they question that there is a Japan to be affected by a China. So the semiotic and historical task of this study is to differentiate the Heian text and court from the Japanese language and the modern nation.

In literary studies, it is not uncommon for scholars to treat poetics as a site of political contestation and to analyze poetics exchanges in which poets air their grievances in a competitive arena. Such competition is often construed by contemporary scholars as a form of resistance — usually to the ruling elite — and is interpreted in terms of the individual versus the group; in effect, they presume a modern apparatus of resistance. In this study, I do not treat such exchanges primarily as a form of resistance but rather as a mode of participation in a poetic order of things. My intention, instead, is to contest the national imagination of poetics and to reimagine the role of poetry at the Heian court. The emphasis is thus on the participation and interpellation of courtiers into the poetic order.

With the national imagination as a central problematic, this study necessarily pursues two lines of inquiry at once. On the one hand, it looks at the emergence and maintenance of the modern "ethnolinguistic regime" of reading Heian Japan. On the other, it explores other possibilities for reading Heian poetics.

The first line of inquiry demands a continual critique of primary and secondary sources, in particular with respect to the problematic of "Japan versus the West" and "modernity and its others." As a point of departure, I resort to a rough chronology to establish a general sense of the genealogy of modern studies of ancient poetry. In the early modern period, the Tokugawa or Edo period (1603–1868), the *kokugakusha*, or nativists, read the ancient texts against (and through) the dominant paradigm of neo-Confucianism. Although there are important medieval commentaries on Nara and Heian texts, the genealogy of the modern regime of reading effectively begins with the nativists, for it is they who begin to isolate a relationship between language and identity. It is not until the Meiji period (1868–1912), however, with the emergence of a modern nation, that we find a disciplinization of language and texts that results in a truly modern regime of reading in which the assumptions of the national imagination become the dominant logic. Later, with the cosmopolitanism of the Taishō period (1912–1926), there emerges the possibility of a more "modernist" reading of ancient texts — modernist in the sense of a search for nonmodern or antimodern modes of reading. Needless to say, a modernist impulse is detectable in the nativist and nationalist modes; with reference to nativism in particular, I look closely at the intersections with modernism. First, however, I provide a rough delineation of the discourses—Edo, Meiji, Taishō—to establish a historical framework for the imagination of early Japan. Finally, rather than referring to the Shōwa (1926–1989) and Heisei (1989–present) periods, I refer to prewar and postwar periods, using the American Occupation of Japan (1945–1952) as the boundary.

This study is not, however, a survey, and these historical moments do not receive equal treatment. The postwar imagination of Heian Japan looms largest in the secondary sources I consulted. In the wake of the Occupation came a shift in the national imagination: there arose a search for a nonfeudal, nonmilitarist image of Japan. The Heian court, somewhat disparaged before the war for both its elegance and its Chineseness, furnished a site for the imagination of a civilized, aesthetic, nonmilitarist Japan— which could assure Japan's historical position in the postwar world order— provided the links with China could be broken. The consequent invention of an isolated, refined, purely aesthetic Heian Japan is one of the major targets of this study. Thus the names of a series of postwar scholars—Yoshimoto Taka'aki, Saigo Nobutsuna, Karaki Junzō, Konishi Jin'ichi, Suzuki Hideo— appear frequently. In the West, English and American research tends to dominate the scholarship and, for the most part, to follow the ethnolinguistic assumptions of Japanese literary scholars. In fact, Japanese and English-language studies work together to consolidate the postwar image of an insular, ethnolinguistic community in Heian Japan. In sum, the postwar imagination of Heian Japan provides the main locus for a critique of the national imagination.

The second line of inquiry involves an exploration of all the features of Heian texts that the national imagination tends to overlook, omit, or suppress. In particular, the figural operations of Chinese characters come to the fore. In fact, this study could be considered a meditation on the question of figurality, one that takes characters as a point of departure. In a general way, what I characterize as the philological or linguistic legacy in Heian studies involves the extraction of vernacular speech from a complex network of signs.[6] The most obvious way to shift attention in this instance is to look at the visual register of the Heian text. In Part One of this study, therefore, I enter into Heian poetics by way of the rebus or picture-puzzle. Although the rebus does not statistically dominate Heian poetics, it offers a way to rethink the overall logic of poetic composition—through such features as word games, image games, pivot words, and so forth. Ultimately, I relate this to an aesthetics of the Chinese character, which is precisely what the philological text strives to omit.

There is a politics to the omission of the Chinese character, one that relates to the national imagination of Heian Japan and presents the Heian court in opposition to China. In order to counter this impulse, I show how a logic of doubleness pervades the Heian order, informing not only poetic composition but poetic competition as well—and poetic competitions are central to the politico-economic organization of the court. Rather than an ethnolinguistic opposition between Japan and China, I find a stylistic differential that literally draws or writes the Heian court into the nexus of the Middle Kingdom.

Part Two deals primarily with calligraphy in relation to Heian poetry. I look especially at the various stylistic and perceptual registers that come into play in the calligraphic poetic text. In the final analysis, the Heian text seems to leave open the gaps or disjunctions between different registers. This allows for diffuse subjectivity and for a particular manner of interpellation or embodiment—a poetics of the "multisensible figure." This disjunctive "openness" of the Heian text is not, however, an indicator of modernist or postmodernist sensibility. It opens poetic practice and subjectivity into a cosmological order, which becomes the subject of Part Three.

By *cosmology*, I mean, primarily, two things. First, in empirical terms, is the ubiquity of calendrics at the Heian court—the sense of established and proper concentric cycles of hours, days, seasons, activities, and so on.[7] In this respect, my usage of the word *cosmology* relates not so much to structures of religious belief as to a form of knowledge that lies between ritual and science. Second, in sociohistorical terms, cosmology is a matter of an order that does not place human agency in the central role. The source of political order for the Heian world does not lie with humans. This is what I call the "cosmological imagination of community." Humans may act with or on the political order, but they do not invent it, for its sources are external to them. The cosmological imagination differs profoundly from modern humanism, and Part Three turns to an archaeology of this nonhumanist order—the song machine of *Kokinwakashū*. The Heian emphasis on the links between calligraphy, figurality, and cosmology thus affords a way to challenge the national imagination of community, which is based on the consolidation of links between speech, ethnicity, and territory.

In effect, this study takes Ki no Tsurayuki, the chief compiler of *Kokin-*

wakashū, at his word when he writes in his preface, "Song is what moves heavens and earth without applying force, draws out the feelings of unseen spirits of the dead, soothes between man and woman, and calms the hearts of fierce warriors." In effect, the movements and interactions of people at the Heian court needed poetry and calligraphy to give them consistency. Which is to say, the ranks, bureaucracies, alliances and genealogies were, in many ways, far too aleatory to ground a stable order. At a certain point, everyone was related to everyone else, and there were too many titular dispensations and alterative ranks. The role of waka poetics, at the heart of the Heian order, was to open the social order out into the cosmological order; and, in the final analysis, it was the cosmological order that assured the stability and longevity of the Heian court.[8] The power of brushwork lay in its ability to yoke sensible forms (and thus courtiers' practices and experiences) to an intelligible order, one that inscribed the Heian court into a larger nexus of resonant centers (other courts and empires), while sustaining the autonomy of different centers. It entailed an order of the senses that allowed courtiers to move intelligibly through the realm of sensible forms, aligning the movements of the senses and emotions with the movements of seasons and constellations, while entering into the larger classical community by way of the synthetic nexus of forms.

PART I. THE INTERPRETATION OF REBUSES

ONE. Revising the Rebus

Syntheses

At the Heian court, poetics permeated all aspects of life. The dexterity of the brush, the style of composition, the fold, texture, and pattern of paper significantly marked the courtier's position in relation to others. Diaries and tales turned around poems; lovers navigated through trysts and alliances with poems; poems punctuated the rites and ceremonies that negotiated the cosmological dimension of court bureaucracies; and poems flowed with major and minor exchanges of wealth. At large-scale poetry contests, the presentation and evaluation of poems meshed with an almost potlatch-like collection and redistribution of ranks and wealth.

The waka, a thirty-one-syllable poem or song, came to prominence in the course of the ninth century, the first century after the removal of the court from Heijō-kyō to Heian-kyō around the year 794. In 905, the emperor Daigo ordered the compilation of an imperial anthology of waka; by around 920, four compilers (Ki no Tsurayuki, Mibu no Tadamine, Ōshikōchi Mitsune, and Ki no Tomonori) had gleaned 1,111 poems from a range of sources and eras. They presented them in twenty scrolls arranged by topic, with two prefaces and brief notes on each poem giving the poet's name and the occasion of its composition.[1] The anthology took the title *Kokinwakashū* or "Collection of Yamato Songs Old and New," and its poetics became the major source for subsequent composition in court circles.

Even this brief overview of *Kokinwakashū* shows that it brought together many forms of expression. (1) The characters of songs spin supplely down the page in calligraphic variations on the cursive or grass style (*kana*), with intercalated titles and topics in the stiff or regular style (*mana*). (2) Songs resonate across the ages: the collection strategically comprises poems from several generations.[2] (3) Twenty scrolls unwind in two major cycles: the first cycle begins with six scrolls that move from the first day of spring of the new year through the last day of winter, then on into congratulations, separations, travels and wordplays. The other cycle winds through five scrolls of love, from a time before lovers meet till the dissolution of their alliance and on into grief followed by miscellaneous forms and styles. (4) Commentaries on the poems speak of ceremonies, exchanges, and competitions, and in these names and notes resides the politics of poetic inclusion, collusion, and competition. In sum, the anthology brought together forms of expression related to the patterns of words, eras, seasons and emotions, and of court ceremonies, competitions, and hierarchies. It implied a tremendous synthesis of forms in the multiple registers of inscription, composition, competition, and compilation.

Many modes of synthesis punctuated the often-chaotic interactions among peoples, languages, techniques, ideas, and forms that traveled and settled within and around the courts at Heijō-kyō and Heian-kyō (Nara and Heian Japan). The synthetic poetics of *Kokinwakashū* did not come out of nowhere, nor was it alone. In fact, the *Kokin* prefaces name *Man'yōshū* or "Collection of Myriad Ages" as a prior site of order in the incessant flow and jumble of things. *Man'yōshū* itself is a vast collection of poetic forms that presents multiple experiments with scripts, events, songs, and commentaries. Apparently, a number of different scribes and poets compiled the scrolls in different eras. By around 759, Ōtomo no Yakamochi had gathered these attempts together and made his own additions to them. The result looks not so much like a form of synthesis as a series of different attempts at synthesis.

Contemporary with *Man'yōshū* there appeared an anthology of Chinese songs, *Kaifūsō* (751), which was followed by three imperial anthologies of Chinese poems: *Ryōunshū* (814), *Bunkashūreishū* (815), and *Keikokushū* (827). Although the synthetic moment of *Kokinwakashū* evokes *Man'yōshū* and borrows songs from it, its formal methods and concepts derive largely from these three imperial anthologies of Han songs, as well as from Chinese poetic prefaces. Thus, even when *Kokinwakashū* summons *Man'yōshū*, it speaks in the language of the Chinese poetics of a particular period.

Presently, modern scholars deal historically with this array of poetic collections by borrowing and transforming the rhetoric of the *Kokin* prefaces. That is, the *Kokin* prefaces attach the rubric "Yamato" to *Man'yōshū*, and this rubric is now read as "Japanese"—Japanese language, Japanese people,

Japanese culture. Thus a synthetic, hybrid text like *Man'yōshū* often is read as if it expressed unity, purity, and homogeneity. Occasionally, it is noted that *Man'yōshū* is a hybrid affair trafficking in a range of Chinese forms and scripts; and yet, even when its hybridity is acknowledged, the tendency is to look for the moment of Japaneseness, in opposition to Chineseness. Likewise with *Kokinwakashū*. The problem is basically this: *Kokin* poetics shows a constant evocation of doubleness, ceaselessly conjoining "Japanese" and "Chinese" forms, and modern histories take *Kokin* doubleness and fit it into a framework of exclusion/inclusion, into a politics of opposition, repression, or negation.

At one time it was common to construe the Chinese poetic anthologies of the early ninth century in terms of a "dark age of native styles" in which the advent of Chinese characters cast shadows on the radiance of native song. More recently, it has become equally common to allude to an "age of adulation of Han styles" and to point out that Yamato song continued to be performed at the Heian court even in the era of the Chinese anthologies.[3] Hence the two stories most often told about Yamato and Han song: (1) Han forms threatened to occlude Yamato forms, but Yamato forms resisted and triumphed over them—*Kokinwakashū* marked the *restoration* of native forms; (2) Han forms presented a challenge to Yamato forms, but Yamato forms successfully absorbed Han forms—*Kokinwakashū* completed the *absorption* of foreign forms. In both stories, there lingers a sense that Yamato forms existed in some pure form before and after the advent of Han forms, invariably in oral form.

Needless to say, for many Japanese scholars as well, these stories of Chinese encroachment and Japanese resistance ring false—yet how can we discuss the Heian coordination/differentiation of Yamato and Han in another way?

The Rebus

A strange character appears on a fragment of an earthenware vessel excavated from the remains of the Heijō capital. Written with ink inside the vessel, this character consists of three common characters 我、君、念. The first two characters are above the latter and somewhat to either side, and the three figures are drawn closely together to form a single character, an "assembled character" (*kumiawasemoji*). A translation of the three components yields three words—I, you, cherish—but the translation says little about the logic or usage of this assemblage. One commentator, Wada At-sumu, turns to a book of charms from the Tokugawa period in which the same combination occurs, with this gloss: "when far away is your heart that I yearn for, neither will you yearn after me, nor I after you." He con-cludes that this assemblage of characters is to function magically to ease the sorrow of lovers who must part.[4]

If there is something magical about this assembled character, it lies in the idea that the parting and joining of characters acts upon the parting and joining of lovers. The operations of characters affect the motions and emotions of people. Across time and space, the operations of words main-tain linkages. This is one kind of magical connection with words. The in-determinate nature of the assembled character on the eighth-century shard allows the modern scholar to work other kinds of magic. For instance, using the assembled character, Wada constructs links among the Heijō shard, an early modern book of charms, and a Tokyo umbrella. He turns to young lovers in contemporary Tokyo who write their names inside an umbrella to inscribe their intimacy. For Wada these are all analogous opera-tions. And at this level, who can say that he is not right? What remains so difficult to articulate are the specific functions of this assemblage of char-acters at the Heijō capital. Is it possible to read the rebus-like operations of the assembled character with any sense of historical and cultural specificity at all? What would constitute the horizon for analysis?

Faced with a nongrammatical assemblage of signs, our critical faculties tend to waver and buckle. We relegate it too readily to an undifferentiated realm of magic and magical forms, precisely because we are at a loss to ana-lyze nonlinguistic or a-signifying forms. This is a general problem, one that contemporary disciplines are not entirely prepared to deal with. How are we to situate the picture-puzzle historically? Linguistic histories of writing tend to place it at an archaic level of signification, one that is subsequently superseded by more rational (less pictographic, more phonographic) forms of inscription. Yet the rebus or picture-puzzle refuses to be buried, con-tained, or superseded; it demands attention. This is precisely the tension that Freud evoked in his discussions of hieroglyphs, rebuses, pictorial in-scription, and picture-puzzles. In *The Interpretation of Dreams*, he tries to deal with the rebus-like pictorial compositions that emerge in dreamwork, only to conclude that this "pictographic script" must be analyzed for its sym-bolic value, not its pictorial value.

The dream thoughts are immediately comprehensible, as soon as we have learnt them. The dream-content, on the other hand, is expressed as it were in a pictographic script, the characters of which have to be transposed individually into the language of the dream-thoughts. If we attempted to read these characters according to the pictorial value instead of according to their symbolic relation, we should clearly be in error. . . . The words which are put together in this way are no longer nonsensical but may form a poetical phrase of the greatest beauty and significance. A dream is a picture puzzle of this sort and our predecessors in the field of dream-interpretation have made the mistake of treating the rebus as a pictorial composition and as such it has seemed to them nonsensical and worthless.[5]

Freud's comments cast light on the analysis of the rebus-like mode of the assembled character. In his opinion, in order to gauge its significance, we would have to read its symbolic relations rather than its pictorial value. There are, however, at least two ways to interpret Freud's insight. On the one hand, the interpretation of rebuses could be construed as an act of linguistic translation. We might translate or transpose the rebus into a grammatical linguistic message, however cryptic, in order to determine its symbolic value. The analysis of symbolic relations, in this instance, would amount to a translation into grammar of the pictographic script.

The assembled character on the Heijō shard, the three characters signifying I, you, and cherish (or yearn), thus allows for various grammatical recombinations of the three component characters, such as "I yearn for you," and "you yearn for me," and "you and I yearn." It seems somewhat absurd to think that these three combinations should exist at once, and so we transpose it into a phrase of great poetic beauty and significance, like that of the early modern book of charms: when far away is your heart that I yearn for, neither will you yearn after me, nor I after you. This method results in a phrase that makes grammatical, even poetical, sense of the simultaneity of the three components and three combinations. It uses translation and transcription to reveal symbolic relations. Slavoj Žižek, commenting on the above passage from Freud, describes such picture-puzzle translation in terms of "secondary revision."

There is, however, a certain distinction between a rebus and a dream, which makes the rebus much easier to interpret. In a way, a rebus is like a dream that has not undergone "secondary revision," whose purpose is to satisfy the "necessity for unification." For that reason, a rebus is immediately perceived as something "nonsensical," a bric-a-brac of unconnected, heterogeneous elements, while a dream conceals its absurdity through "secondary revision," which lends a dream at least superficial unity and consistency.[6]

According to Žižek, the aim of secondary revision is to impart superficial unity and consistency—which satisfies a psychic and grammatical need for unification. Otherwise, the rebus-like assembled character is perceived as a nonsensical assemblage of unconnected elements.

Now, the combinatory operations of the assembled character anticipate many of the operations in Heian poems (which emerge in subsequent discussion). But how are we to revise such rebuses? (By "we," I mean "we who take Japan as an object of study.") Modern scholars usually seem embarrassed by such operations, looking at them as absurd ornaments or bric-a-brac that contribute nothing to poetics, except perhaps a rhetorical flourish or comic gesture. In short, the usual mode of revision tends to dismiss or overlook the operations of rebuses in order to translate the poem into a coherent phrase. Žižek's remarks remind us that the act of translation is an act of secondary revision that satisfies the necessity for unification. Analogously, the modern academic concealment of rebus-like operations in waka poetry is part of a dreamlike secondary revision of the Japanese past. The omission or suppression of rebus-like operations constitutes an attempt to produce a unified symbolic relation from an assemblage of elements that do not immediately or necessarily cohere in any familiar way. Waka studies strive to revise (omit or repress) the oddities of Heian poetic play in order to construct grammatical relations, and these are supposed to constitute a phrase of great poetic beauty and significance. Moreover, the symbolic relation that determines this secondary poetics is that of the national imagination. The dreamlike unity imparted to the archaic rebus ultimately derives from the dream of Japanese unity, of the unity of the Japanese language and nation. Of course, in Žižek as in Anderson, terms like *dream* or *imagination* or *fantasy* do not signal that we can easily debunk or discard this revision. On the contrary, it takes root in empirical knowledge and experience—whence the necessity for disruption, the second path from Freud.

Félix Guattari tries to disrupt the unity and authority of the act of translation (and signification) that would subsume (or sublate) all other modes of expression. His analytics draws partly on Daniel Stern's exploration of the preverbal subjective formations of children. Stern submits that the child does not go through stages in which each stage subsumes the preceding stage; rather, its development results in levels of subjectivization that will be maintained in parallel series throughout the life of the child. As a result, Guattari writes, the subjectivity of the child involves a transversal subjectivity, one that continually crosses these various levels and allows for various modes of consistency.[7] It is no longer a question of a self that mediates and represses or contains prior stages.

Guattari's analysis provides another way of thinking about the rebus in the context of waka studies. Rather than see the pictorial operations of characters as subordinate to the linguistic message or to grammatical signification, we could see them as parallel processes or operations. In other words, secondary revision never subsumes or exhausts the rebus but runs parallel to it. This has implications for how we view the history of writing.

If we transform the logic of stages (an evolution from pictograms to symbols to alphabets) into a logic of coexistent parallel levels, it is possible to think of the role of rebus in Heian poetics without subsuming it within secondary linguistic revision. We could explore the logic of the rebus itself, not as a nonsensical bric-a-brac but as a form of inscription and expression in its own right. But this way of looking at waka poetics demands that rebus-like operations come to the fore. They cannot be treated as prior stages, or as absurd or deviant modes. Only then do other histories and other kinds of consistency become imaginable.

Revising Kana

In the course of the ninth century, in the period between *Man'yōshū* and *Kokinwakashū*, there emerged a style of script known as kana. The poems of *Kokinwakashū* are said to be written entirely in kana. Although we only have the retroactive testimony of later renditions of *Kokinwakashū* to confirm that this is so, I do not intend to contest this view. Nor do I intend to contest the idea that kana writing can transcribe speech phonographically. I do, however, wish to contest the interpretation that the prime goal of kana writing was an attempt to write speech phonetically or phonographically. While kana inscription entailed a phonographic or logographic level, this phonography existed alongside visual or figural levels of inscription that were in no way subordinate to phonography. Figural operations were integral to Heian poetics. (Initially, because I deal with the modern verbal and textual legacy, I approach "figurality"—the qualities pertaining to figures—by way of the visual or pictorial qualities of poems; but figurality is ultimately a site for analysis that lies between image and text, that is neither seeing or speaking and both.)

Why would anyone want to construe kana writing as phonetic to begin with? This phonetic desire goes back to the modernizing impulse of the Meiji period. Karatani Kōjin has written extensively on this topic, pointing out that the Meiji movements for the "unification of speech and script" (*gembun itchi*) did not entail an attempt to write colloquial speech so much as an attempt to eliminate visual or figural elements from writing. Early modern writers, he suggests, knew very well how to transcribe colloquial speech and dialects, and yet they also engaged the play of visual elements made possible with Chinese characters. Karatani submits that the movement for the unification of speech and script aimed to strip away figural elements from language in order to make script appear perfectly transparent to thought. The visibility of writing itself presented an obstacle to transparency, and so Meiji advocates of speech-script unification aimed to suppress the figural operations of writing. Initially, Karatani notes, some advocates actually proposed the elimination of Chinese characters from Japanese writing.[8]

As a result of this antifigural modernizing impulse, certain myths developed with respect to the historical usage of kana. Because the kana script now functioned as the modern basis for phonetic writing (as opposed to the alleged opacity of Chinese characters), the history of its figural functions and its relations to Chinese writing had to be suppressed and revised. This modern revision of the history and figurality of kana script has had profound consequences for the study of Heian texts. These are some of the quasi-mythic stories that arise around kana and waka:

1. Modern scholars posit Chinese characters as pictographic or ideographic, submitting that they presented obstacles to the phonetic transcription of Japanese speech from the dawn of Japanese history. Yet Chinese characters clearly were used phonographically and logographically, in Japan as in China.

2. Scholars typically see the emergence of kana in terms of natural, evolutionary progress—and visual or figural elements as obstacles to progress.

Which is to say, ninth-century kana was posited as the outcome of a natural evolution in writing, an evolution toward phonetic transcription. Those instances in which the ancient Japanese do not resort phonetic usage are seen as retrograde tendencies or as failed efforts.

3. In conjunction with the identification of Chinese characters as obstacles to phonetic evolution, scholars began to posit China as an obstacle to the evolutionary emergence of Japan. In short, narratives of phonetic evolution combined with narratives of national emergence and identity, positing external forces as threats to indigenous evolution.

4. Because kana gradually emerged in the course of the eighth and ninth centuries, scholars could construct a transhistorical homology between early Japan and Meiji Japan: just as Japan confronted and absorbed Western modes in the course of modernization, so early Japan had confronted and absorbed Chinese modes in the course of the emergence of the Yamato court. As a result, it has become almost impossible to think of the interaction of Heian Japan with other courts across East Asia in any terms other than Japan versus a monolithic empire (China or the West). Needless to say, the fantasy involved in this type of secondary revision is that Japan, past and present, successfully absorbs external influences and continues its eternal and immutable native ways. By extension, such stories made it possible, particularly in the postwar period, to posit Heian Japan as somehow modern, indigenous, and self-determined.

5. Conflating script and speech, scholars imagine kana in terms of the triumphant reemergence of native speech or language. In fact, in literary studies, it is rarely acknowledged that courtiers spoke Chinese at court, or that the Korean language had any impact on Japanese dialects, or even that there existed many dialectical and linguistic variations. This denial means that, even when linguists signal extensive linguistic transformations between *Man'yōshū* and *Kokinwakashū*, the possibility of linguistic hybridity never makes an impression on poetry studies: all the transformations remain internal to the development of the Japanese language.

6. Because kana characters are seen as an indigenous invention, scholars often overlook or downplay the fact that, in phonographic terms, kana follow from modes used in Chinese scripts related to Indic phonetics, which was disseminated largely by Buddhist monks; and that, in figural terms, kana closely approximate the Chinese style known as grass writing (*sōsho*). When these facts emerge, scholars do their utmost to transform the singu-

larities of kana into generic distinctions that posit Japanese culture as the horizon for analysis. Thus scholars speak of "kana culture" as distinct from "kanji culture" (that is, Chinese-character culture).

In sum, the image of the ancient scribe or poet is that of an naive yet ingenious native who, threatened and overwhelmed by the encroaching technologies of the Chinese empire, valiantly tries to preserve his indigenous speech, native customs and ethnic identity. Kana script, waka poetry, and the Heian court present the successful outcome in this battle to protect native identity. This dreamlike revision of early Japan derives from the modern fantasy of a national community without social alienation or historical transformation.

I would like to oppose another image to this one, that of a mobile and literate elite versed in Chinese and Korean poetics—many of whom were of Chinese or Korean provenance or descent—who not only used Chinese script with great sophistication but also demonstrated great interest in complex, puzzlelike inscriptions that traversed languages and dialects with an array of vocal and visual operations. This does not mean that early Japan was beset with modern alienation, but rather that the ancient court was riddled with conflicts, hierarchies, peoples and movements. The revision of the rebus affords us a way to contest the national imagination and to imagine what Anderson calls the "classical community"—which is ethnically diffuse, territorially porous, and indifferent to linguistic boundaries.

Žižek's interpretation of Freud calls attention to the mediation implicit in the act of transcription or translation. "In a way," he writes, "a rebus is like a dream that has not undergone 'secondary revision,' whose purpose is to satisfy the 'necessity for unification.'" Žižek tells us that this translation satisfies the *necessity* for unification. In the context of modern Japan, one might well imagine this dreamy act of national translation in terms of necessity—the necessity of constructing a modern nation in a period of Western colonial expansion. Although I do not wish to downplay the historical need for Japanese unification, to speak continually of Japan as a subaltern of the West glosses over its interactions with China, Korea, and other countries of East Asia. So, it is important to recall that in national formations desire operates alongside necessity in unpredictable ways, making a necessity of things that are not always desirable. In the realm of literature, too, the necessity for national unification results in textual interpretations that are something of a nightmare with their compulsion to repeat the phantasm of national unity. In the case of Heian studies, it is not only possible but also desirable to speak of the necessity for disruption, for trans-versality and for different modes of mediation or representation (whence my juxtaposition of Guattari's anarchic desire with Žižek's national theori-zation).

Still, of the assembled character brushed in dark ink on an earthenware vessel, it is difficult to speak. It is easy enough to conclude that there is some belief in the ability of words to produce effects, but what effects are these? Despite their complexity, rebus-like operations do not belong to a realm of magic and unreason simply because their logic is not grammati-cal or linguistic. Nor are rebus-like operations primitive or preverbal in the sense of stages that come before verbal or linguistic operations or scrip-tural evolution. The rebus constitutes a kind of nonverbal operation, which exists with, and crosses through, the elements of linguistic signification. In the case of waka poetics, I will show that rebus-like operations func-tion specifically to open poetic composition into nonverbal, extralinguistic registers.

The layers of textual revision that result in the standard editions of Heian texts consistently suppress or overlook anything like a rebus or pictorial operation. Nevertheless, difficulties linger in many poems. In particular, the poems of Man'yōshū present difficulties, since their scribes often used combinations of sounds, words, and grammars from Chinese, Japanese, and probably Korean. Nonetheless, most scholars relegate the many scrip-tural experiments and figural moments of Man'yōshū to the status of oddi-ties and imperfections, claiming that the overall trend is phonographic. Thus the dreamwork of modern scholarship begins with the phonetic tran-scription of the ancient text. The reigning wisdom is that the script of Man'yōshū was a largely successful attempt at phonography that was evolv-ing in the direction of the kana script by the time of the late Man'yōshū. To emphasize the proximity of the Man'yō script to kana, scholars have coined terms such as manyō-kana (man'yōgana) and "character-kana" (magana).

A poem from the late Man'yōshū illustrates these phonographic revisions and their ambiguities. The poem is one of "two verses that the maiden Awatame sent to Ōtomo no Yakamochi." Because Ōtomo no Yakamochi (718–785), reputed to have been the last editor of Man'yōshū, makes an appearance in the commentary, the poem probably coincided with the late Man'yōshū and Heijō-kyō. It is roughly contemporaneous with the as-sembled character brushed on an earthenware vessel. The first line of characters comes from an original text (although it undoubtedly has seen a number of historical revisions). The phonetic transcription follows in brackets, with a translation.

思遣　為便乃不知者　片椀之底曾吾者　恋成尓家類　注土椀之中
［思ひ遣る　すべの知らねば　かたもひの　底にそ我は
　　恋ひなりにける　土椀の中に注せり］

As one who knows no art to send off feelings,
within the depths of an unclosed vessel
I have come to yearn.
—signed in an earthen vessel [9]

The poetess cleverly combines writing and yearning in a single phrase. She writes that she "knows no art to send off feelings" (*omohiyaru sube*). This phrase combines two ideas: she knows no technique that would dispel her feelings (*omoi wo harasu hōhō*), and she knows no letter that would send her feelings (*omoi wo yaru tayori*). The form of the poem, signed in a vessel, makes this phrase doubly ingenious. On the one hand, her feelings, inscribed in the vessel, are contained therein; she cannot dispel or express them: "within the depths of an unclosed vessel I have come to yearn." Yet, on the other hand, her feelings have flowed into the lidless vessel, and that vessel is to find its way to him; lidless, it openly proffers her feelings. Like the flow of writing, the flow of feeling is at once an outward release (expression) and an inward containment (content). Both expression and content are given form, and the poem entwines the two forms in such a way that the two alternate—superimposed yet not reducible to one another.

Such an interpretation follows well enough from the phonetic transcription, and yet it is the scriptural oddities of the original that sustain it. The transcription transforms 為便 (roughly, in Chinese, "with letter") into *sube* (in Japanese, method, technique, art). Yet the phonetic transcription involves a major dislocation, for the interpretation of the poem may follow as much from the Chinese as the Japanese. The Chinese hint of "with letter" allows the poem to turn in its two directions. Likewise, it is the Chinese characters that reinforce the interpretation of omohiyaru as "to send feelings." Naturally, it could be argued that an emphasis on the Chinese characters constitutes an overinterpretation of the poem. Yet the Chinese level of interpretation dovetails with the Japanese interpretation. Moreover, certain phrases are perfectly consonant with the grammar of classical Chinese: 不知者 (one who knows not) and the remark 注土椀之中 (signed/poured into an earthen vessel). Generally, the commentaries and remarks on poems in *Man'yōshū* are written in classical Chinese, and, as this case demonstrates, it is impossible to keep the remarks outside the poem; they inform its functions and effects.

In sum, even in this innocuous example, there are signs that two grammars intertwine. The rebus is the site of intersection.[10] With such effects, it is easy to see why some scholars have recently suggested Korean readings for the same characters. These rebus-like moments introduce so much play between inscription and vocalization. If two grammars intertwine, why not two vocalities? And if two, why not three? Modern phonetic transcriptions reduce this play as much as possible, and, what is more, centuries of interpretation in Japan consolidate and legitimate this effort, to the point where modern scholars feel justified in claiming that poets really intended to write Japanese phonetically but that Chinese characters got in the way. Nevertheless, even in this slight poem, which seems so settled in its transcription, the play between inscription and vocalization remains. This study takes the stance that such play, evidenced in rebus-like moments of inscription, lies at the heart of ancient Japanese poetics, and that the forms and functions of Heian poetics emerge from this play. It directs attention to the network of a-signifying, nonlinguistic and a-grammatical forms that structure the field of Heian poetics. My point of departure is an image of the early Japanese poetic text as a vast unfurling puzzle that interlocks diverse elements; therein lies its possibilities and its limits.

TWO. *Kana Inscription and Stylistic Differentiation*

Kana and Mana

In Heian manuscripts the word today read as *kana* was often glossed with the characters for "provisional names" (仮字). This gloss has encouraged the notion that the word comes from *kanna*, an altered pronunciation of *karina*. *Kari* (仮) indicates the temporary, impermanent or provisional, and *na* (字) implies Chinese characters or names. Komatsu Shigemi, in his introduction to kana, explains that the first recorded usage of the term *kana*, written with the characters "provisional name," occurs in the *Utsuho monogatari* (ca. 976–983). There are also instances in which *kana* takes the characters for "borrowed names" (借字) or "Yamato names" (和字).[1] It is usually paired with the term *mana* (真字) or "perfected names." Just as provisional names imply Yamato names, so perfected names imply Han names (漢字).

J. Marshall Unger takes issue with the phonetic derivation of the words *kana* and *mana*.[2] He traces mana to a specialized use of the allomorph /mana/ (model), which he then relates to stiff-style calligraphy. He tentatively derives kana from the allomorph /kana/ (unit), which indicates Chinese characters reduced to their smallest recognizable shapes. Unger thus anticipates the distinction that informs this study: that mana and kana are above all differentiated in formal or stylistic terms and are related to calligraphy rather than to semantic or grammatical functions. Unger simply concludes that this is a formal, not a functional distinction. Presumably for Unger grammar and semantics are functional but styles and forms are not. I adopt a different tack: form relates directly to function, and the formal differentiation of mana and kana is the functional differentiation for the Heian court (for which grammatical or linguistic distinctions were secondary).

The formal differentiation of kana and mana involves some practical stylistic differences related to the art of writing. Histories normally signal a general trend from graphic complexity (mana) to cursive simplification (kana). Kana derive from mana by way of abbreviation and cursification of Chinese characters. When writing rapidly, instead of using the complex perfected names, one could brush a simplified version. For a number of reasons, this kana transformation of mana should not, however, be construed as a historical evolution, as it so often is (to wit, kana advance from ideography toward phonography). Kana characters never replace mana, nor are they ever truly unrelated to Chinese characters. The forms of Chinese characters guide the movements of the brush, even when it draws abbreviated or simplified characters. What is more, the term *mana* itself, with its connotations of true, pure, genuine, correct, and so on, points to the continued privileging of Chinese characters in calligraphic simplification: kana are, after all, provisional names. (Unger's derivation of "model" (mana) and "unit" (kana) recalls this calligraphic relation, in which mana constitute the authoritative model or pattern.) Chinese characters and calligraphy assured the prestige of writing, and mana recalled that prestigious realm of formally elaborate characters. Rather than subsume practical stylistic differences within a dubious evolutionary history, therefore, we need to ask, "what are the functions and implications of the kana-mana relation?"

First, it is essential to understand the prestige of mana or Chinese characters. The use of characters at the Heian court entailed practices and concepts other than the phonetic transcription of speech. In the early ninth century, for instance, the notion of "designs/inscriptions to alleviate the land" (*bunsho keikoku*) held sway. This notion of writing informed general formulations of the art of governance, as well as the role of the sage or scholar, whether these formulations were Taoist, Buddhist or Confucian. Kūkai, or posthumously Kōbōdaishi (774–835), who founded Shingon Buddhism and brought this sect to prominence at the Heian court, expressed the efficacy of writing in terms of its ability to follow and align cosmological patterns and forces.

Patterns of writing inevitably arise along other patterns. The heavens clear, pending configurations. People feel, grasping brushes. On this basis, *Eight Trigrams, Tao-te Ching, Odes, Elegies*, moving through the middle, signed on paper. Although it said there is difference between the high ages and today, and no comparison between sage and common man, can one resist putting emotion into words somehow, tracing out the human pent-up feelings?[3]

The passage comes from a tract in which Kūkai discusses the three teachings (Confucianism, Taoism, Buddhism), and so he begins with a statement that passes for general wisdom in each of these teachings: the patterns or designs of writing emerge from and align with other patterns. The sage directs his emotions through the brush in order to align them with cosmological patterns or celestial configurations. The art of writing lies in the production of patterns that align with cosmological configurations; in this way, the sage directs emotions through the proper channels, assuring the alignment of human activity with the cosmos. Now, some forms of writing are already perfected with respect to the cosmos. For instance, Kūkai places the Chinese classics almost on par with the heavens in providing auspicious patterns. He praises the works of sages, for these have already moved through the middle, successfully aligning emotions with the cosmos by way of the designs and patterns of writing. The sagacious patterns of the classics thus serve as models for self-cultivation or self-rectification in the present, bringing order to the realm of human activities. It is in these terms that one can imagine "designs and inscriptions to alleviate the land" in which the art of writing coincides with the art of governing.

Kūkai himself, renowned as a poet and calligrapher at the early Heian court, played an important role in establishing the contours of Heian writing. In fact, although some postwar scholars go to great lengths to downplay the role of Buddhism and Kūkai in the history of writing and chanting, legends attribute the very invention of kana to Kūkai, associating his fluid movements across the land (irrigation projects and temple circuits for pilgrims) with his fluid hand. In any event, the kinds of statements that he makes about the efficacy of forms, designs, or patterns constitute the general framework within which Heian poetics assumed its political and cosmological effectiveness.

Such ideas about the efficacy of writing contributed to the great prestige of Chinese characters (or Han names) at the Heian court. Because Han names had already been established and perfected in accordance with Chinese cosmogony, scribes could enter into practices of self-perfection or self-cultivation as they gained fluency and dexterity with the brush and with the characters of the classics. Naturally, the practices associated with fluency and dexterity in patterns could go in any number of directions. Kūkai, for instance, takes his ideas about designs and configurations in the direction of esoteric rites that evoke the adamantine body (of the Buddha). Waka poetics, on the other hand, juxtapose and superpose various patterns of inscription and vocalization, constructing different bodies and subjectivities in relation to the cosmological potential of writing and singing. In any event, it is clear that mana—perfected names—supplied the sources of, and modes of access to, the cosmological patterns that gave writing its status and efficacy.

As Kūkai's comments about the high ages indicate, the prestige accorded to mana also introduces a historical movement or temporal hierarchy. The Yamato court began to cultivate its lineage and descent from a Han-like high ages (上代). It patterned its growth in accordance with the model configured in other Han outgrowths, such as the courts of the various kingdoms of Six Dynasties, Sui, and Tang China as well as the courts and commandaries on the Korean peninsula: Paekche, Palhae, Silla, Lo-yang, Koguryo. In this historical imagination, the past—in particular the texts or characters of the past—was the ultimate source of authority and perfection from which the present derived its legitimacy. In this sense, there is already a historical lag and temporal hierarchy implicit in the differentiation of mana and kana. The prestige of kana writing would derive not from its autonomy from mana but from its proximity to mana. In fact, "high" kana texts (like imperial anthologies) stress their proximity or equivalence to Han forms. They sing of the resurrection of the high ages.

Frequently, Heian texts associate the high ages with the Han dynasty or legacy, and Yamato modes are paired or compared with Han (漢). In addition, in Heian texts, Yamato is also frequently paired with T'ang (唐), sometimes pronounced *Kara*). The Heian association of Han and T'ang makes sense in so far as the lineage of the T'ang dynasty associated itself with the Han dynasty—just as many other kingdoms after the Han empire (including the Yamato court) would associate their ascendency with the Han model. There were any number of other courts across East Asia that also played roles in the Heian imagination, that informed modes of writing, dressing, singing, ruling, painting, of organizing time and space. Nevertheless, the differentiation of Yamato versus Han/T'ang seems to have provided the operable binarism.

The Heian court tended to design styles and modes that especially recall those of the Six Dynasties, Sui Dynasty, and the early T'ang. The architecture and layout of Heian-kyō differed in some respects from Chang-an, and yet those differences actually point to its similarities with the capitals and outposts of the early T'ang.[4] This stylistic difference can be attributed either to the mediation of the Korean courts in the transmission of Chinese modes, or to migratory movements in northeast Asia during those turbulent years — when refugees or travelers from certain courts might construct or assist in constructing other courts. As both circumstances were perhaps common, it makes sense to think of the Yamato court as contemporaneous with these other formations (rather than to depict it as isolated spatially or temporally).

Still, despite evident parallels, many scholars argue that actual visitors from the continent were few and far between. Kaneko Shūichi, for instance, tries to quantify immigration into early Japan on the basis of ancient references to visitors, travelers, or envoys. He concludes that there were few immigrants — fewer than the number of Chinese tourists in Japan today![5] But there is an element of disingenuousness to his figures, because he never considers the status of such sources. Rather than ask how such texts construct boundaries or represent outsiders and with what goals, Kaneko treats them as immigration records. Amino Yoshihiko, on the other hand, stresses admixture, particularly in relation to sea traffic, in order to undermine notions of a pure and homogeneous Japan.[6] He also questions the ethnic status of so-called clan affiliations, which were political not racial assemblages. In any event, it is probably impossible to speak with any certainty about migration and diffusion between Heian Japan and other courts. What is clear is that the Heian court made great efforts to avoid political subversion by controlling courtiers' relations with the exterior. Amino suggests that the imperial household sustained close yet discreet relations with travelers and other people outside the capital. Benedict Anderson's remarks reinforce Amino's perspective: classical communities envisaged hybridity and hierarchy as central to the political order, not purity or homogeneity.

In sum, the general framework that informs the emergence of Heian poetics involved a binary differentiation of Yamato versus Han/T'ang. This binarism organized various modes of production and types of expression — bureaucracies (ranks, titles, court dress), scripts, poetry, painting, and architecture. It could be schematized as follows:

Yamato (倭、大和)	Han, Kara or T'ang (漢、唐)
Heian-kyō (平安京)	Chang-an (長安)

uta (歌)	shih (詩)
waka or Yamato uta (和歌)	kanshi or Han shih (漢詩)
kana (仮字、和字)	mana (真字、漢字)

This binary schema was fundamental to the Heian imagination of order. It is reprised in different ways in later eras, especially by the nativist scholars of the Tokugawa period. The nativists were really the first to devalue the "China" side of things. For them, *karagokoro*—the Chinese heart or mind—represented all that was artificial, lifeless, and corrupt. Modern scholarship inherits the nativist framework but radically transforms it, introducing narratives of historical progression. As a result, the impulse of Japanese studies is to treat the Heian binarism in terms of opposition, negation, sublation, and absorption; that is, Yamato opposes, resists, negates, sublates, or absorbs Han/T'ang. This way of imagining the Heian order aligns it entirely with the national imagination. In the next section, I present the views of some Japanese scholars on the interactions of Yamato and Han/T'ang in the Heian context. Then, in the final section of this chapter I return to the differentiation between mana and kana to present an alternative way to read the interactions of the Heian court and the Han/T'ang model.

Opposition, Negation, Sublation

Initially, Western histories of East Asia focused on the Chinese dynasties and much of ancient Japan was construed as little more than failed imitation. Needless to say, this stance toward premodern Japan reinforced the idea that Japan was a nation of slavish imitators, first of China and now of the West. In Japan, then, it is not surprising then that modern national studies would generally aim to show that Japan responded actively and selectively to China and the West and to reverse the order of priority implicit in studies of influence. To achieve this reversal, studies of early Japan invariably take the logic of selective reception to its limit, suggesting, in effect, that early Japan not only responded actively to China but also resisted and overturned China. I would like to approach this logic of opposition and resistance by looking at two moments in the modern formation of Japanese resistance in the context of Heian Japan.

(1) In the first half of the twentieth century, scholarship on early Japanese poetry tended to celebrate the lyricism of *Man'yōshū*. Scholars situated its poetics at the moment just prior to, or coeval with, foreign in-

trusion, when native resistance still held its ground. In these studies the Heian court and *Kokinwakashū* tended to be held under suspicion: everything looked and sounded too Chinese, and in general it didn't seem possible to claim outright that Heian poetics resisted or overturned Chinese poetics. This scholarship generally looked at poetics in terms of imagery, themes, and concepts; and in those terms, much of *Kokinwakashū* failed to reveal its native status.

(2) In the postwar period, the stance changed considerably, and scholars posited *Kokinwakashū* as a moment of native absorption of the foreign. This shift emphasized the emergence of kana: phonetic writing that cast off foreign obstacles to native expression, thus liberating the people's voice and enabling a transparent link with the pure Japanese of *Man'yōshū*. This scholarship tended to classify and quantify rhetorical devices and tropes. It either entailed a linguistic focus that could establish links between preforeign and postforeign styles of expression, or it simply assumed that the rhetoric devices of early poetics constituted a cultural and linguistic boundary between Japan and China.[7]

In short, prewar studies tended to elevate *Man'yōshū* and hold *Kokinwakashū* in suspicion, whereas postwar studies show greater confidence in the Japaneseness of *Kokinwakashū*. Still, *Man'yōshū* remained an important site of Japaneseness, and postwar studies assume (or strive to establish) transparent links between *Man'yōshū* and *Kokinwakashū*. The maintenance of such transparent links involves a desire to see ancient Japanese poetry in opposition to Han forms, but now opposition is assumed to be successful—and takes the form of absorption, domestication, or sublation of the foreign.

There is, then, a common problematic in prewar and postwar studies, that of influence and reaction. The major collections of poetry are situated with respect to a history of external influences, which were met with internal reaction, resistance, opposition, negation, and so forth. The songs of *Man'yōshū*, especially the early ones, are said to constitute a native poetics (associated with orality). Subsequently, Han/T'ang script and poetics came to dominate the Yamato world, resulting in the three imperial anthologies of Han-style poetry in the early ninth century—the so-called "dark ages of native styles and customs" (国風暗黒時代). Prewar and postwar studies have somewhat different sensibilities with respect to the "dark ages." Prewar studies are often pessimistic about *Kokinwakashū* and its hold on Heian poetics, as if the dark ages still continued. Postwar studies are mostly confident that, in the early tenth century, native forms surged out of the dark shadows cast by Chinese forms: *Kokinwakashū* revived or restored native poetics in the form of an imperial anthology of waka (Yamato uta). More recently, this confidence in native forms has gone a step further: it suggests that there really was no dark ages and that native forms continued alongside the foreign.

To anticipate and situate my own take on this problematic—I see in this latest permutation of the history of influence and reaction an opportunity to challenge the logic of the native versus the foreign. There were no natives versus foreigners, nor were there dark ages. Instead, out of a heterogeneous field, there emerged a binary machine that could synthesize and organize multiple forms of expression and production: the Yamato-Han or "wa-kan" assemblage.

I begin with an overview of the histories of influence and reaction with Saigo Nobutsuna, who provides a bridge between prewar and postwar studies (as I have characterized them). Not long after the war (1951), Saigo published *Nihon kodai bungakushi (The History of Ancient Japanese Literature)*. In a chapter on waka and kanshi, he writes about early Japanese poetry in terms of its historical and technological development.

> At that time, there existed great disparity between T'ang society and Japanese society in their degree of historical development. . . . Accordingly, since the culture of the former functioned freely and powerfully with respect to the latter, this naturally could only lead to a process of cultural subjugation and assimilation of the latter by the former. In this way, beginning with Japan (even though a phenomenon of the ruling classes), a state of affairs arose in which the less developed folk who inhabited the great T'ang empire nevertheless became colonies of the T'ang empire culturally, and offered tribute as well.[8]

Saigo declares himself a Marxist, and he writes of historical subjugation and liberation, of peoples and empires, of cultures and ideologies. For him, the T'ang empire posed the threat of cultural subjugation and assimilation, although he briefly reminds us that this cultural imperialism addressed not so much the people of the Japanese archipelago as the ruling class. Note, however, that Saigo already assumes the existence of a unified people in the eighth century, despite stratification by social class or caste. As a result of this logic, the ruling class comes to stand for Japan. Once he establishes the idea of cultural imperialism, he turns to the significance of that imperialism, not in terms of class struggle but of cultural mentalities.

What soon becomes problematic are the contents of the so-called advanced culture. It was truly not a healthy popular culture but a decadent, degenerate, aristocratic culture, intellectually overripe, centered on Buddhism and Confucianism, and as a result it held the potential to dissolve the youthful folk mentality with its poison. Since we/they did not universally adopt foreign culture, we must grasp the concrete substance of that culture of foreign mentality which they did accept.[9]

Saigo deals with the content of the advanced culture of the T'ang empire, signaling that he wishes to champion the spirit of the people or folk. His is an unusual type of Marxism. He displaces modern class struggle onto the archaic state; then, in order to sustain the anachronistic unity of the Japanese people, he shifts from class struggle to a battle between cultural mentalities. Saigo thus posits the early Japanese as a subjugated class, and it becomes obvious that his account of the archaic state is not so much Marxist as nativist. His concern is not for the material subjugation of the peoples within the ancient empires but for the cultural subjugation of Japan. Only when he has established the latter does he bring in the question of "concrete substance" — under the aegis of cultural imperialism.

He asks, how were we/they concretely affected by decadent foreign culture? In 1951, this was surely a loaded question. Yet for all its possible resonance with the Japanese empire in Asia or the "reverse course" of American Occupation of Japan, it clearly draws the line between the Japanese folk and empire: empire is external to the native spirit of the people. In this respect, Saigo makes clear that he does not truly intend to discuss "the concrete substance of that foreign mentality" — that is, he wants to explore the native purity and innocence of the Japanese folk. Not surprisingly, then, he turns to the mental purity and vitality of the ancients.

Yet fortunately in the hearts of those courtiers of ancient Japan, the vitality of an artless, healthy folk mentality resolutely lived on, one which could not be defeated even while being assimilated to a decadent foreign culture. . . . Seen in terms of culture, the tragic quality of Hitomaro constitutes a vehement expression of dissent against the foreign culture continuing to dissolve the folk mentality. What sustained the particularly superior quality of the early *Man'yōshū* was the great soul of a youthful folk mentality yet undefiled by Confucian prosaism and Buddhist pessimism. . . . in the depths of their hearts pounded, in some form, the tradition of folk mentality which, unperturbed, lashed back and turned against foreign intellect and education.[10]

It is initially difficult to say what Saigo himself intends to make of folk resistance. His notion of ancient folk resistance may be a way to promote local resistance to the alignment of postwar Japan with the American military-industrial order. Yet his story partakes so fully of nativist *cum* nationalist scenarios. He insists that the spiritual vitality of the folk is not some magical force, it "originates in the folk independence which our ancestors won through their battles in the heroic age." He then writes of the artificiality of the court bureaucracies, singing the praises of Otomo Yakamochi, who resisted to the death the plans of the Fujiwara clan to move the capital from Heijō-kyō to Heian-kyō.[11] The shape of Saigo's national fantasy emerges more clearly when he strives to establish a contradiction between excellence in literature and the establishment of class society.

Saigo claims that the foreign-derived class society of the *Man'yōshū* period merely furthered bureaucracy and solidified prosaisms: "It did not enable a fertile womb for literature in the truest sense; it only furthered a cold intellectual numbing of the poetic mentality of the people."[12] The imperialism of class society, then, is foreign to Japan, and the proletarian revolution must pass through the ancient literature that truly expresses the original classless spirit of the ancient folk. In particular, because literature in the truest sense is lyric poetry, the revolution against class society must pass through the songs of early Japan, restoring the purity and vitality lodged in the womb of ancient Japan. (Note that the "mothers" of this native womb are doubly erased, for they do not possess the lyric spirit, they bear it and guarantee its continuity; they are channels in which the blood and spirit of heros flows in lofty independence.) In sum, Saigo combines the logic of a classless society with the logic of ancient poetic purity, and the resulting *Gemeinschaft* is far closer to racialized nativism than to Marxism.

Even though Saigo's attempt to politicize ancient poetry tended to align him with fantasies of native purity and unity, his account is of interest because it engaged the political framework of waka studies. His turn to Marxism constituted an attempt to revise the prewar ideologies of native purity in the direction of classless society, and his account of waka showed an awareness that poetry studies need to address the ideological legacy of Japanese militarism and nationalism.

Two other studies of ancient Japanese poetry are central to this study:

Suzuki Hideo's *Kodaiwakashiron* (*On the History of Ancient Waka*) and Yoshimoto Taka'aki's *Shoki kayō ron* (*On Early Song*). Both Yoshimoto and Suzuki are cultural spokesmen as well as scholars; Suzuki, in particular, is a key figure in the study of Heian literature and in national literary studies generally. Sometimes considered the country's leading postwar intellectual, Yoshimoto is something of a maverick in his account of early song. He constantly challenges certain nativist assumptions about ancient poetry and strives to link song to political formations; his analysis, however, does not work as close to waka scholarship as Suzuki's. For this reason, I treat Suzuki as representative of the ways in which postwar waka studies consolidated the image of Heian Japan. A newer generation of scholars in Japan have begun to articulate their interpretations through or against the scholarship of Suzuki's generation (which includes Akiyama Ken, Konishi Jin'ichi, and others)—as the example of Yoshino Tatsunori, discussed in the next chapter, attests.

Suzuki takes up the Chinese sources of Heian waka, acknowledging the importance of dynastic China: "No matter how much we insist, it is impossible to stress the point enough, that Japanese culture was cultivated on the soil of T'ang styles and customs." Subsequently, however, he proves the autonomy of Japanese culture. How exactly does the flower of waka prove independent of its soil? It is interesting that Suzuki does not attempt to establish Japanese autonomy on the basis of waka themes, images, or concepts. In fact, he frequently notes the Chineseness of waka sentiments and expression. In this sense, his account is consonant with prewar interpretations of *Kokinwakashū*: with respect to themes and images, its waka fail to reveal their native status. But Suzuki mobilizes another narrative for autonomy, one that only emerged fully in postwar scholarship: kana enable a native speech community and, hence, an autonomous culture. Thus kana— or rather, kana culture—becomes his emblem of autonomy: "Within the wide-ranging sphere of kanji culture in East Asia, it so happens that kana culture came to life while taking in kanji culture—all the more so because kana culture was continuously encompassed by it." [13]

The way Suzuki writes of kana culture versus kanji culture evokes a logic of decolonialization. Which is to say, when local peoples are surrounded by an imperial power, a national culture emerges. So it is that kana—which he styles "the phonetic characters unique to our country"—"formed as one part of an independent Japanese culture in the latter half of the ninth century, in the same period that saw the inauguration of the regency system." [14]

It is hard not to read this as an allegory of modern Japanese nationalism: Japan, beset by Western imperialism, shaped a nation in order to preserve its autonomy and integrity. Suzuki's account seems to draw, in particular, on the parameters of Japanese nationalism in the wake of the Occupation. For instance, he insists on the Heian regency as a marker of an autonomous Japanese culture, which recalls the politics of the symbolic emperor in the immediate postwar period. The regency provides him with a vision of a culturalist, nonmilitarist Japan in which the emperor serves as a symbol of the people rather than a militarist dictator. In short, his account of kana turns into a rather comforting political allegory: what is uniquely Japanese is a symbolic emperor and culturalist isolation from international, even imperialist forces.

Now, even though it is hard to agree that the Heian court responded to the dynastic classical community by forming an insular nation, nonetheless it is interesting that Suzuki sees the national community as a response to imperial encroachment rather than a result of internal consensus or organic development. His account potentially prepares the background for a very different view of the relations of the Heian court to its past; in it, prior forms are not so much realized or restored as overcoded and alienated. Yet Suzuki does not take this route. He does not pursue the implications of his narrative of decolonization but turns instead to a narrative of phonetic evolution. It is this narrative that erases any conflicts and difficulties that could be associated with the emergence of kana culture.

> The very beginning of kana in the Heian period consisted of something called the masculine hand, in the regular or semi-cursive style. Although there are differences owing to the disappearance of characters from the ancient period and to linguistic currency of varying purity, there is a direct succession from the *man'yōgana* of the previous period. Around the end of the ninth century, this advances one step further into the feminine hand (*hiragana*) — grass kana in the grass style, and in this series of stages in formation of kana, vowels become restricted to some extent, and there is a gradual purification into phonetic characters of one character for one sound. In this way, prayers, proclamations, songs, waka — pure Japanese so to speak — came gradually to be recorded.[15]

If we omit changes in character usage and linguistic impurities, one can detect a gradual purification of writing and speaking, in the direction of pure Japanese (so to speak). Suzuki asks us to discount actual changes in the structure of the spoken language—the vowel shifts that occur between the Man'yoshū and Kokinwakashū—in order to perceive continuity.

Paring away the heterogeneity of songs and scripts, Suzuki arrives at a single line of transmission between the Man'yoshū and Kokinwakashū. "In the reception of old poems," he writes, "I think that, although there are differences between oral transmission and the medium of written records, we should think of them in terms of one world, one space of transmission." [16] This too is an important moment for Suzuki: although there are differences, we should think of them in terms of one world. If we do as Suzuki thinks we should, we see the emergence of kana and waka around Kokinwakashū in terms of direct transmission, a single line and a process of purification. If we do not, we have to face a heteroclite field riddled with scriptural oddities, with figural operations, vocal impurities, and poetic and political experiments. Yet Suzuki continually assures us that it is reasonable, and maybe not undesirable, to ignore discrepancies and differences.

> We get a better handle on the process in which the waka of Man'yōshū went from indigenous songs to court songs subsequently to settle in as imperial poetry, in terms of a single thread of logic through the history of literature in the early Heian period. The stages of formation in which kana originally generated among the people went on to be perfected as court culture can also be seen to correspond with that logic, for the most part. [17]

Suzuki mentions two movements, one of speech—from indigenous song to imperial poetry; one of writing—from the people to the court. He passes over this ground so quickly that, in a blink of an eye, he arrives at an indigenous, populist, imperial court (one that is really a culturalist nation).

Nonetheless, it should not be supposed that Suzuki blindly falls into ideologically charged statements about Heian Japan. On the contrary, what is striking about his discussion is that it is frankly ideological in its claims, and it so clearly uses Heian poetics to champion a certain vision of modern Japan. In this respect, Suzuki makes possible a political reading of waka, one that has consequences for the imagination of modern Japan. Suzuki's approach merits comparison with another Japanese scholar, Karaki Junzō, who merely bypasses the questions that Suzuki feels compelled to finesse. In *Nihon no kokoro no rekishi (The History of Japanese Heart/Mind)*, Karaki demonstrates complete confidence that Chinese forms simply did not matter. A prime example is his discussion of inscriptions that simultaneously register Han and Yamato modes of notation.

> Using diacritic marks to read Chinese by omitting the Chinese reading of characters and reading them in Japanese is probably a unique phenomenon, without parallel in the world. And whenever the Japanese wrote Chinese poetry, they wrote using diacritic marks, adding Japanese inflections in their hearts. Although its form may have been Chinese poetry, it was actually Japanese poetry.[18]

Karaki's fantasy involves the complete transparency of writing, and he arrives at the point where it makes no difference at all whether courtiers actually wrote in Chinese: in their hearts they read and wrote Japanese. Such a fantasy would naturally be impossible without the mediation of modern editions in which both Han and Yamato songs are transcribed and translated into classical Japanese. If the Japanese heart shines forth for Karaki, it is because, in modern editions, inscription becomes completely immaterial.

The use of diacritic marks demands some explanation. Such marks, derived largely from the sutra exegeses of Buddhist monks, were used to gloss pronunciations of Chinese and Sanskrit characters and to edit, punctuate, and indicate grammar. One form of kana stemmed from diacritic marks that transformed and explicated the flow of Chinese characters (much later systematized as *katakana*). In the ninth century, however, diacritic marks and kana did not constitute homogeneous or autonomous systems, and it is difficult to see how they could have transmitted a homogeneous language. What is more, there exist few documents that actually show the poetic use of diacritic marks, and these do not date from the ninth century. Karaki insists that, because all Chinese texts used diacritic kana, no one actually read or wrote Chinese—he never entertains the idea that some spoke Chinese. And if they did, he tells us, they really felt and thought in Japanese. He invents an ideal or mental continuity by insisting on the immateriality and transparency of writing. Actual usage, however, does not support his claims.

There is no doubt that Heian courtiers worked to ensure the intelligibility of inscription. In fact, intelligibility might be called the first principle of calligraphy. Nevertheless, intelligibility is not the same thing as transparency or immateriality or phonography. On the contrary, the intelligibility of Heian writing, whether kana or mana, related directly to figurality; as a result, it called attention to operations that, by the standards of modern linguistics, could only be considered opacity or materiality. Heian poetic inscription, in this respect, followed a turn that Wallace Stevens aptly calls "making the visible a little hard to see." [19]

For Karaki, it is no longer a matter of establishing Japanese resistance to Chinese forms. He assumes successful resistance. He simply negates Chinese forms and presumes the triumphant and transcendent radiance of the Japanese heart. In comparison, the engagement of Saigo and Suzuki with T'ang-Yamato interactions raises questions, not only about Heian Japan but also about the ways in which our imagination of Heian Japan affects our imagination of modern Japan. Both Saigo and Suzuki were interested in native purity and autonomy, but for Saigo it was a problem of imperial encroachment and indigenous revolution, while for Suzuki the underlying narrative was one of colonial response and national evolution. Moreover, because Suzuki's discussion of Heian Japan versus T'ang China draws on the cultural dynamics of postwar United States–Japan relations, it poses a certain challenge with respect to how we imagine Japan in the world. His account shows an imagination of Japan in terms of a kind of decolonization—akin to Oe Kenzaburō's notion that Japan, in the wake of the American Occupation, remained a third-world nation culturally. But Suzuki pushes this in the direction of the naturalness of, and necessity for, national unification as far back as the Heian court, where he sees it prefigured in the phonetic evolution of kana.

This study aims to challenge two notions that are consolidated in Suzuki's work. First, by reading kana in terms of figurality rather than phonography, I question whether the Heian waka constituted a speech community. Second, by questioning the notion of an ancient speech community, I challenge another extension of the national imagination: that the Heian court constituted its subjects in the manner of the territorial nation.

E. J. Hobsbawm describes the concept of the territorial nation in his book on the rise of modern nationalism. After the First World War, he writes, the peace treaty attempted to redraw the political map of Europe along national lines by applying Wilsonian principles; national frontiers were to coincide with the frontiers of culture as defined by language. The Wilsonian principles made explicit certain assumptions that were inherent in modern national structures; namely, that political formations, cultural or ethnic identities, and linguistic structures should coincide. The coincidence of these three established natural, objective boundaries for nations. The Wilsonian world order, however, did not work. Hobsbawm notes that "the main change was that states were now on average rather smaller and the 'oppressed peoples' within them were now called 'oppressed minorities.' The logical implication of trying to create a continent neatly divided into coherent territorial states each inhabited by a separate ethnically and linguistically homogeneous population, was the mass expulsion or extermination of minorities. Such was and is the reductio ad absurdum of nationalism in its territorial version, although this was not fully demonstrated until the 1940s." [20]

As terrible and absurd as this image of community is, it remains the inevitable point of departure for discussions of kana, waka, and the Heian court.

Stylistic Differentiation

The act of inscription provides another way to conceptualize the material interaction of Han and Yamato forms at the early Heian court. Above all, inscription breaks the myth of linguistic transparency and ideal continuity between Man'yōshū and Kokinwakashū. It allows one to imagine a network of sounds, signs, images, and languages and brings into consideration the diverse forms and transformations that swarmed between Man'yōshū and Kokinwakashū. It expands the waka form beyond the confines of internal linguistic evolution or oral transmission and undermines the maintenance of exclusive, transparent links between the two collections.

Nonetheless, Heian poetics made all kinds of claims for continuity. The two prefaces to Kokinwakashū positioned waka poetics in the lineage of Man'yōshū. One preface to Kokinwakashū even called it a "Continued Man'yōshū (shoku Man'yōshū). What did continuity with Man'yōshū mean in the Heian context? One way to re-imagine this claim for continuity is to look at the claims made by another, roughly contemporaneous, anthology, Shinsen man'yōshū (ca. 893), which posed as a "newly selected Man'yōshū."

The compilation of the poems of Shinsen man'yōshū is often attributed (wrongly) to Sugawara no Michizane (845–903), a high-ranking courtier, poet, and scholar who wrote primarily in Chinese and had great influence at court under emperor Uda (r. 887–897).[21] Yet the false attribution of this collection to Sugawara no Michizane, together with its style of inscription, suggests that the aim of Shinsen man'yōshū was to assure the prestige of waka by making them look like Han poems. After all, Sugawara no Michizane had a reputation for attempting to promote and maintain the prestige of Chinese modes of singing, writing, and governing. *Shinsen man'yōshū* may have been attributed to him because it takes a number of waka from a poem contest and transliterates them into mana-style writing, in effect rendering Yamato poems in something like Han forms.[22] In any case, around *Shinsen man'yōshū* there arose a certain conflation of *Man'yōshū* and Han forms. The prefaces to *Kokinwakashū* made a similar gesture: the poetics of *Man'yōshū* are consistently conflated with the poetics of the three Chinese anthologies. In sum, both continuations of *Man'yōshū* confused it with Han forms at some level. How did such confusion arise?

The scriptural difficulties of *Man'yōshū* encouraged a conflation of forms that we have come to separate linguistically. Courtiers certainly knew that the *Man'yō* script was intelligible, but who could read it? In the tenth century, the emperor Murakami ordered a translation and explication of the poems of this collection. The imperial translation of *Man'yōshū* suggests that the complexities of its scripts had made it almost unreadable. Apparently, it was the difficulties of *Man'yō*-style inscription that made it possible for the courtiers to see it as analogous to Han-style inscription. They came to see mana as any characters that appeared in their perfected form and emerged in the regular or stiff style (or its companion, the current or cursive style, *gyōsho*)—whether these were used phonographically or logographically and whether they implied Han grammar or Yamato grammar. Unger reminds us that, "there is no evidence that graphs used in this bizarre manner were any less mana to the writers of the Heian period than were the graphs used in more conventional ways."[23] What mattered was the look or style of poetic inscription, its grid of figural intelligibility, not its language or grammar. In this way, the emergence of kana tended to force *Man'yōshū*, on the basis of stylistic differentiation, into the same space as Han poetics.[24]

On the level of inscription, the differentiation of kana and mana did not appear as an act of opposition, negation, or sublation. Take, for example, this mana-style inscription of a waka, which appears in *Shinsen man'yōshū*. The first line gives the mana poem in its original form from a standard edition (in modern characters). In brackets is the Japanese transliteration.

冬来者　梅丹雪許曾　降粉倍　何礼之枝諸　花砥折申
［冬来れば　梅に雪こそ　ふりまがへ　いづれの枝を　花と折るべし］

When winter comes
on the plum tree snow
　　　falls and flocks in confusion:
from which branches one might pluck flowers?[25]

In their notes, the editors of the modern edition point out the difficulty of knowing how to transliterate the mana inscription. There is no simple way to extract a single Japanese pronunciation and grammar from it. The first phrase (冬来者) reads oddly, as do the other segments; the phonetic transliteration adds elements to them to render the waka syllabic count. Of course, Heian poets were surely competent in such matters, since they often transformed Han phrases into Yamato phrases. Still, it is significant that *Shinsen man'yōshū* does not attempt a phonographic inscription of Yamato phrases: it takes waka from a poem contest and transforms them with the elements of Han-style mana inscription. The resultant inscription vacillates between phonography and logography, as well as between Yamato and Han grammars. Or, rather, there is an oscillation between rhythms: the rhythms of mana characters (3-5-3-5-4) are out of sync with the expected rhythms of syllables (5-7-5-7-7). Are these twined rhythms not part of the art of the poem?

Typically, the kana script is thought to be phonographic (inscribing sounds), while Chinese characters are thought to be logographic (inscribing words). Of course, because Chinese words are monosyllables in this context, it could be said that Chinese characters are simultaneously phonographic and logographic. In this respect, creating equivalencies between kana and Chinese characters does not require incommensurable operations. In fact, kana inscription derives in part from a phonographic usage of monosyllabic characters typical of Chinese writing. Despite its phonographic potential, however, an inscription like the above does not use phonography to differentiate linguistically between Han and Yamato forms. It uses both phonographic and logographic modes and is at once both and neither. It stands at a point where Yamato and Han names are reversible and interchangeable—at a site where rhythms overlap. As such it calls attention not to the phonetic transcription of sounds but to the figural operations of sounds and images. Even in the modern typographic text there linger rebus-like traces of a writing that vacillates between two styles and two rhythms.

Naturally, it is possible to push this vacillation in the direction of phonographic transcription in order to extract a single linguistic phrase. But why then did the scribe or scribes bother to produce such complex rebus-like inscriptions? Some commentators would say that the scribes would surely have used a purely phonographic transcription had the difficulties of Chinese characters not stood in their way. Yet such an assertion cannot explain the ubiquity of puzzlelike inscriptions, which suggests that scribes either delighted in such figural play or were not particularly disturbed by it. Calligraphic texts, of course, make figural operations all the more apparent, and it seems likely that the logic of the brush played a central role in determining the forms and functions of poetry. In any case, even this modern transcription hints that poetic inscription used both phonographic and logographic characters not primarily to transcribe speech but in order to produce figural operations through which Yamato and Han names and forms could conjoin and coincide in the manner of a rebus.

The overlap or coincidence of forms also occurs in the images of the poem. The poem employs a technique called *mitate* in which two things are deliberately mistaken for each other, visually conflated: snow on the plum branches resembles the white flowers that burst forth on spring branches. The poet vacillates between two readings of this sight; snow or flowers? Both are white, both collect on branches, both scatter and fall. Amagasaki Akira writes that mitate functions much like a cinematic overlap dissolve, since in mitate two images are visible at once.[26] The difference lies in the temporal movement; in cinema, one image slowly dissolves into another, which slowly resolves. The art of mitate, on the other hand, comes when two images overlap, and yet the viewer does not temporally pass from one into the other; instead, vision remains posed at the moment of dissolution and resolution, oscillating between images in an eternal rebus. And so, in the mixing of plum flowers and snowflakes, the temporal passage from winter to spring halts eternally, suspended upon the reversibility of images — and this suspended oscillation leads into the next poem. It is not entirely unlike cinema, and yet the movement of forms and images in waka belongs to cosmological configurations; they are fixed poses and moments in a cycle of seasons, days, hours, and so forth.

Then there are the characters, whether in the Yamato or the Han style: both styles run down the page, both entail figures that flock and scatter as they inscribe a poetic rhythm and allure the reader. The brush traces the oscillation of each character, then opens into the next. Which branch might the poet break off as flowers? Which style might he delimit as Yamato, and which as Han? The confusion and conflation of Han and Yamato forms operates at the stylistic level of inscription, much in the manner of mitate. It is as if mitate—visual overlap or double vision—is extended from poetic imagery to poetic inscription (or vice versa) and to doubled rhythms as well. Thus mitate reminds us that there is something profoundly performative about the play of images, rhythms, and figures in Heian poetics.

Visual overlap or double vision affords a way to conceptualize the emergence of kana. When a Chinese character is written rapidly, fluidly and cursively, its strokes take on new speeds and contours, becoming more rounded and sinuous. The calligraphic mode in which the brush reaches its greatest fluidity and rapidity is called grass style (sōsho, 草書), for characters move so supply down the page that they appear as pliant and twining as blades of grass.[27] A Chinese character like 安 with six strokes gradually comes to appear as something like the modern kana あ. And the character 知 becomes ち, and so forth. Kana is a calligraphic style that consists of variations on the grass style. Sometimes kana are dubbed "grass-kana" (sōgana). It is important to keep in mind that, in Heian calligraphy, kana characters never gain complete autonomy from Chinese characters in practical or stylistic terms. The movements of the brush render a form that falls between 安 and あ or between 知 and ち. There is no crisp typographic distinction between the two, and there are many intermediate forms of cursification. (It is not a matter of genre or species but of variety.) It is a matter of practical and performative differentiation, which evokes a kind of double vision in the space of the character: one sees the "base form" as well as its kana double.

The above poem oscillates between two styles, two rhythms, two images, and two moments. Suddenly the disingenuous rhetorical style of the poem (so typical of Kokin poetry) makes sense in another way; the riddles, feints and rhetorical questions of waka replicate the logic of the overlapping images and interlocking styles. The poem is a puzzle that traverses rhetoric, image, sign, and rhythm—it is riddle, double vision, and rebus. The art of poetics thus consists of operations that facilitate reversibility, exchangeability, or comparability between two forms. With respect to Han and Yamato forms, then, the art of poetics shows not a strict opposition-negation but a performative differentiation-coordination. This mode of mediation (in some respects a form of nonmediation) affords another perspective on the interaction between so-called Japanese and Chinese modes at the Heian court and on the role of poetics in that interaction.

The interaction of Han and Yamato forms, with its mode of differentiation and coordination, could be tentatively described as one of mimicry. The courts of early Japan mimicked continental modes (as with kana and mana, waka and kanshi, etc.)—however much their diverse components were rearranged. Walter Benjamin gives a tentative definition of such a mimetic faculty when he writes that, for the ancients, "the sphere of life that formerly seemed to be governed by the law of similarity was comprehensive; it ruled both microcosm and macrocosm. . . . 'To read what was never written.' Such reading is the most ancient: reading before all languages, from the entrails, the stars, or dances." [28] Of course, Benjamin was not really interested in generating descriptions of ancient modes of mimicry. His interest lay in making a general historical delineation that would help explain the "resurgence of the primitive" within modern mass culture.[29] And Benjamin's evocation of mass culture primitivism serves as a reminder of the fine line that lies between delineations of historical difference and outright exoticism. My own use of the notion of mimicry is intended to delineate the relations between mana and kana and to indicate how styles of inscription replicate the historico-cosmological structures of the Heian court. I do not argue that Heian use of inscription is somehow "primitivist"—any more than cinema or photography are—even though the Heian mobilization of the mimetic faculty differed profoundly from that of films or photos.

Most commentators are uncomfortable with the idea of mimicry, for the tendency is to think of it as a debased mode that strives for exact identification or resemblance. From this perspective, the differences of the Heian court from T'ang China appear only as failures. This is surely why Heian studies distance themselves so quickly from the mimetic faculty. Moreover, the notion of mimicry provokes anxiety because it suggests that culture is not internal and autonomous but external and relational.

I would argue that mimicry is a mode of interaction that operates from a ground of difference (rather than from the unified, homogeneous ground of monolithic nations or empires such as China and Japan). Mimicry reminds us that entities like Han, T'ang, or Yamato were not unified in their operations in the cultural and linguistic manner attempted by modern nations. In short, there was no Japan or China in the modern sense. Moreover, the ground of difference evoked through mimicry reminds us that singing and writing were acts of cosmological significance. The sources of the human order lay outside the court, not really in Han or T'ang China but in perfected patterns. Finally, it is necessary to recall that the archaic state—Anderson's "classical community"—did not see purity and homogeneity as the source of authority and productivity. A question then arises about the kind of hybridity specific to the Heian court—in this case a binary machine of scriptural differentiation.

In the grass style that forms kana characters, the brush still follows the contours of perfected names and thus enables the writer to evoke past resplendence. The art of calligraphy demanded that one know the forms of perfected names even as one simplified and cursified their contours. Perfected forms guided the motions of the brush, operating as a virtual form that always showed through the brushwork, assuring its intelligibility and efficacy. In this sense, provisional names could never oppose, negate, or dispense with perfected names. The very authority of the provisional names depended on the virtual presence of those perfected forms.

The models of perfected names crop up in Heian poetics on a number of levels. Sometimes, poems explicitly evoke the rebus-like operations of the Chinese character. Take, for example, this *Kokinwakashū* poem (6:337) that turns explicitly around the picture puzzle of a Chinese character.

> 雪の降りけるを見てよめる　紀友則
> 雪降れば木毎に花ぞ咲きにけるいづれを梅とわきて折らまし
> Seeing that snow had fallen, Ki no Tomonori composed:
> When snowflakes fall,
> on every branch petals open:
> might one not pluck snow-white plum petals
> from snows plum-petal white?

The poem recalls the example from *Shinsen man'yōshū*, in which winter snows and spring plum flowers created visual confusion. But this poem relates visual confusion even more directly through the figural operations of characters. The poet literally discerns or parses the "plum" (梅) from "every branch" (木毎). He questions whether one might not read the snows on "every branch" as "plum" (木 + 毎 = 梅). It is as if a series of words—snow, plum, flower, white—lost their grammatical connections and lent themselves to recombination. A character is taken apart and pieced together, two images overlap and oscillate, and the rhetoric of the poem takes the form of a riddle. The poem thus pauses at the moment when winter has not yet turned to spring but spring can almost be seen. It pivots on the moment of seasonal change and sets the pivot into motion with the oscillating components of a Chinese character. The operations of characters, images, rhythms, and seasons thus come into alignment.

Naturally, one could construe such operations as protogrammatical or metagrammatical, or protolinguistic or metalinguistic, or in some way could bring their logic back into the fold of heightened speech. In that event, one would have to add that speech is heightened to the point where it disperses into figures, patterns, and images that no longer operate by the rules of speech or grammar. In fact, that would seem to be precisely the point of such poetics: to evoke various registers of expression (image, inscription, vocal rhythm, etc.) and to align them in such a way that they correspond with the auspicious and efficacious patterns of celestial bodies and seasons. None of this has anything to do with the Japanese language, or with the Chinese language for that matter. It might be possible to extract a classical Japanese phrase and treat the Chinese character rebus as mere ornamentation, but such a gesture misses the point of such poetics—that figures and patterns are what make poetry work.

Modern waka histories deliberately downplay the figural logic of kana in order to create the impression that the emergence of kana constituted a linguistic and ethnic opposition to Han forms. Or they tend to posit the Japanese language as the sole resource for poetic expression. Nothing could be more at odds with the logic of kana inscription. Kana allowed a stylistic differentiation that provisionally manifested the order of things implicit in Chinese writing. As Kūkai notes, the goal of writing is to double or mimic those forms that have already proved efficacious. Writing does not merely retrace the patterns of the past; it makes those patterns manifest. Therein lies the goal of waka and kana: to make manifest the poetic forms of the high ages, provisionally, in the present.

It is not surprising, then, that superposed images, twofold rhythms, rebuses, riddles, and double vision should play such important roles in Heian poetics. A regime of doubleness emerges around kana and traverses the Heian order of things. During enthronement ceremonies, for instance, two types of folding screen came before the emperor, to manifest the lands he ruled. There were Yamato-style screens and Kara-style screens, which had somewhat different dimensions as well as different styles of brushwork. On the Kara screen appeared a Han poem (or at least something written in mana), and on the Yamato screen was a waka written in kana.[30] This ceremony utilizes the same logic that governs the production of provisional names: two forms are simultaneously differentiated and coordinated in such a way that the authority or priority of one form manifests itself in the other. The act of differentiation and coordination constructs a zone of indeterminacy in which doubles are comparable, exchangeable, and reversible, and in which there is yet no chance for one term to replace the other. Kana and mana are destined to march side by side, sustaining the productivity of a perpetual contest of doubles.

THREE. *Composition and Competition*

The Heian acrostic or *woriku* is literally a "broken verse" (をりく, 折句). The broken verse breaks a name into pieces and conceals them within the lines of the poem. For instance, the syllables of the name *kakituhata* (iris) are scattered into the verse rhythmically—one syllable at the start of each line (or at the end of a line, or both, as we will see). The acrostic thus introduces a figure, a layer of pattern that both disrupts and meshes with the flow of the poem. There are a couple of ways to think about the texture of the broken verse. Often, because of the similarity of the verb *break* (をり) to *weave* (おり), the broken verse is thought of in terms of a textile: a name is woven into the fabric of the poem. Weaving implies a woof and a warp, a top and a bottom, a gridlike orientation of threads. Thus the analogy to a textile suggests that the broken name intertwines with the poem in an ordered and orientated fashion. Yet, an analogy to paper would be equally appropriate. In the manufacture of paper, fibers of heterogeneous size and shape are swollen and frayed until their microfibers intertwine, forming a dense mat in which elements cohere without horizontal and vertical orientation. The broken name is also like the unorientated mesh of microfibers: it is a wandering, asymmetrical figure that arises on the microaesthetic level of beats and accents. From a micropoetic beat to a macropoetic figure, the broken name emerges from the poem, at once a source of order and disorientation.

One of the best known acrostic poems of the Heian period illustrates the broken-verse operation. Attributed to Ariwara no Narihira and recorded in *Kokinwakashū* (10:410) and in *Ise monogatari* (dan 9), this poetic line breaks and scatters the word *iris* (written with the syllables *ka-ki-tu-ha-ta*).

| 唐衣 | kara koromo |
| きつつなれにし | kitutu narenisi |

つましあれば　　　　tuma si areba
はるばるきぬる　　　harubaru kinuru
旅をしぞ思ふ　　　　tabi wo si zo omohu

I continue unwinding into the distance
Roaming in the familiar folds of a Kara robe
I linger with regret on my journey
Stitched with longing for my long-worn wife.

Any annotated edition gives the details of the pivotwords (kakekotoba) that induce a kind of doubled narrative, but rather than linger on the pivotwords (they turn up later in this section), I look at how the doubled images in the poem repeat the play of the acrostic.

There are two images, one that describes distance and separation, one that describes proximity, familiarity, and attachment. The poet appeals to reattachment over a distance. He recalls her who is far from him as he travels; his robes recall to him the wife who stitched them. The operations of the broken verse thus enable an enactment of the process of recollection. The poem takes apart the word iris, only to re-collect it, literally. The broken verse thereby enacts a re-collection of elements, and this performative re-collection of elements enables the poet's recollection of his wife. Note that the operations of words or names are central to the poetic act. The breaking and re-collecting of names (or words) underlies the act of reminiscence itself. Images and acts align with the operations of words. The name is broken and re-collected, the wife is separated from him yet recalled. The distance between man and wife is the distance between syllables in the name kakituhata. In addition, the poem evokes the finery of the Kara robes in which he travels; the stitches that the wife kindly sewed are akin to the bonds that bring the word back together. Words or names hold together with a kind of affective force; syllables may be sundered but the name tends to, even longs to, collect and coalesce—just as lovers do.

The force that binds words is something other than grammatical or linguistic: it lies at the heart of an attachment at once erotic and cosmic. It is for this reason, no doubt, that Ki no Tsurayuki claims that poems soothe relations between man and wife; he also submits that poems move between heaven and earth, calm the ferocity of the warrior and pacify the spirits of the dead. If poems have such cosmological potential, it is because they deal with the forces implicit in words.

The linguistic treatment of waka, however, tends to push analysis in a very different direction. It passes over the erotic and cosmic bonds of words in order to stress a purely rhetorical space. The rhetorical treatment of poems pretends that Heian poets believed in the ethnolinguistic boundaries of speech, not the cosmic and erotic affinities of words. Akiyama Ken, a prominent postwar scholar, established such an interpretation of *Kokin waka*. He claims that, whereas *Man'yō* songs dissolve into nature, the *Kokin* poems construct a world of words at a remove from nature. Akiyama relates the construction of a world of words to the courtiers' ability to write with kana, which he construes as a phonetic script. Thus the poetic construction of rhetorical space is conflated with the construction of a speech community, and he aligns waka expression, kana inscription, Japanese speech, and Japanese community.[1]

It is this movement from poetic space to ethnolinguistic community that must be challenged. That is why I center my account of waka composition on the broken verse, to call attention to certain suppressed aspects of waka. The broken verse reminds us that the Heian imagination of signs did not exclude the operations of Chinese characters. On the contrary, it works with them. Moreover, it places the emphasis on the cosmological forces at the heart of words. The broken verse shows how Heian poetry deals with the dynamic forces implicit in signs, how it harnesses their generative potential. Heian poetics does not promote static, ethnic particularism or phonetic, linguistic boundaries. What would it matter what language one speaks when one cultivates cosmic forces through signs?

The operations of the broken verse rely on (what one might call) nonlinguistic, nongrammatical operations. Broken verse uses combinatory operations, and the poetic interest of such operations lies precisely in their ability to link microlevel events (breaking and re-collecting the elements of names) with macrolevel events (travel, separation, reunion, etc.). These operations derive from an aesthetic of the Chinese character. This is not the only way in which Chinese characters can be imagined or deployed, but it is the trajectory that informs the Heian imagination.

Within Chinese poetics, poems that take characters apart and put them together are called "poems of parting and joining" (離合詩).[2] The parting-joining poem is one in which a character or name is separated or parsed into components in order to recombine them. The last chapter gave some examples from Heian waka and kanshi, including the *Kokinwakashū* poem that disassembles the character 梅 (plum tree) in order to ask whether the snow on its every branch (木毎) could not be spring flowers; it thus enacts a parting and joining of winter (snow) and spring (plum flowers). Likewise, the "iris" poem enacts a separation and a re-collection of kakituhata, but in a manner that recalls a journey's partings and recollections.

Appropriately, the "iris" acrostic appears in the scroll of travel poems in *Kokinwakashū* that follows the scroll of poems of separation, which use similar conceits, such as how to remember the one who is far distant. The "iris" poem uses kana to enact the journey's distance and remembrance, graphically and in its composition. Its operations are not unlike those of the "assembled character" brushed inside the earthenware vessel discussed in chapter 1), which was supposed to comfort lovers during a separation: assembling the characters 我, 君, and 念 into a single character enacts a joining together at the moment of parting. This is an art of arranging things, and of combining or composing elements. Even though the broken verse uses Yamato names (kana), it frankly duplicates the compositional or combinatory operations of Han names (mana).

The parting and joining of names brings into play the relations within words, between words, between words and humans, between humans, between humans and places, between humans and seasons, and so forth. Poetics thus uses names or characters to align relations and forces that arise on different levels: as in names, so in humans; as between names, so between humans and between seasons. Take this example of a Han-style acrostic from a later Heian collection, *Wakanrōeishū* or "Collection of Yamato and Han Cantillations" (ca. 1013).

物色自堪傷客意　宜将愁字作秋心
[物の色は自ら客の意を傷ましむるに堪へたり
　　宜なり愁の字をも秋の心　に作れること]
Autumnal hues, autumnal passions, as a matter of course,
weather and grieve the traveler's heartfelt thoughts:
truly the word "downhearted" is made of a "fall" of the "heart." [3]

This poem discloses the secret wisdom of the name or character for grief, sorrow, lament (愁). The character comprises two other characters, autumn or fall (秋) and heart or mind (心). The poem unfolds a purely conventional scenario, that of a traveler who misses a loved one and notes the passing of summer into autumn. The poem doubles this autumnal story with the lament for a passion that fades even while its colors linger; a memory that fades even while its shape lingers.

Remembrance in this poem has none of the qualities of internalized trauma that a Romantic reading of this poem might evoke. There is no expression of an interior realm, but rather a parting and joining of forms and surfaces: superimpositions and afterimages. Remembrance takes place through a literal re-collection of characters. The ability to do things with words prevails. This is one reason why such poetry (and the waka of Kokin-wakashū in particular) often receives criticism for being overly mechanical and rational. Such poetry seems to display little interest in personal profundity but rather emphasizes the mechanics and materials of writing, for it is through signs that greater forces are cultivated.

The above acrostic gives the most conventional of Heian poetic sentiments: autumn is sad. Its creativity lies in its assemblage of names, rendered in translation as fall (秋) + heart (心) = downhearted (愁). Its effectiveness stems from the way in which the act of parting and joining characters aligns relations over vast scales. The components of 愁 move apart—but only so far—and then rejoin. There is a figural economy, a limit to the dispersion of the character; the character promotes motion between elements but only just so much. (For instance, the character 心 does not disband into scattered strokes.) Only in this way can it implicate the movements of seasons and asterisms. There is movement between summer and fall, between fall and winter, but only so much. The forces that direct the paths of constellations cause motion but not dispersion. The microcosm of the character can enact the macrocosm because a similar economy of forces—that of channeled or directed motions—informs both.

The emotions of humans move along the same path as words and seasons. The sad and fond recollections of the traveler (for what he leaves behind) twine with his sorrow for the autumn colors that mark the passage of the seasons. (One might think of emotions literally, as e-motions or outward motions.) Indeed, autumn captures the motions of seasons and emotions of the traveler in one passion (with a vibrant erotic charge). The poem thus situates and directs human emotion along a specific path, one that follows the lines of force implicit in words and seasons. On all levels—the force that binds words, the force that spurs humans, the force that links seasons—the poem allows for separation and thus for motion but prevents dispersion by sustaining "natural" bonds. This is poetics on an intimate, material, immanent level and on a vast, cosmological scale. For this reason, interpretations that center the poem on the expression of human emotion miss the mark. This is not a human-centered poetics. If it calls attention to human actions, motions, and emotions, it is to make these resonate with the forces implicit in words and the motions of stars.

It is common knowledge that the convention "autumn is sad" became prominent at the Heian court in the late eighth and early ninth century, largely through the Six Dynasties poetics, which informed the three imperial anthologies of Han shih (or kanshi) at the early Heian court. Suzuki Hideo, in his study of waka, discusses in detail the Chinese forms, sources, and channels that established "autumn is sad" in Heian poetics.[4] Nonetheless, even though such links between waka and kanshi are acknowledged on one level (influence), they are denied on another level. We recall that Suzuki acknowledges the Chineseness of themes and images but finds linguistic purity and autonomy in the emergence of kana.

Since new terminology alone (say, Middle Kingdom and Heian court) does not overturn this bias, I wish to underscore the idea that "autumn is sad" is not a mere poetic convention that can be subordinated to the emergence of native language or the indigenous mind. "Autumn is sad" evokes a network of forms and forces that cannot be subsumed or excluded by the dimension of language (that is, language narrowly defined as speech).

The second scroll of autumn poems in *Kokinwakashū* opens with an acrostic-style verse by Funya no Yasuhide (KKS 5:249) that turns on the breaking and re-collecting of a Chinese character (嵐). Ki no Tsurayuki, in his preface, complains about the paucity of its sentiment but praises its skilful use of words.[5] He lauds the play with Han names, which, together with the verse's prime position at the head of a scroll, should overturn any claims that *Kokin* waka strived to distance themselves absolutely from Han script. As for Tsurayuki's comments on sentiment, it is true that Yasuhide's play on characters allows little room for the articulation of human sentiment. Yasuhide's poem does not even clearly say "autumn is sad." Yet we should not suppose that Tsurayuki wants the poem to center on human emotion: what he points to is the poem's failure to relate emotions to the motions of words and seasons. The poem uses the forces of words and seasons but fails to sandwich emotions between them. The poet asks, is it because mountain (山) and wind (風) together compose tempest (嵐) that we call a wind from the mountains a tempest?

是貞親王家歌合の歌　文屋康秀
吹くからに秋の草木のしをるればむべ山かぜをあらしといふらむ
A poem from the poetry contest at Prince Koresada's residence, Funya

no Yasuhide

With gusts that blow, autumn Pampas and bUSHES are PUSHED
down: is this not why one calls Gusts from the dALES GALES?[6]

Naturally, it is impossible to render the character play in translation, because it moves so deftly from kana to mana (deftly as the brush shifts the
contours of styles). The play on the character 嵐 moves in between kana and
mana. The mana name 嵐 appears in kana as あらし, and only when one
converts between kana and mana does one see the logic of the riddle-like
question about mountain gusts (山風).

This style of word play recalls what Wittgenstein calls "seeing as." For
Wittgenstein, seeing entails a description, a copy, or an indication—I see
this. "Seeing as," however, entails likeness or resemblance. "I contemplate
a face, and then suddenly notice its likeness to another," he writes. "I see
that it has not changed; and yet I see it differently." Wittgenstein calls this
experience "noticing an aspect."[7]

So too with the characters in Yasuhide's poem: one contemplates the
characters 山 and 風 then suddenly notices their likeness to 嵐; or one contemplates the characters あらし and recollects the character 嵐 and then 山
and 風; or some combination of these events occurs. The rebus-like style
of composition or combination is not about seeing (description, representation, indication) but about "seeing as." Wittgenstein's remarks thus call
attention to the proximity of the operations of acrostic verse and those of
"visual overlap" (mitate): both constitute modes of "seeing as."

In a general way, Wittgenstein uses "seeing as" in order to question
whether language is a picture of reality, and he concludes that language
does not picture things. To understand an utterance is not to know what
it pictures but to explore what it does, how it functions, what purpose it
serves. Likewise with the "seeing as" of broken verse or visual confusion: it
is a way for the poetic utterance to show its functions, purposes, and operations. The waka utterance does not try to depict things or paint pictures; it
strives to do things with words.

So far I have discussed two specific operations: (1) how to make kana resemble mana (to make kana and mana into aspects of the other) and, thus
(2), to channel the cosmic forces implicit in Han names and forms.

We have seen that Yasuhide's poem, as Tsurayuki notes, falls short in the
realm of sentiment or emotion. In Tsurayuki's own poems, on the other
hand, the operations of words act directly on human emotions, bringing

order to their mobility and intensity. An acrostic poem Ki no Tsurayuki wrote for a flower contest (Suzukuin no wominahesi ahase) held in 898 appears in *Kokinwakashū* (10:439). Its style recalls the "iris" poem; as I did with that poem, I translate freely in order to mimic the acrostic, rendering the name *wominahesi* as "ladyflower." The flower *wominahesi* (*Patrinia scabiosae-folia*) is often rendered as "maidenflower" in translation (*womina* implies maiden). Of course, these aspects of the name do not paint a picture of a maiden or a flower. They evoke the functions of words.

朱雀院女郎合の時に、をみなへしといふ五文字を、句のかしらにおきてよ
　　める　　つらゆき

小倉山	wogurayama
峰たちたらし	mine tatiratasi
鳴く鹿の	naku sika no
経にけむ秋を	henikemu aki wo
知る人ぞなき	siru hito zo naki

On the occasion of the cloistered emperor's contest of ladyflowers,
Tsurayuki recounted this, placing the five characters for ladyflower at
the head of each segment of the verse,
Longstanding, lovelorn,
Along the peak of Ogura the stag
Does bellow, passing
Year after year of autumns unknown, unrequited.[8]

Tsurayuki presents a stag bellowing in the autumn hills, a stag who yearns for, yet cannot find, his mate. She is missed and missing, this lady. Yet, as other aspects of the poem emerge, she appears, encrypted in the name wo-minahesi, lost yet re-collected. L-A-D-Y hovers on the verge of emergence and disappearance. The forces that bind words hold the L-A-D-Y together in her dispersed state. Likewise, the forces of longing—that recall her to him—conjure forth the vanished woman. The stag bellows forlorn for his mate, and his calls recall her. His crying summons her, just as the words of the poem summon forth wominahesi. The final phrase *hito zo naki* suggests both "there is no one" and "someone cries." Is she not there? Or does she cry out in response? Is the lady(flower) hidden in the poem or summoned by it?

Tsurayuki's poem hovers between loss and re-collection in several registers, across which the operations of words mesh with those of the seasons. Human emotions are caught between the two, and their motions are thus directed or channeled. As in the "fall of the heart" poem, the time of Tsura-yuki's poem is autumn, when summer slips away like a beloved left behind. For the bellowing stag, seasons pass, fading one into another, and years pile up. In the moment of autumnal passage, all other autumnal passages recur. Autumn upon autumn, year upon year, the stag continues his lovelorn quest, his love unknown and unrequited. What prevents his emotions from passing, from dispersing and diminishing with the years? Because each autumn is every autumn, the emotion hovers undiminished in the space of words.

Tsurayuki's acrostic also evokes the pattern of the "iris" acrostic attributed to one of the Six Poetic Immortals of the mid-ninth century, Ariwara no Narihira, in the same anthology in the scroll on travels. And so, its pattern thus recalls (or re-collects) another poem. In this way too, poems harness eternity, with a literal re-collection of other eras, poets, and signs.

Each autumn is every autumn, because its signs or names are fixed. This is the great project of *Kokinwakashū*: to fix the relations between words, emotions, occasions (not in order to inhibit motion but to channel it). The two scrolls of autumn poems establish the sequence of signs that aligns with the cycle of autumn: cool wind, brilliant moon, cricket chirps, bush clover, wild geese, bellowing deer, maidenflowers, suzuki grasses, colored leaves, autumnal mist, chrysanthemums, scattering leaves, and so on—a network of signs and sensations that in various combinations repeats the moments of autumn. In this way, signs intersect and unfold in accordance with the movement of asterisms: the scrolls of autumn begin with the encounter of two constellations in the sky. In accordance with Chinese cosmology and mythology, on the seventh day of the seventh month, the "herd boy" (Alstair) and the "weaver maid" (Vega) cross the celestial river (the Milky Way)—the two constellations meet, only to part again. A series of poems sings of the moments of their reunion and separation, establishing on several levels—of sign, sensation, asterism, and so on—the breaks and links that activate the turn of the season. Signs and asterisms move in syncopation, and emotions emerge in alignment with specific signs and sensations, recurring in accordance to (in time with) cosmic rhythms. The order of signs is not an arbitrary system of expression but a form of knowledge that follows from contemplation or observation of the spatiotemporal nexus of celestial and terrestrial events.

It is a Han-derived form of cosmological knowledge that informs the unfolding of signs and poems, most obviously in the seasonal scrolls of waka. Tsurayuki's poem, however, occurs not in the seasonal scrolls, but in the scroll on "names of things" (*mono no na*, 物名). The compilers of *Kokinwakashū* (among them chief compiler Tsurayuki) organized the 1,111 waka into twenty scrolls, and these twenty scrolls are divided roughly into two cycles of ten each. The first ten scrolls move through the four seasons, from the first day of the new year in spring to the last day of winter (in six scrolls); winter then leads into scrolls on congratulations, separations, journeys, and finally, names of things. After the names of things, scrolls eleven through fifteen begin the cycle of love poems, and these move from the moment before lovers meet, through their union, and to its subsequent dissolution. The love scrolls segue into scrolls on grief and miscellaneous poems, forms, and styles. Names of things (scroll ten) thus arise at the fulcrum of the two major cycles (seasons and love), presenting another register of poetic knowledge and practice, which clearly overlaps with the logic of seasons and emotions. In this respect, the scroll on names of things lies at the heart of the logic of poetic signs or names.

Names, characters, words, signs—synonymous in the Heian order— have an energy and consistency that is not simply external (derived from the celestial order) but also internal (constitutive of their elements). Like Chinese characters, kana names can be disassembled and reassembled, but there are limits to the deconstruction of the sign or name. The figural play allowed by the movement of the elements of the sign shows that it does not have, and does not aim at, logocentric or phonocentric consistency. Nevertheless, it is not a site of sheer dissemination or differentiation: only because forces bind together the mobile elements of names or signs can these elements be re-collected. Because the forces within signs mimic or repeat the mobile consistency of asterisms, I will call them "constellar." The sign mimics constellar forces and arises at their juncture; the sign manifests constellar forces. Ultimately then, because the forces associated with signs or names are at once internal and external to them, I propose that we think of them as "transversal." In sum, the waka utterance uses signs or names to manifest the consistency of things (to "constellate" them as it were) and to align various levels of action and interaction, motion and emotion (i.e., to "transverse" them).

Because the logic of acrostic-style waka overturns the simplistic notions of language and script that underlie the cultural and national essentialism of numerous postwar waka studies, it is not surprising that many scholars do not know what to make of them. Helen McCullough, in her study of *Kokinwakashū*, simply bypasses the logic of "names of things" by asserting that it deviates from the usual *Kokin* aesthetic standards. She concludes that the poems of this scroll are "negligible as literature" because they consist of nothing more than literary games rather than serious literature.[9] By writing off poetic play as trivial, however, McCullough is dismissing more than acrostic styles; she is also refusing any attempt to discuss the language games of waka in their own terms.[10]

The poetic games of acrostic verse are worthy of critical attention, not only because they demonstrate the logic of the poetic signs but also because they overlap with other politico-poetic games. The last two acrostic-style verses in *Kokinwakashū*, for instance, come from matches or contests (*awase*). Yasuhide's acrostic is attributed to a "contest of poems" (*utaawase*), and Tsurayuki's broken verse to a "contest of things" (*monoawase*). I return below to the structure of these games and their relation to the poetic composition. First I wish to review how the logic of the constellar, transversal sign relates to the general structure of Heian waka.

Fortunately, there are commentators who, unlike McCullough, do not force poems that deal with names of things into the margins of Heian poetics. The linguist Tokieda Motoki relates these acrostic-style waka to the structures deemed most characteristic of waka poetry—kakekotoba or pivotwords. The pivotword is a kind of double entendre in which one word calls another—for example, the word *kiku* evokes both *chrysanthemum* and *to hear*—and because the double entendre frequently shifts between two grammatical elements (noun and verb, or adjective and noun, or verb and adjective, etc.), the structure of the waka tends to pivot or turn, moving syntactically in two directions.

Categories like "pivotword" do not appear in Heian criticism (which uses terms like *kokoro*, *kotoba*, and *sama* or *sugata*, that is, *heart*, *word*, and *form*). The panoply of modern critical terms applied to Heian waka often derive from the late medieval or early modern periods: for example, *makurakotoba* or *pillow-word*, *utamakura* or *poem-pillow*, *joshi* or *preface*, and *engo* or *kinword*. These are later attempts to parse court poetics, and, as such, their purveyance of Heian poetics entails a particular perspective. A great deal of waka criticism directs its energies toward defining and quantifying these categories, as if doing so would forever decide and resolve all problems of interpretation. Yet such categories provide no more than hints and clues for analyzing waka. Frequently, scholars devote so much attention to the quantification of a figure that they omit any analysis of its operations. Tokieda, however, offers a way to cut to the quick of such rhetorical categories, approaching the pivotword in terms of its general structure and aesthetics.[11]

He diagrams the structure of the Japanese utterance in terms of a series of nested boxes. He sees the pivotword as part of this nested structure, and yet the pivotword also opens the nested boxes, which then overlap like interlinked sets. He identifies three aesthetic modes in which the poetic utterance opens into such interlinked segments: the aesthetics of pleasantry, of harmony, and of melody. Tokieda situates the names of things, together with pivotwords, in the aesthetics of pleasantry. To some extent, he tends to lead everything back into the Japanese sentence, which leads to a flattening of the differences between classical and modern Japanese. Nevertheless, his nested-box approach opens the possibility for other discussions of poetic language games by providing the impetus to look at the operations of broken verse in relation to the general operations of waka.

The scroll on names of things includes a series of poems that conceal the name of a bird, flower, insect, or place. Tsurayuki's broken verse on wominahesi is one example. The majority of name poems, however, do not follow the style of broken verse with the name parsed in syllables at the head of each segment. Most conceal the name within the poetic line, as a hidden topic, whence the other designation for such poems—*kakushidai* or "hidden topics."[12] There is a poem by Fujiwara no Toshiyuki (10:423) that encloses and discloses the word *hototokisu* (cuckoo). Somewhat whimsically and anachronistically, I render hototokisu as *nightingale* in order to simulate the play of the poem. The first line is a transliteration from an original calligraphic text, and a modern transliteration follows in brackets.[13]

> ほとときす　　　　藤原としゆき
> くへきほととききすきぬれや万ちわひてなくなるこゑの人をとよむる
> ［来べきほど時過ぎぬれや待ちわびて鳴くなる声の人をとよむる］
>
>   Nightingale　　　　Fujiwara no Toshiyuki
> Is it from waiting for one who should come,
> passing the night in gales of crying,
> that grief sings out?

Although the technique of such a poem is dubbed "hidden topic," the name hototokisu is far from hidden: it functions as the topic for the poem as well as a response to the riddle it poses. The poet awaits the arrival of something or someone long overdue. The encrypted name discloses that arrival: the hototokisu, which signals the arrival of summer. (The scroll of summer poems begins with a poem that sings of anticipation for the hototokisu.) The poet waits for the resonant call of the cuckoo, and when at last the cuckoo cries, its voice mingles with the forlorn cries of the poet who waits.

Seasonal interpretation dominates the commentary on this poem; and yet, like so many waka, the erotic charge of the poem renders it a love poem as well. The cry of the cuckoo in the night is the cry of one who awaits its mate. The utterance might be that of a woman, listening to the plaintive call of the cuckoo, who passes the night in tears waiting for a lover who does not show up. As in the broken verse, the style of the hidden topic depends on the coherence of the name; the figure of the name emerges from the message of the poem and turns the poetic utterance back on itself and beyond itself. The figure of the name answers to the mysteries posed in the utterance: what or who cries out, and why? The answer resounds (*toyomu*): the cuckoo. Yet even as the cuckoo clarifies the scene of the poem, it complicates its voice. The poem at once cries out for the cuckoo and cries out in response to it. From this double cry, this moment of ventriloquy, emerges two possibilities: (1) The poet waits anxiously for the arrival of summer till the cry of the cuckoo signals its arrival; (2) the poet waits, and in a state of anxiety, cries out.

As in so many *Kokin* waka, it is hard to say why this poem should be considered a seasonal poem rather than a love poem. Once narratives are doubled in this way, the poem seems to extend in both directions: the arrival of summer and the arrival of a lover are indistinguishable, as likewise are the cries of the bird and of the one who waits. That is precisely the function of poetic signs in waka: to act at various levels and to align them. The anticipation of a lover and the anticipation of summer are aspects of one force, a force at once emotive and cosmological. It is the poetic name that enacts those forces, because the name oscillates between two aspects. In this instance, hototokisu oscillates between a noun, cuckoo (時鳥) and a kind of adverbial fragment, passing time as (程時過). In this way, the poem disperses the consistency of the name into a grammatical fragment; and yet, to read the poem, one must reassemble or recollect the name. The operations of the sign simultaneously evoke and align verbal, emotional, and seasonal levels: between elements of a name, between seasons, between lovers arises a force that makes all these levels consistent and coherent.

The pivotword operates in a similar fashion, through the ventriloquy of the poetic sign or name. The three syllables *nagame* evoke "gazing" and "long rains"; the three syllables *mirume* evoke "seaweeds" and "eyes that see"; the two syllables *oki* evoke both "settling" and "rising." Because these figures rely on operations of sound rather than image, accounts of the pivotword often stress the importance of speech. Akiyama Ken relates the pivotword to the emergence of kana. Because he sees kana as a mode of phonetic transcription, he claims that the pivotword depends, first and foremost, on the transparency of writing. Only with phonetic transcription could the pivotword emerge; only phonetic writing, he assumes, can make sound play possible. Overall, his is an attempt to ground the pivotword in native speech. It is an attempt to tie rhetoric to national language and to an ethnolinguistic community. However, the proximity of the pivotword to the acrostic mode suggests that the pivotword is not particularly concerned with Japanese speech. It concerns the production of a specific kind of figure, related to the operations implicit in Han names. It is equally characteristic of the Chinese poetic forms then in vogue at the Heian court. In fact, Chinese poems also use characters that, like the pivotword, simultaneously evoke a place name and a human state.[14] Still, it is not necessary to seek a one-to-one correspondence between Yamato and Han poetic devices. One need only recall the performative and figural qualities of waka and kana. These inevitably lead away from the nationalist closure of current studies of waka rhetoric.

Amagasaki Akira, for instance, takes an unusual stance vis-à-vis the pivotword. He adopts a structuralist view of waka and emphasizes their performative elements. He relates the pivotword to mitate, the poetic operation of visual confusion (or seeing as), which he describes in terms of a cinematic overlap dissolve. In his opinion, pivotwords and visual overlap call for greater efforts on the part of the recipient, particularly with respect to characters. He suggests that, rather than an easy two-stage movement from perception to comprehension, double vision in waka adds a third stage in which there occurs an "objectification of the form of the character," a stage that comes between perception and comprehension. In short, he denies the transparency of the kana character. Amagasaki follows the linguistics of Jakobson, finding a reification and objectification of words in waka: waka render language opaque by means of doubleness, and that is what makes waka into nondaily speech—that is, poetic speech.[15] His remarks are very much to the point, but I would add that aesthetic reification should not mark the end of analysis. Amagasaki is content to have shown the nondaily literary status of waka through formalist analysis, but the nontransparency he finds in waka then demands some account of the functions of those opaque or reified signs.

Yoshino Tatsunori takes the discussion of the pivotword in the direction of the materiality of writing. He begins his account by challenging Akiyama Ken by asking, Can phonetic writing alone explain the emergence of pivotwords? After all, he argues, plenty of poems in *Man'yōshū* incur a similar "conceptual evocation of doubleness." There are, for example those place names that evoke a sense of doubleness, as with the name Furuyama in which *furu* (to wave) relates to rituals of sleeve-waving that summon souls. Yoshino claims that, by the time of *Kokinwakashū*, this ritual use of words has given way to conceptual or metaphysical operations. In *Kokinwakashū*, he suggests, there occurs a "mutual adaptation of vocality and the materiality of *écriture*." [16]

Yoshino uses an example from the start of the first scroll of love poems in *Kokinwakashū* (11:470), a poem composed by Sosei, a poet of Tsurayuki's generation. In order to mimic the operations of the pivotwords, I use "a rose" for "chrysanthemum" because "a rose" suggests "arose," a play on words that breaks the syntax into two lines, and also because it allows a second pivot around "lying" (in both senses of *to lie*). I add the word *mum* as gesture toward the chrysanthemum.

> 音にのみきくの白露夜はおきて昼は思ひにあへず消ぬべし
> Sounds, rumors of him,
> arose in the night with dewdrops lying mum
> in the sun will vanish
> unable to endure such longing.

At the start of the first scroll of love poems, the future lovers have not yet seen each other or met; they know each other first through rumors and then through glimpses. In this waka from the early love songs, there are two images and two stories: dew that beads on flowers during the night only to vanish in the light of day and a woman who lies awake in the night, hearing rumors that he will visit her. He does not visit, and by the time day arrives, she can no longer bear her longing—it becomes so intense that she is on the verge of vanishing like the dew in the morning sun. A series of pivotwords twine these two narratives. Kiku evokes both "chrysanthemum" and "to hear or harken." *Okite* combines the person who "lies awake" with the dew that "settles." Whence the two stories: (1) dew settles on the chrysanthemum at night, and (2) she lies awake at night, harkening to rumors of him. The last phrase twines and completes both scenarios, with the phrase "unable to endure, vanishes" (*ahezu kinubesi*). Note, too that, the male poet Sosei speaks in a feminine voice that doubles itself with the dew, engendering two levels of ventriloquy: he speaks in her, and she speaks in the dew.

The English translation attempts to mimic some of these twists and doubles. The words *arose* and *lying* allow a number of pivots: "sounds arose, lying" (I heard he would come, but he didn't); "arose in the night" (I lay awake); "a rose in the night with dewdrops lying" (I lay like beads of dew gathering on chrysanthemums); "dewdrops lying in the sun will vanish" (like dew I will vanish in the day, just as these rumors lied and brought nothing).

Yet this is all very awkward. Yoshino explains that the double narratives of "dew" and "me" create confusion; there is a breakdown in logical order, a pivoting, twisting movement of signification—so much confusion that only the fixed syllabic pattern—5-7-5-7-7—ensures the verse's consistency. In short, Yoshino arrives at the importance of rhythm and figure in his account of the pivotword and links the rhythmic figure to writing. It is the materiality of writing (which he styles écriture) that makes the structure of the pivotwords apparent. This is an extremely important point: Yoshino relates the consistency of waka to writing by asserting the figural and rhythmic status of the pivotword.

His analysis rests with this insight, however, leaving a somewhat ambiguous sense of what nuance he wishes to give to writing. What is more, a great deal of ambiguity remains with respect to the status of Chinese characters. These points demand closer attention.

Yoshino concludes that "kana may have abstracted and extracted the ideographism from Chinese characters, but the method of reading and writing kana gave linguistic substance to a standard that goes one step beyond the level of transcribing sound." [17] He says that kana strip away and simplify the "ideographism" of Chinese characters but concludes that kana, nevertheless, do not entail a mere transcription of sound—the kana standard moves beyond phonographic transcription. How then do the material and figural functions of kana relate to Chinese characters? It is difficult to pin down Yoshino on this point. His remarks suggest that kana move away from Chinese characters, and then move beyond phonetic transcription into the realm of écriture. Kana seem to gain a special privilege: they outdistance Chinese characters and outstrip phonetic transcription. On the one hand, I agree with Yoshino that kana usage is neither ideographic nor phonographic: it is figural, it relates to writing more than speech. On the other hand, I would not sever the linkage to Chinese characters, for this is where we can approach the specific functions of kana figurality.

In Yoshino's account, it is the notion of écriture that leads to an impasse. Roland Barthes, for instance, used écriture specifically to question certain modern notions of writing (such as the referential illusion, the readerly, and the naive realism that would treat writing as transparent and immaterial). If Heian writing seems to dovetail nicely with écriture, it is because its treatment of signs is not modern. Nonetheless, to equate kana with écriture leaves no room for a historical articulation of kana usage and waka practice. Barthes himself created much of this confusion with his deliberately fantastical account of contemporary Japan, in which he conflated Japanese writing with écriture. In any event, to associate kana with écriture simply equates Heian poetics with modernist or postmodernist space. Such an approach is defensible if modernity is identified as the site of critique, but historicization then becomes essential. Yoshino aptly debunks phonetic fantasies about waka and kana, but he fails to explain what kind of materiality kana do entail. The interpretation of kana demands two gestures: the notion of écriture serves to deconstruct the phonetic text and to remind us that kana entail material and figural operations (Yoshino does this nicely); but it is then imperative to broach the specific construction of that materiality or figurality.

In some texts, kana border on pictography—as in the calligraphic style known as the "reed hand" (ashide). In the grass style, the brush moves through the series of characters so fluidly that elements of signs begin to look like supple blades of grass; in the reed hand, characters actually merge with images, taking on the form of a crane, or a leaf, or a bug. Poem and picture continually intertwine. It is a common subject of debate whether the reed hand constitutes a style of writing or of drawing; commentators usually conclude that it is impossible to differentiate between writing and drawing in this context.

Joshua Mostow, for one, sees many examples of the interpenetration of poem and picture in Heian texts. One, a waka from the first scroll of Kokinwakashū on spring (KKS 1:27) by Henzeu, the rector of monasteries, is about the green strands of spring willows. The poem winds its way over an illustration of a monk standing by the gate of a temple beneath a willow tree. The picture presents the topic for the poem: "composed of the willows near the West Great Temple." Initially, it would seem that the calligraphy of the poem simply moves over the picture, but then some of the kana take on the forms of the birds and leaves on the tree. Such reed-hand kana oscillate between sound and image. In another example, the intersection of sound and image takes the form of a rebus or riddle: three birds in flight are to be read as *midori* or green—from *mittsu* (three) and *tori* (bird). For these types of sound-image interactions, Mostow coins the term "visual pivot." [18] His account provides an insight similar to Yoshino's: kana and waka cannot be explained in phonetic terms alone. Whereas Yoshino arrives at the rhythmic qualities of kana, Mostow stresses the visual dimension of waka.

In the Heian period, the figurality of waka inscription was subject to any number of regulations. The art of calligraphy itself imposed certain limitations, one of which, the requirement for legibility, demanded knowledge of Han names or characters. In addition, Heian poetic criticism directs attention to the repetition of characters (*moji*) in waka. Fujiwara Kintō, in the *Shinsen zuinō* (ca. 1004–1012), warns of "character maladies" (*moji yamai*). It is important, he writes, to avoid certain types of repetition in waka, even in the use of characters. It is permitted to repeat the same kana character, provided it is used with different "heart" in the two instances. Kintō uses the example of the character 久 deployed in three different ways. But he also advises against repetition when the words differ yet the heart is the same: his warning refers specifically to a poem using both *nagisa* (water's edge) and *migiha* (water's edge). The same prohibitions about words extend to kana: he warns against a poem in which the character 久 appears twice with the same intent (both times as an honorific). [19] Note that he treats words or names as if they were characters, and vice versa. Moreover, his advice on repetition treats kana characters and kana words in much the same way as it does Chinese characters.

To point out the overlap of kana and Chinese characters is, in some respects, nothing new. Yoshimoto Taka'aki, in his study of early Japanese songs, declares that, no matter how far back one looks, everything Japanese bears the mark of the Chinese character. He even finds the Chinese character at the heart of those forms most associated with native expression (early prayers and such). He also declares that the nature aesthetic of early Japan, so long deemed native, derives from Chinese aesthetics. [20] His remarks run counter to the usual nativist bias. And yet, a certain emotionalism pervades his account, an emotionalism that often glosses over the history that could be specified or differentiated. "Look to China," he insists. Yet what in China are we to look to? This is not exactly clear.[21] For this reason, it is important to call attention to the Heian logic of the poetic sign.

Thus far, I have traced a sinuous path through various poems in order to look at the operations of signs in Heian poetics. In opposition to the currently entrenched equation of kana with the transcription of speech and the demarcation of ethnolinguistic boundaries, I have stressed the figural operations of names within waka. Often, in the secondary literature, figural operations are ignored or denied. On the other hand, when scholars turn to visual, rhythmic, or rebus-like operations, they seem content to merely indicate the existence of these overlooked qualities; there is little attempt to explore their functions or implications, or to challenge the linguistic model. I propose that the figural operations of names relate to a constellar and transversal logic of the sign, which in turn relates to a cosmological imagination of human activity and society. Much of the third part of this book deals with that cosmological imagination of community. At this juncture, however, I would like to present one of the primary sites of waka composition: *awase* (contests, competitions, or matches).

A brief overview of awase will highlight some of its relations to waka poetics. First, the rise of waka poetry paralleled the rise of poetry contests, especially during the reigns of the emperors Kōkō (884–887) and Uda (887–897).[22] *Kokinwakashū* includes a number of poems from poetry contests. In the late ninth and early tenth centuries, the production of waka was apparently closely related to poetry contests. (The acrostics by Yasuhide and Tsurayuki discussed earlier in the chapter are attributed to awase.) While there were a number of occasions and sites for poetic composition, contests seem to have provided a format in which poems from a variety of other sites could be brought into a common space—a space of competition. Second, a strong analogy can be drawn between the logic of pairs and comparison in awase and that of stylistic pairs and comparison around kana-mana and waka-kanshi. This analogy suggests a certain structure common to the composition of waka and to the interaction of courtiers. I take these structural analogies as evidence of a kind of discursive field—a middle ground between poetics and politics—that informs the Heian order and grounds a regime of doubles. Finally, because awase are, above all, competitions, they remind us that the cosmological imagination of community does not entail some holistic sense of belonging to the cosmos but, on the contrary, involves intense struggle for ranks, titles, goods, and so forth.

A number of poems survive from the match of maidenflowers in 898 at the residence of the retired emperor Uda. The manuscript includes, after the twenty-two poems presented at the match, additional poems that were not recited or included in the contest, probably because of time restraints or unsuitability. Among these poems are several acrostic poems, some of which apply the operations of broken verse twice; that is, they encrypt wominahesi at both ends of each line or segment. The following poem uses the variant *wominatesi* (which I again translate freely with the acrostic L-A-D-Y).

をる人を　　　　　　woru hito wo
みな怨めしみ　　　　mina uramesimi
なげくかな　　　　　nageku kana
てる日にあてて　　　teru hi ni atete
しもにおかせじ　　　simo ni okasesi

Lament we all feeL
At one who plucks a patriniA
Desiring to keep it from frost so colD
Yearning to keep it in the sun of daY [23]

By now, these operations may seem familiar. The poem plays with the dispersion and re-collection of a name, which emerges as a rhythmic figure (in this case doubled). Moreover, as with other acrostic poems, the ability of the name to hide and appear serves to mimic the movement of the seasons.

The moment of the wominatesi flower is early autumn, recalling the movement from summer sun to fall frost. Because "autumn is sad," the poet duly includes a sense of sorrow for the passage of time. This sorrow takes the form of an impossible effort to make time stand still. Someone plucks the flower to keep it from the frost, to keep it in the summer-like warmth of the sun. The flower will fade nevertheless—it is impossible to hold back the passage of seasons. Thus the poem oscillates between summer and fall, enacting the motion between seasons in a way that holds time at the moment of passage. While the wominatesi still blooms, the fullness of summer is not entirely gone, and the fullness of autumn is not entirely arrived—such is the essence of early autumn.

This poem might not be considered particularly good by Heian standards: the repetition of the acrostic, for all its rhetorical rigors, imposes an overly rigid structure that allows for little dispersion or motion, and without a bit of rhetorical divagation there is no sense of human emotion, and thus no way for the poem to link words, emotions, and seasons. (The poem emphasizes the constellar potential of signs yet cuts short the transversal potential; it clumps, as it were.) Nevertheless, such a poem serves as a reminder of the ubiquity of acrostic-style composition, particularly at contests. In addition, the very clumpiness of its structure recalls the intent of the first stage of contests: to pull courtiers together.

Courtiers were not drawn into competitions in a random fashion but in carefully chosen doubles. The general structure of an awase consisted of a number of rounds in which two teams, left and right, brought forth for comparison objects of a particular kind fixed in advance. A monoawase or contest of things, for example, might compare examplars of a certain flower, or sapling, or insect, or some other object deemed characteristic of the season. In an autumn contest of things, the object of comparison might be the chrysanthemum. At the match, each team would present a chrysanthemum, and the qualities of each would be discussed and evaluated, and then two more chrysanthemums would be presented and evaluated, and so forth, round after round, till the contest was ended or a winner was declared.

Since contests were elaborately prepared and organized, other forms entered into the fray. As the poems cited above indicate, poems often accompanied the comparison of things. In such case, a poet might cleverly conceal and disclose the name of the contested flower, as Tsurayuki does with wominahesi. Many of the poems in the scroll on names of things appear to have come from contests of things. Thus utaawase, contests of poems, could run parallel to contests of things. Things and poems were not the only forms to enter into the structure of awase. Large-scale awase organized the efforts of a great number of courtiers and artisans and involved elaborate dress, musical concerts, banquets, manuscript preparations, religious offerings, and exchanges of gifts. The Eawase or "Picture Contest" scroll of The Tale of Genji illustrates the stages and levels of preparation that went into a large-scale awase. In addition there are the passages from the Fukuro no sōshi (Book of Folded Pages) of Fujiwara no Kiyosuke (1104–1177) in which he outlines the regulations and preparations for a poetry contest (which are largely consonant with those that appear in The Tale of Genji).

Once the topic was established, courtiers selected the leaders and supporting members of the two teams. Then began the selection of poems, the preparation of prayers and offerings at shrines for victory, and the commissions for artisans to design tables and scoreboards. In particularly elaborate contests, small gardens were constructed for the presentation of calligraphed poems (suhama). Following the contest, a banquet, with music and dance, accompanied the presentation of gifts in accordance with the excellence of performance. In short, there was an element of potlatch to these large-scale competitions, in which each team strove to outdo the other in lavishness of expenditure and which resulted in a redistribution of wealth and status. As the "Picture Contest" scroll of The Tale of Genji makes clear, the most basic distributions of rank and wealth were caught up in the outcome of large-scale awase: when Genji's team wins the picture contest, his rise to the position of regent to the young emperor is assured, as is his consequent advancement to the rank of "quasi-emperor" (juntennō).

The structural analogy between poem and contest begins with the two-sided impulse to gather and disperse. In the poem this involves the dispersion and re-collection of names or signs. In the contest it entails the collection and redistribution of wealth or status. Significantly, just as the poem relies stylistically on the production of doubleness within the sign, the contest functions through the production of doubles within the court. I have shown that the logic of doubles around kana and waka is not one of opposition, negation, or sublation but rather one of differentiation and coordination. Similarly, the awase causes a mode of doubling that foregoes negation and sublation in order to sustain an incessant confrontation of doubles. Poetics furthers the productivity of endless doubles around kana versus mana, waka versus kanshi, Yamato versus Kara, whereas the productive site of doubles for contests is that of emperor versus regent, right ministries versus left ministries, and right teams versus left teams. These points demand some introduction.

Yoshimoto Takaaki, in his account of the rise of waka, describes the conflicts that arose between various factions at court throughout the ninth century and calls attention to the problem of the double court. When an emperor retired and his successor took the throne, the retired emperor retained wealth, prestige, and an aura that could continue to influence events at court; courtiers therefore aligned their fortunes with different emperors and imperial lineages.[24] In the doubled court, there was always the question of who would advise the young emperor: should this task fall to a retired emperor or to a regent? In the latter half of the ninth century, the northern Fujiwara clan gradually tied itself to the throne by marrying a series of daughters to a series of emperors. When the empress (his daughter) gave birth to a crown prince, her father, the prince's maternal grandfather could become regent by forcing the early abdication of the emperor and enthroning the young prince. As the Fujiwara family succeeded in producing a number of empresses and crown princes, it could effectively control the throne by serving as advisor or regent to young emperors.

In his extensive studies of Heian poetry contests, Hagitani Boku relates the history of awase to the political maneuvers of the Heian court, describing how emperors Kōkō and Uda used large-scale awase to resist the emergence of the regency system of governance. He links the emperor Uda's promotion of grand awase to an effort to restore the authority of the throne by using poetry to maintain the unity of courtiers around the emperor (and so lessen the influence of the Fujiwara clan).

Of course, Uda's struggle against the Fujiwara regents was an attempt to confer regentlike status upon the retired emperor (himself); he did so to resist not the regency but the ascendancy of the Fujiwara family. Hagitani, however, tries to translate the emergence of awase into a story of resistance to the dissolution of the unity of the emperor and his subjects. Writing in the mid- to late 1960s, he spoke against the manipulation of the emperor by a bureaucratic elite. It had become the common wisdom about World War II that a feudalistic military elite had led the Japanese emperor and people astray. Thus Hagitani sustains the sanctity of the emperor and his people, even in the ninth century. He also relates awase to kana inscription and speaks of a revival of native expression after the dark ages, thus linking the imperial bid for unity to the (re)emergence of an ethnolinguistic community.[25] His is the usual impasse: in national literary studies, the Heian court and the Japanese nation are incessantly conflated because no attempt is made to distinguish the political ground of Heian Japan from that of the modern nation. It is assumed that the field of forces on which Heian strategies emerge is identical to that of the modern nation, and that the sources of the modern order are found in the distant past.

Yet what is astonishing about the awase is that its regime of doubles is indifferent to the ethnolinguistic concerns that characterize the national imagination and haunt Japan studies. It is not simply that awase could be traced to poetic banquets and imperial ceremonies that derive from Han/T'ang models; but they also involved forms of mediation and organization that did not involve the negation, elimination, or absorption of one element by another. An awase is an assemblage that sustains doubles and, in the incessant competition of doubles, locates a way to achieve the distribution and redistribution of rank and wealth around the figure of the emperor (rather, as I have said, in the manner of a potlatch).

To cite again the example from *The Tale of Genji*: Genji's team wins the match, and he becomes a regent figure—regent to the young emperor. Subsequently, as Genji's fortunes wax, he raises the emperor-regent double to a new level, becoming a quasi-emperor whose position lies between the emperor and his regent; the emperor, however, remains emperor. Why maintain the figure of the emperor if his authority and genealogy were always so thoroughly comprised? Why does a man like Genji not simply declare himself emperor? One might almost expect modern scholars to cite the emperor's sanctity, authority, legitimacy, purity, and even ethnicity. Yet nothing is more questionable. If the emperor remains, it is because the logic of doubles emerges from the ways in which the field of forces were configured in the Heian imagination of community. Of course, the emperor sits at a site of cosmological authority; yet it is essential to remember that the sources of political order were, therefore, forever external to him. The cosmological ground involved a mode of continual mimicry and manifestation, which results in the differentiation and coordination of doubles, which in turn grounds a system of hierarchy and distribution that centers around potlatch-like moments like the large-scale awase.

Unlike the logic of opposition and negation (which tends toward elimination or sublation), this politico-poetic logic allows for greater indeterminacy in the arena of human relations and competition. For instance, the final judgment at Uda's poetry contest in 898 wavered: "With respect to flowers, the right proved inferior; with respect to poems, the right won."[26] Who really won the whole contest, the right or the left? That would depend on whether we rate flowers or poems higher; but in the logic of the awase, we can only compare the comparable (and a comparison of flowers with poems does not constitute a proper comparison). This is not to say that all is indeterminacy, but rather to indicate that the logic of awase does not call for the elimination of one team by the other, nor the absorption of one by the other. Its logic keeps doubles in a state of permanent provocation (agonism), the maintenance of doubles—and, even more, in an alignment of doubles that gains its productivity through resonant tensions.

Doubles—in agonist pairs—fairly overwhelm the Heian court. In addition to emperor and regent, court bureaucracies entailed a right and a left, with a whole series of right and left positions (that often related to the right and left teams of awase). Naturally, with such a preponderance of doubles, at any one time not all doubles could be aligned; therein lies the potential for political intrigue, variation, and transmutation. Amid this perpetual doubling, comparing, matching and contesting, did *Kokinwakashū* further the interests of the emperor or of the regency? It is difficult to say, precisely because it stabilized the logic implicit in poetic sign, deploying its transversal and constellar forces in ways that resulted in a perpetual contest of doubles.[27]

This order, like any other, had its limits. By the end of the Heian period in the twelfth century, the perpetual breaking of figures into doubles reached the point where doubles emerged that could not be re-collected nor brought into resonant alignment. There arose the dissonant voices of those who lived beyond the capital, the discordant cries of warriors with their "tent government" (*bakufu*), and the disconcerting speeches of new religious movements. The court attempted to bring its own manner of composition to bear on these transformations and even tried to explore the aesthetics and politics of these new patterns, which were so dissonant in courtly terms. Yet, at this point, it proved impossible to align doubles across levels. The hierarchical distributions of the Heian court verged on the edge of collapse, generating the possibility for the nonhierarchical and provisional alliances of a new age.

PART II. INSCRIPTION AND SENSATION

FOUR. *Toward a History of Styles*

Inscription and the Imagination of Community

Histories of calligraphy in early Japan point to a shift in Buddhist styles of writing around the time of the Heijo court (710–794): by the end of the eighth century, sutra had became flowery and ornate, designed for stylistic effect rather than practical usage. Earlier, Buddhist sutra had been easier to read; they were written in the stiff style (楷書), with symmetrical characters of regular size and with even application of ink and measured rhythms. The stylistic effects of calligraphy occurred largely in the application of bold points of attack in the brush strokes, resulting in well-defined, frank characters. This balanced and forthright style, writes one commentator, reflects an age of scholastic activity and intellectual understanding.[1]

Oddly, however, by the time the Heian court emerged and Buddhism had become thoroughly enmeshed with affairs of state, the so-called practical styles had already given way to ornamentation and stylistic effects. Subsequently, throughout the Heian period (794–1185), the interacting Buddhist sutra and court styles of calligraphy became ever more lavish and sensational.[2] Compare figure 2 with figures 5 and 6.

Mutations in the realm of calligraphic styles raise a general question about the formation of the Yamato courts. What do stylistic effects—the use of forms that appeal to the senses—contribute to the formation of the Heian community? Again, we should see the Heian community in this context as part of a larger classical community, a local precipation within the dynastic nexus of communities and courts that coalesced, fragmented, and dispersed across East Asia in the eighth and ninth centuries.

One common model for the formation of the Yamato court insists on its increased rationalization and centralization. Central to this project was the reconciliation of clan lineages such as in Kojiki (ca. 712), in which diverse mythic accounts were loosely combined, chiefly through juxtaposition of divergent myths, but with intermittent narrative bridges—the god of one clan defers or cedes land to another (although later they are at odds again). In such a record, not the power of narrative to coordinate and predicate events but the power of writing to list and juxtapose names comes to the fore—whence the seemingly magical tangibility and effectiveness of signs in Kojiki. Genealogies are traversed through cosmological forms and forces that allow for strange gaps and links among genealogies—strange, that is, from the standpoint of rationalized records.

Buddhism as well, it would seem, functioned largely to further the bureaucratic network. After all, it was reputedly through Buddhism that technologies of inscription took root on the Japanese archipelago; and if numerous clans erected and patronized Buddhist temples, it was because temple scribes kept records of taxes, levies, properties, rice stipends, and domiciles. One might conclude that writing acted primarily as a tool or instrument for recording or exchanging information, for consolidating a community on the basis of rationalized symbols. Yet it is precisely this assumption that is disrupted by the prevalence of stylistic effects. Suddenly, one faces the question of the role of sensible forms, sensation, and performance in the emergence of community.

The question is not whether writing contributes to the emergence of this community (it does), but rather what kind of center, boundary, and consistency is involved in the development of the Heian order. This question cannot (or at least has not) been asked in current histories of writing in early Japan. At present, there are two common ways to tell the history of inscription around the courts at Heijō and Heian. One is a history of rationalization and centralization, in which inscription is seen exclusively in terms of its instrumental potential, its capacity for practical or rational transcription. The other is a history of inscription as a form of cultural expression, in which case certain styles of writing are construed as markers of a particular culture—to wit, characters are Chinese, alphabets are Western, and kana are Japanese. In this tradition, scholars speak of kanji culture versus kana culture.[3] These two histories often work together, and their individual and overall effect is to collapse the differences between early Japan and modern Japan. In effect if not intent, they impose the national imagination on history.

Seeley's recent history of Japanese writing is a good example of the rationalist approach. In the context of *Man'yōshū*, he describes many examples of rebuses and other character puzzles and figures. He then comments, "This type of studied, jocular usage suggests that by the time of *Man'yōshū* there were Japanese who were very much at ease with the Chinese script."[4] This remark is a welcome antidote to all those histories that posit the script of *Man'yōshū* as a frustrated attempt to use characters phonetically. Seeley points, instead, to an intelligent and intentionally playful use of characters. Yet, in the end, he tends to relegate the stylistic complexities of inscription to the realm of retrograde tendencies. All that does not fit the model of the rational evolution of script (from pictures to ideograms to phonetics) falls by the wayside. In particular, when he turns to the complex use of characters in manuscripts of *Kokinwakashū*, he asserts that this constitutes a "reverse tendency" that "was by and large restricted to texts in which there was a prominent aesthetic element."[5] Yet how is it possible to write a history of Heian inscription if the prestigious court anthologies are passed over as retrograde because they contain aesthetic elements?

The culturalist approach, on the contrary, lingers over the aesthetic elements but speaks unabashedly of "our nation" and "our script." A good many (if not all) of the Japanese histories of Heian calligraphy adopt this paradigm. A prime example occurs in a book written in 1966, which prefaces its account of Japanese calligraphy with a story about the word *gofuku* (呉服)—dry goods, piece goods, draperies, and so on—which originally refers to "clothing from Wu" (an ancient state in southern China). Thus the author, Ayamura Tan'en, gives the common word an exotic charge and awakens a sense of the foreign amid the familiar. He writes that, in ancient times, "we Japanese" lacked an independent culture yet gradually adapted foreign clothes to suit our body—this is our tendency, he explains, to adapt the foreign. Ayamura makes cultural transformation seem easy, friendly, domestic, and natural. Such comfort depends, of course, on recognition of a common body of a single people that extends throughout history—"we" put on foreign clothes and tailored them to "our" bodies, and now they are no longer foreign—the assumption being that we all share the same body, tastes, and so forth. In brief, the goal of this type of history is to demonstrate corporeal (ethnic and racial) resilience and independence.

Still, such culturalist histories of inscription present other possibilities. Perhaps because their materials are less settled and more fragmentary, histories of Japanese calligraphic styles never attain the same degree of rhetorical or conceptual consistency as waka studies. In a sense, they are easier to critique, for their impulse is frankly nativist. To borrow from H. D. Harootunian's discussion of Edo nativism, "nativism directed its attention less toward developing a methodology to decode settled inscription than toward demonstrating how writing perverted and suppressed genuine meaning. It was less interested in approaching texts with a theory of reading than in showing conclusively how writing failed to convey the experience of presence and immediacy promised by speech."[6] Culturalist histories of writing simply displace nativist notions about the perversions of writing to the realm of foreign styles.

Histories of Heian calligraphy do not really have a theory of reading. Although they strive to show the inadequacy of foreign forms and to demonstrate the independence of native styles, their materials are themselves so heteroclite that no settled method of reading results from them. Moreover, when difficulties arise and stylistic contradictions become rife, modern histories of calligraphy resort to oppositions between speech and writing. In the wake of Derrida, such reliance on voice as presence should be subject to doubt and critique, because from the outset it presupposes a metaphysical stance vis-à-vis inscription. Nonetheless, it is important to note that nativist histories of Japanese inscription do not ever attain metaphysical consistency; even when they use speech to guarantee (racial) presence, they are rhetorically and logically diffuse. It is the national imagination (with its disciplinization of language) that ultimately serves as the proof of the integrity and eternity of the Japanese body, and this national identity is constructed and grounded in a lived experience of the nation. For these reasons, for all its proclamations of independence, the culturalist or nativist approach to writing does afford a way to open the study of Heian waka into another kind of analysis in which the relation of speech and writing remains far more ambiguous.

Histories

Histories of early Japanese writing confront a truly heterogeneous collection of fragments, all of them organized around the emergence of *wayō*— *wa-style* or *Japanese style*. The term *wayō* could also be translated as "court style" or "Yamato style," but, because it is consistently equated with Japanese style, I often refer to it as wa-style or Japanese style. Usually such histories discern three to four stages:

1. Nara: In the seventh and eighth centuries, the primary documents are sutra copies with their easy-to-read styles. See figure 2.

2. Early Heian: By the end of the eighth century and throughout the ninth century, T'ang styles, centered on the calligraphy of Wang Hsi-chih (303–361), came to the fore.[7] See figure 1. Characteristic of this stage are the "Three Brushmasters" (三筆), Kūkai (774–835), emperor Saga (786–842), and Tachibana no Hayanari (d. 842).[8] See figure 3.

3. Mid-Heian: In the tenth and eleventh century, the Wang-centered style was gradually transformed, and wa-style began to emerge. Characteristic of this era are the "Three Precedents" (三跡), that is, the three masters or exemplars: Ono no Michikaze (894–966), Fujiwara no Sukemasa (944–998), and Fujiwara no Yukinari (972–1027).[9] See figure 4.

4. Late Heian: The twelfth century saw the maturation of the wa-style, and certain schools began to consolidate their own distinct styles and to circulate treatises—for example, Sesonji-ryū and Hosshōji-ryū (the school, lineage, or current of the Seson temple and the Hosshō temple, respectively). See figures 5–9.

The first transformation (from stage 1 to 2) is usually described in terms of a shift from pragmatic to aesthetic modes: that is, from the easy-to-read Buddhist sutra described at the beginning of the chapter (sometimes called *tempyō style*). Hirayama Mitsuki thought this balanced and forthright style reflected an age of scholastic activity and intellectualism. As Ayamura puts it, there is no emphasis on heart. Sutra copyists did not adopt velocities, twists, turns, or rhythms that imitate the leaps and bounds of the calligrapher's heart.[10] The emphasis apparently favors legibility over sensibility.

A problem arises from such descriptions, which prepare the ground for a historical narrative about a movement from pragmatics to aesthetics, from intelligibility to sensibility, from intellection to emotion, from imitation to expression, and so forth. The resultant narrative has it that the popularity of the Wang-centered styles of the T'ang court gradually opened up calligraphy to the possibility of expressing the feelings and that, at the Heian court, the Three Brushmasters followed suit. Subsequently, calligraphers transformed and adapted this sensibility to express the Japanese heart (as exemplified by the Three Precedents). This is a serviceable history, but it is important to question the way in which it constructs a dichotomy between intelligibility and sensibility, imitation and expression, and China and Japan. There is a tendency to treat earlier forms of calligraphy as so much heartless or mindless imitation, followed by an apprenticeship in heartful (ethnic) expression. Japan is thus associated with heart and emotion, while writing forms that are clearly from the Middle Kingdom (and therefore legible as Chinese) belong to the realm of instrumental signification and intellectual exercise. It is necessary to see some of the stylistic complications that trouble such an easy division.

For one thing, sutra copies involve a good deal of expression and sensation. Ayamura remarks that the speed and continuity of their brushwork was suited to the act of recitation or intonation; thus the life of the sutra copy lay in the swell or undulation that is felt before the eyes in the course of reading it.[11] In brief, there was a figural quality to calligraphic performance, akin to recitation or cantillation or chant, as in figure 2. Then, too, other forms of inscription existed before and alongside sutra copies. Archaeologists in Japan in recent years have unearthed an array of mokkan (narrow strips of wood on which records are written), as well as earthenware vessels brushed or incised with characters (like the assembled character discussed in part one). Tono Haruyuki points out in a recent book that histories of writing tend to overlook these sources (because of the separation of the fields of archaeology and history). He centers his history largely on mokkan, for their historical value is, he says, more evident. The pottery inscriptions, he tells us, though far more common, are more difficult to discuss because they use only a couple characters, apparently as talismans or incantations. He concludes that though these inscriptions are doubtless of great cultural value, they are too difficult to parse and understand.[12]

Tono's history offers some background to the emergence of the easy-to-read sutra. The mokkan, from prior to the early eighth century, mostly present hard-to-read, somewhat peculiar and ancient styles of inscription. The subsequent shift to the even and symmetrical styles of the eighth century followed directly from a shift in China from the styles of the Six Dynasties to those of the T'ang. T'ang modes of measurement and scales were adopted about the same time, as well as T'ang styles of dress and coiffure. About this time, two stylistic streams also arose in mokkan inscription: near the capital city the newer styles prevailed, while at the periphery the older styles persisted. These different characters and styles serve to remind us that there existed a range of uses of inscription, many of which defy our attempts to interpret them in terms of signification. Furthermore, with different styles of inscription came a range of modes of expression, production, and circulation, and these were not spread uniformly throughout the empire or the capital. Various divisions resulted from the diffusion of inscription and the differentiation of styles. In the final analysis, however, style changes did not draw a line between China and Japan, or Korea and Japan. Nor did they mark a facile transformation from pragmatic to aesthetic uses, or from intelligibility to sensibility.

There was, nevertheless, a shift from the easy-to-read sutra of the eighth century to the styles of the Three Brushmasters. We could think of the sutra copies not so much as easy to read as designed for recitation, for they involved a specific relation to vocal expression. In the late eighth and early ninth centuries, however, sutra appeared that were not intended primarily or exclusively for recitation. Emori Kenji points out that Heian sutra began to show some occasional errors in characters and to omit some characters entirely—one sign that sutra were being used primarily for dedications and oblations rather than recitation.[13] In addition, it was at this time that the use of flecks of gold and silver started to change the qualities of scriptural space. At about the same time, the calligraphic styles of the early Heian court, directly indebted to Wang Hsi-chih, introduced new forms of expression. I analyze the effects of these two aspects—space for inscription and modes of expression—in the next chapter. First, however, further historical information is needed here.

Histories of Japanese calligraphy see the works of the Three Brushmasters as representative of an overall transformation in calligraphic styles from the eighth to ninth centuries. The styles of Wang Hsi-chih, and his son Wang Hsien-chih (344–388), were at the heart of an epochal transformation in Chinese calligraphy. During the course of the Six Dynasties (in the third to the sixth centuries), writes Lothar Ledderose, new developments that shaped the course of calligraphy for centuries to come occurred: "calligraphy was elevated to an art form that was practiced by the educated elite, calligraphic pieces were for the first time collected as works of art, theoretical treatises of calligraphy began to be written." Ledderose concludes that these events constituted a "shift of emphasis from religious quality to aesthetic quality." [14] Similarly, Emori Kenji emphasizes that the Three Brushmasters of the Heian court were not professional writers (copyists) but artists, monks or officials who loved letters.[15] While it is true that a transformation is occurring in both the sites and styles of calligraphy, as well as in its modes of expression, production, and reception, it is nonetheless important to question what we mean by "art" and "aesthetic" in this context; the initial impression given by these terms is that of art for art's sake, of disinterested production, or of purely secular expression. Yet we know that the Wang styles were at the heart of the consolidation and unification of states and kingdoms within the T'ang dynasty—as Ledderose's historical overview makes clear.

One of the achievements associated with the Wang tradition was the standardization of three styles of script, which came to dominate all subsequent calligraphy:

—Stiff or regular script (in Japan, *kaisho*; in China, *k'ai-shu*)
—Current or running script (*gyōsho*; *hsing-shu*)
—Grass or fully cursive script (*sōsho*; *ts'ao-shu*)

For some two centuries, the Wang tradition was confined largely to South China, where it had emerged among families of statesmen and officials in the Eastern Chin (317–420). Only with the drive to unify various states under the T'ang dynasty at the end of the sixth century did the Wang style became widespread and established as a standard throughout the empire. The second T'ang emperor forcibly propogated the style of Wang Hsi-chih during his reign (626–649). Thus, the standardization of styles played an important role in the consolidation and centralization of empire—for the T'ang dynasty and, later, for the Yamato court. This macrohistorical perspective should not be lost in discussions of the T'ang or Heian shift to art or aesthetics. The aesthetics of calligraphy affords us a way to explore the operations of the senses and the formation of subjects; it is not only a question of the imposition of standards and boundaries but of the ways in which discipline can elicit participation, shape subjects, and induct perception (interpellation, subjectification, embodiment).

There is no question that the Three Brushmasters of Heian-kyō directly followed the T'ang styles derived from Wang Hsi-chih, both calligraphically and orthographically. Histories of Heian calligraphy make no attempt to place Kūkai or the other two Brushmasters under the aegis of Japanese styles. Generally, the early ninth century is thought of as the era of greatest prestige for Han or T'ang styles. Unlike histories of poetry, however, which lay claim to the native voice hidden behind forms, histories of calligraphy cannot so easily call upon the problematic of occluded native speech. The work of the Three Brushmasters in classical Chinese do not differ significantly from that found in T'ang documents. Kūkai (by far the most important of the three) traveled to Ch'ang-an to study Shingon Buddhism and learned the Wang styles then prevalent in the T'ang capital. Upon his return to Heian-kyō, he established a close relationship with the throne, performing rituals of pacification and offering instruction in esoteric rites. He instructed emperor Saga in calligraphy and poetry and gained renown at court for his abilities.

The work of the Three Brushmasters presented some important differences from the previous sutra copies. In earlier, easy-to-intone styles, characters were in the stiff style, of regular size; ink was evenly applied, and the rhythms were constant. The boldness and frankness of this symmetrical, balanced style came from the emphatic points of attack in brushstrokes. The turn to the style of Wang Hsi-chih, however, culminated in a style in which the size of characters was more variable and there were marked shifts in the energy and speed with which characters were written. *Fūshinjō*—a letter by Kūkai to Saichō (767–822, founder of Tendai Buddhism at the Heian court)—is a fine example of such effects.[16] The style falls between the stiff and the current styles. Overall, the brushwork tends toward the current style (gyōsho); each character is inked with broad, dexterous attacks and closes that sometimes fluidly link two characters; yet it stays rather close to the stiff or regular style (kaisho). The result is a higher degree of stylistic individuation among characters; some characters are highly cursive, some only slightly so. Likewise, the size of characters varies: there are intermittent transitions between larger and smaller characters. This style calls attention to each character as an individual component. See figures 1 and 3.

The turn toward Wang showed greater attention to the gestural and compositional dimensions of calligraphy. Which is not to say that these works could not be read, chanted, or intoned—on the contrary Kūkai's poems and letters closely followed the tonal rules of Chinese prosody, and sutra could still be recited—but rather that there were other registers of expression that accompanied vocalization of the text. Style became a matter of the interplay of visual, gestural, and vocal registers.

It is with the advent of the Three Precedents—Ono no Michikaze, Fujiwara no Sukemasa, and Fujiwara no Yukinari—that historians make a concerted effort to assert the emergence of Japaneseness in Heian styles. In his overview of the calligraphic styles of the Heian period, Horie Tomohiko boldly claims that these two centuries of the mid-Heian constituted a golden age that saw the birth of wa-style as well as kana. "It would not be an overstatement to say that, in our long history of calligraphy, it was only in this period that was realized a beauty in complete opposition to that of China where characters originated," he writes. The term he uses for opposition—*taikō*—suggests antagonism and opposition as well as emulation and rivalry, and he plays it both ways, hinting at a kind of defiance to China as well as a desire to produce an aesthetic equal to China's.[17] His account enables us to see mid-Heian calligraphy as strategically parallel with the agonist logic of styles in Heian awase described in Chapter 3. Horie, however, has grander designs. He looks for proof of Japanese autonomy and, as do many scholars, points to the court's decision to cease official missions to T'ang China in 894. Unlike other scholars, however, he asserts that this decision did not simply encourage the formation of an independent culture but resulted from the prior birth of a pure Japanese culture.[18]

The extant documents do not confirm his confidence. Horie turns to the specific works of the Three Precedents, yet is hard pressed to locate the particulars of the Japanese style. He looks at the draft for a (Han) poem to be written on a screen by Ono no Michikaze (*byōbū dodai*) but concludes that, rather than Japanese style, it shows the dense elaboration of the old fashions of Chinese styles. Likewise with Fujiwara no Sukemasa: Horie looks at his poems and commentary, *Shikaishi* (ca. 969), which was written on pieces of paper that the courtier folded into his pocket to have a handy way to record poems and people's comments on them, giving the topic, then the rank and surname of each composer. This was a T'ang practice.[19] In the final instance, although he considers all three calligraphers to exemplify the wa-style, the real honors go to Fujiwara no Yukinari.[20]

At one time, scholars could cite several examples of grass-style kana (*sōgana*) attributed to Michikaze or Yukinari. They provided a sense of the proximity of the Three Precedents to a truly Japanese style through its special relation to kana and, thus, to Japanese speech. Yet as it turns out, the attributions of these kana exemplars have been shown to be mistaken or unverifiable. Thus a number of scholars have sounded a note of caution. Emori, for instance, enumerates what he calls the "phantasms that surround famous kana works." He reminds us that there are no extant kana works by Michikaze and Ki no Tsurayuki, and that there is no proof of the attributions to Yukinari. Finally, he submits, we have no idea what kind of kana were used in this period.[21]

Nevertheless, the pattern of thought has become fixed: the Japaneseness of the Three Precedents is said to derive from their link to kana, and the histories look for qualities common to both kana and the styles of the Three Precedents. Usually, it is a matter of roundness and softness. Along those lines, Komatsu Shigemi gives a nice description of Yukinari's calligraphy:

above all it emphasizes symmetry and the arrangement of forms, but is also characterized by broad, open attacks in the formation of the characters, which imparts delicacy and energy to the flow of the lines. "An elegant and lively style of writing was the formal ideal of the Yamato style," he writes. "It is a style of writing first established by Yukinari."[22] See figure 4. We might add Ayamura's observation that the narrowness of characters and their high shoulders recall kana calligraphy.[23] But histories of Heian calligraphy encounter a basic problem: it is a field of styles and variations upon which scholars project species and genres. Rather than distinct boundaries, we find zones of indiscernability. The styles of the Three Precedents did not actually construct a new zone autonomous from Chinese styles; one bleeds imperceptibly into the other.

I insist on this zone of indiscernability because it tells us something about the way boundaries and spaces in Heian aesthetics are imagined that has consequences for the imagination of community, especially in so far as Heian works were communal efforts that related directly to court hierarchies and competitions. What is striking about histories of Heian calligraphy is the frequency with which they encounter the bleed between supposedly autonomous styles. When Shimatani Hiroyuki delineates the scribal functions of the Three Precedents at the Heian court, it becomes evident that scribes' styles always shifted deftly between Han and Yamato styles: scribes wrote the poetic strips for screens (shikishi) in the palace and for enthronement ceremonies; they wrote Buddhist memorials and prayers, government documents, letters, and inscriptions for gates and portals. Moreover, Shimatani discovers that the calligraphy of one of the Three Precedents, Fujiwara no Sukemasa, was cited in a Sung dynasty chronicle, which suggests some degree of continuity with the continental courts.[24] All in all, there was a spectrum of calligraphic variations, in which it would be impossible to speak of opposition, negation, or even dissolution of Chinese forms. In fact, "China" itself cannot be fixed or bounded in any self-evident way.[25]

There are indications of other ways to construe Heian styles in the accounts cited thus far. Komatsu, for instance, stresses that the ideal of the age of the Three Precedents resided in the orderly regulation of forms. Emori reminds us that the wa-style of the Heian court is commonly called the "style of the ancient era" because it "still retained its form." This point could be extended to kana calligraphy and waka poetry as well: the regulation of forms dominated the organization of expression and production.

Indeed, the differentiation of Yamato from Han/T'ang could be seen to play into the regulation of forms—which is the direction I take in this study. How is it, then, that histories of Heian calligraphy avoid an exploration of the regulation of forms? They do so by associating regulation with Chineseness; the realm of emotion and sensibility therefore fall to Japaneseness.

Komatsu Shigemi, whose numerous articles, books, and edited collections make him one of the most important scholars of Heian calligraphy, offers a good example. In a volume dedicated to Heian and Kamakura calligraphy, Komatsu and his collaborators continually elevate wa-style calligraphy to the status of Japanese sensibility and mentality and take pains to link it to kana. The watchword of this volume is opposition or resistance (teikō). Kuboki Shōichi, in his account of the emergence of kana, sketches out different histories for the peoples of Japan and of China and depicts the advent of Yamato forms in terms of the autonomy of Japan from China. He sees the movement away from China toward Japanese autonomy in the realm of arts, letters, politics, and culture; and he relates this movement to a shift from "ideographism" (表意文字) to "phonographism" (表音文字).[26] Thus in an attempt to prove Japanese autonomy, the culturalist approach resorts to the authority of phonetic evolution.

In the same volume, Shimatani Hiroyuki centers his analysis on the Three Precedents, describing their styles in terms of the formation of wa-style culture. He writes of a steady movement away from the T'ang styles manifested in the work of Wang Hsi-chih. From Michikaze through Sukemasa to Yukinari, he detects a turn away from the T'ang-derived emphasis on order and correctness and toward the direction of flow and self-abandon. He construes Heian variations on the styles of Wang as departures from the T'ang ideal and then elevates these variations or departures to the status of opposition or resistance. Ultimately, Shimatani's interest in Heian calligraphy has little to do with the Heian court, but it has everything to do with calligraphy's legacy as defined retroactively in Edo Japan. This is most apparent when he describes the later influence of the Three Precedents.

Emperor Fushimi (1265–1371) learned the writing styles of Michikaze and Yukinari, and among successive generations of emperors they also were extolled as prominent exemplars of excellent calligraphy. A sixth-generation descendant, Prince Son'en, inherited them and established a style of writing called Son'en style (or Shōren-temple style). Between the Kamakura and Muromachi period, numerous styles and schools formed in confusion. Then, in the Tokugawa period, the Son'en style, transmitted by each priest prince of the Shōren temple, became the public style of the shogunate, and spreading under the name o-ie-ryū, again widely flourished and continued in factions. Other diverse methods of wa-style calligraphy appeared, but it is no exaggeration to say that all of them emerged from the styles of Yukinari. The calligraphy of the Three Precedents is not merely a precious legacy from the Heian period alone, but its influence and role in achieving the development of wa-style ways of writing was extraordinarily great.[27]

A subtle form of confusion creeps into Shimatani's account of the Three Precedents: although he writes of Heian Japan, he has actually used Edo Japan as a point of departure. He adopts the perspective of an already-unified court tradition. In the Edo period, at a nearly millennial remove from Heian-kyō, the wizened descendant of that court (at Kyōtō) resorted to all manner of assimilation and consolidation of hundreds of years of courtly forms of expression. Then, in their opposition to the neo-Confucian ideology of the shogunate, nativists posited these forms in opposition to Chinese forms. Shimatani uses these genealogies in order to shore up his story of the Japanese divergence from China.

Komatsu writes of the subsequent maturation of the Japanese style. He outlines a history in which the golden age of Yukinari goes into decline in the twelfth century, with a surge of individuality, personality, and stylistic abandon within wa-style writing; the surge accompanies the development of a wilful masculine style related to the emergence of samurai. It might seem odd to present the decline of the golden ideal of a formal order in terms of stylistic maturation. How does he resolve this apparent paradox?

Komatsu's account closes with descriptions of the styles of the Hosshō temple—Hosshōji-ryū—which was established around Fujiwara no Tadamichi (1097–1164). The Hosshōji school arose almost simultaneously with the styles of the Seson temple (Sesonji-ryū) and contested their ascendancy. The school of the Seson temple established its lineage in direct descent from Fujiwara no Yukinari, laying claim to his elegance and finesse. The Hosshōji style, with its darker, thicker elements and tilted brush, often stands in opposition to the delicacy and symmetry of the Sesonji style.[28] For Komatsu, both styles are wa-styles in so far as they abandon the formal regulations that link Heian calligraphy to Chinese styles. The decline of order and correctness severed the links to Chinese calligraphy and resulted in the emancipation and maturation of the Japanese sensibility—which is born of a marriage of masculine vigor and feminine delicacy. Naturally, because both feminine and masculine poles are attributed to Japanese styles, Komatsu imagines the pure, almost virgin birth of an offspring that lives far from dynastic China. See figures 7, 8, and 9.

In these nativist stories of order and abandon, of regulation and dissolution, there arises a division between China and Japan grounded in and supported by an opposition between reason and emotion, or intellection and expression, or intelligibility and sensibility. It always falls to Chinese forms to be rational, intellectual, ordered, while Japanese forms flow with heartfelt abandon. This is how Edo nativism has been reconfigured within modern histories of Japanese writing. The modern nativist sees Chinese forms (regardless of era or court) as constituting an empty order, devoid of expression or sensibility, diametrically opposed to the Japanese heart. Never is it imagined that so-called Chinese styles are also forms of expression, or that so-called Japanese styles also relate to modes of regulation or restriction aside from the boundaries of national culture.

It is true that the Heian court differed from the T'ang court in that it tended to place much of the administrative control of lands and stipends in the hands of estate managers outside the capital. By the late twelfth century, this situation had encouraged the emergence of samurai who arrived from the eastern plains, forcibly splintered the court's authority, and contested its supremacy. The samurai erected a *bakufu* or "tent government" at Kamakura; its arrival marks the advent of a new era—the Kamakura period (1185–1333). Under these conditions, Heian courtiers struggled to consolidate their lineages and styles and to retain and reaffirm their wealth and status. There arose at Heian-kyō an ever more intense focus on the resplendence of the court legacy, with greater emphasis on expenditure and contests. Furthermore, many courtiers thought they were living in the "latter days of the Buddha's law" (*mappō*) when the human order would inevitably disperse into disaster and discord. They devoted themselves to the production of elegant copies of Buddhist sutras as well as lavish editions of poetic collections—calligraphed over pictures of flowers, birds, grasses, and insects; on papers of various hues, pieced together, rubbed or printed with patterns, and strewn with dust and flecks, bits of gold and silver frayed or cut in an array of sizes and shapes.[29] See figures 5, 6, and 8.

About this time, the Sesonji school constructed its calligraphic lineage and laid claim to certain styles. In his discussion of the political dimensions of calligraphic lineages, John Carpenter opts for an historical and sociological analysis of the role of copying and transmitting calligraphic forms. He looks in detail at the comments made about the Sesonji school and explores these in the calligraphic styles of *Genji monogatari emaki* (the picture-scrolls of *The Tale of Genji*). He concludes that the Sesonji style is the most sophisticated, elegant, and meticulously produced of the calligraphic styles: its "strokes are finely delineated, turns are naturally rounded, and the overall flow of the columns is graceful."[30] Nevertheless, in some respects, the Sesonji school's genealogical claims for stylistic consistency can be seen as fictitious. In fact, it is possible to situate some works in either the Sesonji school or the Hosshōji school.[31] Carpenter's analysis thus suggests that the tension between styles involves a kind of permanent provocation between lineages and schools—rather like the dynamics of awase. Indeed, awase became sites of production for resplendent manuscripts: as in figures 5 and 6 the "Hongan Temple Edition of the Collection of Thirty-Six Poets" (*Honganjibon sanjūrokunin kashū*, ca. 1112), which unfurls a kaleidoscopic collage of patchwork papers, colors, patterns, figures, and poems derived from an awase based on copybooks (*sōshi*).[32] So it is not surprising that certain works turn up in both currents, Sesonji and Hosshōji. What counted in the political arena was the perpetual contest between contenders, which enabled the potlatch-like redistribution of wealth and status at court.

The dynamics of awase affords another way to think about the links between calligraphic styles and the construction of boundaries. It signals that Heian poets and writers situated stylistic differences within the political arena of the competition, rank, and lineage at court. But what made writing so important to the contests of the court? On the one hand, there was the matter of transmission of the bonds that arose within groups through face-to-face instruction and replication of models. To learn the brush was to enter into relations of authority and solidarity. Through the brush, the courtier was inducted into the Heian order, for much of its authority was invested in the instruction and transmission of calligraphy and poetry. In this respect, writing involved a negation of the subject, one that ultimately derived its authority from affiliation and from replications of models. On the other hand, writing also entailed an affirmation of the self, a kind of self-cultivation that enticed and interpellated subjects, to allow for the contests, interests, and strategies that constituted life at the court. Writing with the brush bestowed certain pleasures and controls—the ability to couple Han and Yamato forms, or to couple feminine and masculine styles, which could at once affirm forms of intimacy and hierarchy within the act of writing. Finally, the play of forces evoked in writing—the evocation of the self, its pleasures and its interests—also derived in great part from the cosmological order.

These two aspects of Heian calligraphy (and poetry)—its subjection of the subject and its cultivation of the self—form a complex and changeable subjectivity. One could insist on negation and on the despotism of the Heian order, or one could stress the aesthetic pleasures and the delights of the courtiers. The truth of the Heian order (the subjectivity it constructs) lies somewhere in between. For this reason, I place an emphasis on a kind of ethico-aesthetic or historico-aesthetic analysis. Rather than trace the rivalries that attend the transmission of styles and copies within factions at court (which is one way to get at the political dimension of calligraphy), I explore how Heian calligraphy, as a form of aesthetic expression, constructs certain kinds of boundaries, relates to specific types of consistency, and imagines a particular sort of community. This is a strategy that takes seriously the aesthetic appeal of Heian expression (and opens the possibility of extending it past its historical delimitation) without endorsing rationalist or culturalist-nativist histories of inscription. Aesthetics, however, is not in this instance an evaluation of beauty but an analysis of the operations of the senses, an analysis that leads directly to questions about historical formations of knowledge, perception, and power.

FIVE. *Heian Calligraphy*

Papers

The surface for inscription is not neutral. Heian aesthetics calls attention to its qualities. Calligraphy begins with papers made from vegetal fibers of various types. Different types of fiber result in papers that differ greatly in texture, that absorb ink differently, and that affect the style and allure of brushwork. The fibers teased from husks, barks, or other materials are first swollen in water and pulped; then the water is removed and the fibers are matted together into a sheet. Heian paper differs profoundly from contemporary paper (such as that used for printing or photocopying), which are products of a concerted effort to diminish the visual and textural irregularities of the fiber mat by using flocculation aids, titanium dioxide, starch, sizing, and so forth during machine production. The makers of Heian papers not only had little concern for diminishing the effects of fibers but tended to augment them as well. The result is a surface without horizontal or vertical orientations: fibers overlap any which way, twining and meshing wherever attractions between teased-up microfibers spring up. A sheet of paper may be square or rectangular, but there is no way to determine an up or down, a right or left, amid the entwined, matted fibers. It presents a decidedly "smooth space"—that is, a space that does not impart vertical and horizontal orientation. Its manner of organization does not involve the partition or striation of space.[1]

Paper formats do very little to introduce an orientation. Sometimes sheets are joined together to form longer scrolls; sometimes individual sheets are folded and glued; or many leaves are folded and bound with threads.[2] Such scrolls and booklets are not like modern books; theirs is an art of patchwork or piecework, closer to that of a quilt than a treatise.

Moreover, there is only the slightest anticipation of horizontal or vertical orientation; their formats function as borders rather than frames and have borders and intersections that cross through the work itself.

With the application of color and pattern to the paper, two stylistic poles begin to emerge. On the one hand, these elements can be used to bring as much orientation or striation as possible to the smooth surface of the fiber mat. At this extreme there are papers that bear vertical lines to create columns for characters. Many canonical texts (such as Buddhist and Taoist sutra) adopt such measures to assure in advance that writing will follow and impart a strict orientation. Even when lines are not drawn or printed in advance, the style of inscription tends to create well-defined columns for characters. See figure 2.

At the other extreme are papers that amplify the random variations of smooth space. Flecks of gold or silver scatter, dyes seep and swirl, or papers of various color are pieced together like a crazy quilt with fluid-edged patches. The papers used at the Heian court for poetic inscription—particularly for important occasions like contests, banquets, and ceremonies—typically deploy such techniques, and frequently deploy all of them at once to amplify the smooth potential of paper. The result is a fantastical "paper-scape": trails of dark ink run over lavenders, greens, yellows, and reds that pool and stream, dotted with showers of gold and silver. These paperscapes are characteristic of most of the texts that we classify today as literary. Many of the oldest manuscripts of poetry collections, tales, and letters deploy such surfaces and call on multiple levels of production and expression. The smooth space of these paperscapes—with dyes that seep and swirl, with flecks of colored paper scattered, with figures and designs that twine and creep—seems to anticipate or prefigure poems that sing of celestial and terrestrial movements: petals fluttering, rivers flowing, autumn leaves scattering, bugs chirping and susurrating, lovers meeting and parting, moons waxing and waning. Yet this resonance between the poetic "naturescape" and the paperscape does not belong to the realm of representation: the scattered flecks of color are like petals, leaves, snowflakes only insofar as they betray an analogous motility and play of variation. Likewise with the currents and eddies of dyes, or the layers and patches of papers: this is a mode of mimicry, not of pictography or illustration. There is a mode of expression common to the naturescape and paperscape, one that delights in the possibilities of nonstriated spaces—spaces in which hearts and words wander and cross paths. See figures 5 through 8.

Some papers show admixtures of smooth and striated space. They may have patterns applied to the surface that replicate embroidered silk to impart a sense of vertical-horizontal orientation, with emblems and motifs that echo the woof and warp of textiles. There are also papers rubbed or printed with distinctly oriented designs, or painted with grasses, trees, bugs, or birds. Such figures are not as strictly striated as the vertical columns of, say, a sutra. In fact, on the whole, even though these mixed papers introduce less random variation than the fluctuating paperscapes, they nonetheless impart only the slightest sense of orientation; rarely are their patterns or images used for partition or striation. In the case of cloud and flower patterns, printing, rubbing and painting frequently introduce patterns that run over the edge of the page, give way to other patterns, or involve images without strict orientation. They tend to the smooth pole. Nevertheless it would be misguided to think that the Heian aesthetic has no relation whatsoever with striated space. Of particular importance are the points of intersection between smooth and striated spaces, especially the intersection of paperscape and inscription, where inscription often introduces striation in its fundamental form.

At one level, the differentiation between smooth and striated space might seem to replicate a distinction between scholarly (canonical, or even practical) and literary modes of production and expression. It is often remarked that Heian courtiers favored aesthetic over intellectual production and showed scorn for those who addressed themselves primarily to Buddhist or Confucian learning (though they never failed to call on their services). Such a distinction is misleading, for it all too easily leads to a simple reiteration of modern assumptions about literary versus other modes of expression. Such a distinction presumes a historically specific type of social organization, one that has been both delineated and deconstructed rigorously in recent years.[3] In considering questions of paper and inscription, one has to contend with continual stylistic interactions between so-called scholarly (particularly Buddhist) texts and literary texts. For instance, in chapter 4 I opened with some remarks about the Nara shift in Buddhist sutra from easy-to-read styles to those of lavish ornamentation whose intensity came to define the court style of poetry collections as well as sutra. Certain Buddhist texts, in other words, adopt similar strategies for the production of smooth space. A good example is *Heikenokkyō* (ca. 1164). This is a copy of a sutra with elaborate papers and designs that often contains acrostic-style hidden-word poems at the head of scrolls, a strategy for combining different regimes of reading and writing and conjoining different modes of production and expression. And so, rather than impose simplistic generic distinctions upon Heian texts, we need to think about the strategies that combine different regimes and modes.

In sum, at the level of paper production and expression, the differentiation between smooth and striated space suggests that the Heian aesthetic used smooth strategies not as a refusal of striated spaces but as a way to situate them. This provides some potential answers to my initial question, that of the relations between the political consolidation of the Heian court and the emergence of stylistic and aesthetic effects. The paperscape aesthetic of poetry collections prepares a space of synthesis in which various modes of production (and forms of expression) can be linked while retaining a degree of autonomy without becoming distinct genres.

The paperscape aesthetic also has implications for the way we think about written expression. Typically, the onset of inscription has a particular hold on the modern imagination: the moment when brush or pen encounters the blank page is the moment of ultimate, originary creation—out of the void emerges order; on a field of possibilities arrives the mark, the sign, the word. The fantastical paperscapes in figures 5–8 defy the notion of an originary mark. The nuance and texture of paper are central to calligraphic expression, and the Heian aesthetic works to amplify the variations and qualities already afforded by color, pattern, fiber, dye, and ink. Similarly, poetic expression is not an art of creation ex nihilo, and the poet does not inscribe herself or himself at the center of creation. Poetics is an art of following signs and precedents.

At the level of production, there are indications that calligraphy and poetry together constitute a kind of crazy-quilt economy of the palimpsest. Inscriptions on used papers could be partially erased by soaking away the inks, then covering them with dyes; or the unused margins or scraps could be pieced together; or entire sheets could be shredded, repulped, and matted with other fibers. All these practical ways to reuse paper continually recycle texts into texture and in this respect the Heian art of text emerges from an art of patchwork.[4] See especially figure 6.

Patchwork also affords an excellent analogy for the art of poetic composition and compilation. Composition is an art of piecing together a song from various bits of other songs and poems, and the art of compiling anthologies adds another layer of patchwork composition as songs are pieced together from various sources. Thus, Heian poetics is an art of patching together (composing or compiling) bits and pieces with skill and style. As with the aesthetic production of smooth space at the level of paper, skill in Heian poetics could be said to entail the ability to detect and enhance the texture of bits and pieces by way of juxtapositions, overlays, inlays, complications, and alternations that create new resonances. The emphasis falls not on creation or expression as a form of origination but on expression as a process of synthesis—a disjunctive synthesis that follows patterns of dissonance or diffraction that arise between and across striations and partitions.

Characters

When the tip of the brush moves down the page, it usually traces a vertical column of characters, and column after column unwind across the page from right to left. In this respect, writing always constitutes a striation of smooth space as it introduces distinct orientations. Of course, striation need not always proceed vertically. Characters are sometimes written horizontally from left to right, or right to left (as on temple gates). Still, regardless of variations, writing itself tends to striate, to establish orientations and directions. Or rather, this is what usually happens. There is, in Heian texts, a sometimes astonishing impulse to smooth out even the striations of writing. The *ashide* or reed-hand styles confound orientation with characters of a poem that "hide" in a picture. Characters can be dispersed into a pictorial matrix, in order to be read in a rebus-like fashion, as in the example cited in Chapter 3: three birds on the wing are read as "green" (three *mi* + bird *tori* = green *midori*).[5] In other examples of the reed hand, the characters sprout leaves, spread wings, or stretch legs, entwining with pictures that underlie the written columns—the eyes move freely between lines of characters and traits of images in the zone where the brush blurs the edges of striated inscription, as in the reed hand of figure 9. In the "Branch of Plum" (*Umegae*) of *The Tale of Genji*, one calligrapher writes in such a way that the vertical strokes of characters resemble reeds, while other strokes suggest currents of water or rocky outcroppings.[6] We encounter modes of inscription that do not distinguish between pictures and texts—or, to be more precise, between seeing and reading.

"Calligraphy is simultaneously visual and verbal," writes Naoki Sakai in his study of eighteenth-century Japanese discourse. "It cannot be reduced to verbal representation or to visual experience. After all, is calligraphy a text to see or is it a drawing to read? If it is both, then how should we understand the kind of seeing that is also reading? Or should we insist that seeing is always reading, so that visual perception is in fact an experience of reading the world?"[7]

Heian calligraphy implies a specific experience of the world, one in which reading and writing are vastly important in the construction of human order and are inseparable from other forms of perception. There are so many instances of a kind of "will to smooth"—paperscapes, reed-hand calligraphy, rebus-like poetry—and yet, these modes of expression are related to strategies of orientation and organization. Most of the extant poetic collections deploy styles that striate space in the usual fashion: a series of vertical columns winds down and across the page, superimposing a sense of order on the swirls and eddies of paperscapes. This does not mean that we should think of the reed hand, or paperscapes, or rebus-like poems as exceptional and thus marginal to Heian poetics. On the contrary, they show that poetic inscription hovers between smooth and striated space in a specific way. On the one hand, the brush imparts a distinct orientation; as if ineluctably, inscription tends to striation—whence the mythic status of writing as a bearer of order. On the other hand, the Heian brush introduces a great deal of nuance between the lines of inscription and textures, images, and figures—to the point that striation fairly vanishes. At the point of disappearance, however, the character always retains some measure of integrity. It always guarantees a legibility at once intelligible and sensible. It never vanishes. The character only roots itself more securely in the senses and the world, and the world becomes a vast field of signs, appearing, dissolving, and reappearing.

Characters themselves sustained a degree of organization and orientation in the Heian text. This was not entirely due to properties inherent in characters, however. If there were specific operations that attend characters, it is because various usages had deposited a characteristic constellation of operations around them that came to appear entirely natural. The process could be thought of phenomenologically (in that signs rely on specific configurations of bodies and senses). The bilateral symmetry of characters, for instance, calls on the bilateral symmetry of the human body, which is but one aspect of the general sense of analogy between body and sign; treatises on calligraphy frequently speak in terms of flesh, sinew, bone, heart, and so on.[8] Such corporeal analogies suggest that, although the operations deemed characteristic of characters can be thoroughly historicized (i.e., seen as contingent), they nevertheless come to seem non-arbitrary because they construct and express bodies. They lay claim to nonarbitrary nature different from that inherited from the Enlightenment tradition.

The theoretical point of departure for this study is historical, and thus it looks at the construction of perception, sensation, knowledge, bodies, and so forth in that context. Still, it should not be forgotten that the character does not pose itself as arbitrary but secures itself firmly in a natural world. One way to imagine the Heian "nature" of the character is to turn to the early treatises on writing from East Asia.

In the Han dynasty, particularly in the latter half (the Eastern Han, 25–220), scholars began to classify Chinese characters in accordance with the "six scripts" (六書). Hsu Shen (ca. 58–147), in the "Postface" to *Shuo wen ch'ieh tzu*, formulated and provided examples of the six scripts that became the basis for subsequent theories of writing. First among his formulations for characters are those that "indicate things" (指事). These are characters that visually diagram their intent, such as 二 (two), 三 (three), 上 (up) or 下 (down). Second are characters that "model form" (象形), such as 日 (sun), 月 (moon), 山 (mountain), 木 (tree) or 川 (river). These entail a kind of pictography. Third comes the characters that combine "form and sound" (形声), in which half of the character classifies its form and the other half presents its sound. Characters for birds, for instance, use the bird character (鳥) alongside its sound: 鳩 (dove), 鷄 (chicken), 鶉 (quail), and so forth. (In many instances the sound mimics the call of the bird.) Fourth are characters that "join intents" (合意), in which the intents of two forms are combined: two trees make a forest (木 + 木 = 林), the sun behind a tree makes east (日 + 木 = 東). Fifth are characters with "interchangeable glosses" (転注), in which two different characters derive similar form and intent from a precursor: 老 and 考 both indicate "aged." Sixth are characters derived from "loan and borrow" (仮借), in which a character such as that for "wheat" (来) is used for "to come" (来) because the two have the same sound.[9]

Hsu Shen's classification makes it clear that signification relates both to visual and vocal elements. Characters are formulated in terms of their ability to make diagrams, to present forms, to join sounds and forms, to join forms, to exchange forms, or to exchange sounds. "Fundamentally, then," concludes Jean-François Billeter, "Chinese writing is a combinatory art permitting a virtually unlimited number of compounds to be drawn from a limited number of elements." [10] To this idea of a combinatory game with visual and vocal elements, I would add that the forms of characters tend to mimic the forms of the sensible world. Mimicry does not, however, involve a realistic depiction or pictographic representation; the forms of characters make manifest the sensible forms of the terrestrial domain in accordance with celestial configurations—whence their play between immanence and transcendence. Even sounds enter into this logic of mimicry: sometimes, as with the bird characters, vocal figures mimic the world of sensible forms (bird calls)—which is to say, there is no ideograph in the sense of a communication of ideas that lacks a sensible apparatus.[11] Yet it is easy to understand how, in the (neo)Platonic tradition of forms and ideas, Chinese characters could be dubbed ideographs because the "heart/mind" of characters is always linked to forms.[12]

Early Japanese writing came out of this complex of sounds and diagrams in which form plays an integral role in the articulation of ideas and the expression of emotions. In fact, the various modes announced in the *Shuo wen ch'ieh tzu* can be found in the character-games of *Man'yōshū* or *Kokinwakashū*. What is a broken-verse acrostic but a game that evokes the style of characters that "join intents"? What are kana acrostics but plays between "form and sound"? And the kana characters in the reed hand that transform into birds and grasses—are these not similar to the characters that "indicate things"? And, in *Man'yōshū*, there are "play readings" (戲訓)—for instance, the characters 喚鶏 or "chicken clamour," which designate the *tutu* (mimicking the clucking) of chickens. An example of characters that "indicate things" in *Man'yōshū*, is the sequence 山上復有山 or "on a mountain atop another mountain." The visual juxtaposition of a mountain 山 atop another mountain 山 gives the character 出, which is uttered as *idu* and names an action (go forth) by way of a picture puzzle: a mountain atop another mountain.[13] Finally, the "loan and borrow" characters recall the phonographic dimension of kana (as 仮字 or 借字). Needless to say, these graphic and acrostic games do not correspond exactly to Hsu Shen's formulations, nor do they occur in every type of inscription. Nevertheless, early Japanese poetics often resorted to various combinations of these operations for making diagrams, indicating things, linking sounds and forms, and exchanging sounds and forms.

To understand why ancient poetics would resort to such a seemingly difficult style of inscription, it is necessary to recall that ancient poetics did not envisage ease of reception. Paul Saenger summarizes some of the sociohistorical characteristics of medieval European texts that remind us that the modern regime of reading, with its drive to transparency and accessibility, is relatively new. "Stated summarily, the ancient world did not possess the desire, characteristic of the modern age, to make reading easier or swifter because the advantages that modern readers perceive as accruing from ease of reading were seldom viewed as advantages by the ancients. These include the effective retrieval of information in reference consultation, the ability to read with minimum difficulty a great many technical, logical and scientific texts, and the greater diffusion of literacy throughout all the social strata of the population."[14]

In the case of Chinese characters used in Heian poetics, readers were expected to mobilize a variety of complicated perceptual movements through the text—and different figural operations positioned readers and writers in the world in specific ways. Even though the Heian text treats the visual and vocal forms of characters as arbitrary at the level of representation, illustration, or narration, there is nonetheless a level at which their elements and combinations are not entirely arbitrary—a level that one could describe as prior to or underlying representation—that of the figural. At this level, the forms and sounds of characters echo, mime, or make manifest traits of the phenomenal world. Legends place the source of characters in the tracks of birds on the sand. Tracks and traces, signs, and signatures abound in the world. And the use of characters is not a game of arbitrary combinations, for signs are traversed by forces that make them echoes and mimes of a cosmological realm.

The Dynamics of Heart-Mind

There are three standard sources for discussions of Heian calligraphy: (1) remarks by Kūkai in his treatise on poetry and prose, *Henjō hokki shōryōshū* (usually called *Shōryōshū*); (2) passages in Heian tales, especially the "Plum Branch" chapter of *The Tale of Genji*; (3) treatises from the Kamakura period, in particular *Saiyōshū* (late twelfth century) and *Jubokushō* (1352).[15] Kūkai's remarks follow directly from the tradition of calligraphic treatises as framed in T'ang China, which speak of heart, expression, and their relation to authoritative models. The "Plum Branch" enumerates various calligraphic styles and papers produced for the presentation of Genji's daughter at court. Genji lavishes attention on the production of perfumes and manuscripts because he intends his daughter to become the consort (and future empress) of the crown prince by dint of his wealth and style. Thus the tale positions styles within the arena of contests for political ascendancy. Finally, the two Kamakura treatises might be said to fall between or to combine the preceding two stances. *Saiyōshū*, which is the focus here, deploys the conceptual framework of Chinese treatises but also situates calligraphy with respect to court contests. It champions one school over others, and one court over others.

Saiyōshū, like many treatises, devotes careful attention to the spatial balance of characters. For instance, one side of a character should not be larger than the other. The idea of calligraphic balance conjures up a kind of Cartesian grid, as if the space for the character were a square that is bisected horizontally and vertically. The character is to be balanced around the center of the square. Balance then is a question of weight and shape. The top should not look heavier than the bottom (or the reverse); likewise with right and left: they should not be disproportionate, nor should they drift apart or squeeze together too much. Such considerations of balance extend to the thickness, speed, and density of strokes. *Saiyōshū* includes advice on drawing out strokes, on making strokes energetic (not weak or rough), and on tilting the brush—which is improper when rivals apply it as a general stylistic mode, but acceptable in some instances. Overall, on this level, characters seem to do little more than surround a center in accordance with a sense of proportion and balance.

Balance and proportion, however, give way to other concerns. When *Saiyōshū* suggests that the overall allure of the character should be respected—that taller or wider characters should not be deformed to fit an overzealous sense of uniformity—he reflects the T'ang legacy of Wang-based styles. There is a compositional sense of balance that assures the individuation of characters, and therein lies the essence of style in the Wang legacy. The balance of a character depends not merely on its "coordinate center" (its balance as so much mass) but on its dynamic center (its center of motion) as well as on the resonance that arises between different centers of motion. Characters are not so much mass and proportion as they are motion. See figures 1 and 3. Characters evoke a sense of animate movement; just as we recognize different people by their gait on the basis on patterns of tension between their center of motion and their center of gravity, so characters and styles impart characteristic signatures, for there is a tension between the coordinate center and the dynamic center. The tension between proportion and motion can be thought of as the site where the character opens out to the fluxes of the "heart-mind." (The term *heart-mind* or *heart/mind* is often used to translate the Chinese word *hsin*—in Japanese *shin* or *kokoro*—because it relates to intellectual as well as emotional qualities.)

In his study of Kūkai's brushwork, Hirayama situates him in the larger framework of calligraphy and outlines two notions fundamental to calligraphic practice and theory. First, he tells us, writing shows the organization or composition of things. This is what I have called mimicry: characters echo and mime the patterns of things. Hirayama describes this as a mode of manifestation: calligraphy makes manifest the way in which entities are put together and interact. Such a notion of inscription does not allow for the ascendancy of the subject over objects. The writer, as subject, does not control objects and introduce order but, rather, follows the traces of phenomena. This is Hirayama's second point. He reminds us that calligraphy presents forms of movement. It shows the movements of the heart-mind that make manifest the nature or character of the writer; and, at the same time, it shows the movements of the natural world. Calligraphy thus makes manifest the workings of things.

It is difficult to discourse on this link between the movements of heart-mind and the movements of things. Borrowing the terminology of traditional commentaries, one might think of the heart-mind as an aperture. In calligraphy, the heart is an aperture that is sensitive to natural movements; it dilates and contracts with them, adjusting the flows and responses of the writer's body. The brush, then, is not so much a tool of conscious expression as a kind of seismograph. It feels the vibrations and oscillations of the world that affect the heart. It twitches in response. Writing is a medium in the occult sense. It delivers signs from other realms through the human body, that is, via the heart-mind. The mark of the sage is that his expressions are attuned to natural movements and cosmological configurations. The heart-mind is truly that which moves through the middle.

The relations of old models to new expressions is much like the relations between proportion and motion in characters: that is to say, one could copy the ideal proportions of the classic models, carefully balancing and composing, yet never attain (their) heart-mind. Kūkai, for instance, writes that it is with calligraphy as it is with poetry: one must follow the authoritative models but not too carefully, for one must introduce heart-mind.[16] It is in the realm of motion and dynamic centers that one reaches for heart-mind. This is what the T'ang legacy around Wang Hsi-chih brought to the fore: a sense of the individuation of characters on the basis of their dynamics and mutual resonance. It was no longer enough to balance and coordinate characters through their uniform sizes and shapes. It was no longer enough to compose pages by lining up characters in tidy columns and rows. There must also be the play of the brush that comes from contractions or dilations of the heart-mind.

Yet there are strict limits to individuation in the calligraphic expression of heart-mind. Although the writer is self-consciously involved in the discipline required to master calligraphy, the goals of stylistic individuation are quite different from expression of individuality in the contemporary sense. The writer's heart-mind leaves its signature, and so calligraphy is often said to reveal the moral nature of the writer—which relates principally to the calligrapher's ability to bring composure or rectitude to her or his calligraphy. Inscription is, in a word, discipline. It provides a normative model. It is not possible to be a good person and a bad writer—just as in Heian aesthetics it is good people who produce good poems. Naturally, criteria for good character are variable historically and geopolitically, and there is a good deal of latitude for the able writer with respect to self-cultivation (this is discipline not disciplinization). Nevertheless calligraphy involves a normative model for expression (not a psychological or a Romantic one). This can best be imagined as a metaphor for expenditure.

Kūkai links writing to scattering and dispersing. It is as if the emotions involved in the act of calligraphy were literally e-motions, that is, outward fluxes or expenditures. It is not surprising, then, that calligraphy demands ritual cautions and devotions: one would not want to exhaust one's resources. Ritual observance and stylistic discipline involve a transversal flux—a flux through the writer's body from the cosmos or from prior masters. The writer's heart-mind thus enters into a realm of proper and productive forms. This is the goal of the calligraphic regulation of forms (previously mentioned in Komatsu's account of kana).

We have seen that histories of Heian calligraphy tend to locate the autonomy of Japanese styles in the context of a dissolution of regulated forms by stressing the suppleness, flow, abandon, and emotion of wa-styles. Heian tales would seem to confirm this dissolution or abandon. There are innumerable examples of women characters who seem to push beyond the regulated structure of feeling; in states of distress, their poems slip from their brush as fluidly as tears from the eye, and finally the women vanish, leaving behind a trail of poems brushed in abandon. Nonetheless, even if it is possible to see signs of the dissolution of order in a narrative like *The*

Tale of Genji (especially as it winds into the final scrolls), no alternative order is represented. Aesthetic judgments continue to present the regulation of transversal flux via the heart-mind as the paradigm for order. In the "Picture Competition" for instance, when Genji's team (the left) wins the day with the presentation of picture scrolls from his exile on the Suma coast, the commentary concludes:

> Then in the end, the left side had one last number, and when the Suma scrolls came forth, the counsellor's heart bounded. Although on the other side they too had mindfully set aside a particularly exceptional selection as their final scroll, it could not compare with such a thoroughly superior hand as this one that had brushed so calmly and composed the feelings of a heart at extremity. Beginning with the prince, no one could stop their tears. Even beyond what they had thought sad and painful about that world appeared—as if here and now—the movements that he would have made as well as the things felt in his heart; with the brush he had made manifest without obstruction the strands and inlets that had not yet been seen. Written in the grass hand, blended with kana—it was not the usual diary of details—he infused it with moving songs, which urged one along from one to another. No one thought of other matters, and the attraction to various other drawings all shifted to this one, so moving, so compelling. And so it came about that the left won, all and sundry yielding.[17]

These comments are of a different nature from those in Shōryōshū or Saiyō-shū, and yet they indicate that the ideal for practice is composure, which allows one to attune the heart-mind to natural movements. After his triumph, Genji speaks to his brother, the arbitrator, and his remarks celebrate not just the expression of heart-mind but also its regulation. (Recall, too, that his composure during his exile at Suma involved all manner of ritual observances.) Genji, who is radiant and illustrious by nature, seems able to regulate and express heart-mind almost spontaneously:

> Because I wasn't one to make certain distinctions, it was only in drawing, by some strange design, that there were occasions when I felt I might depict things, as though my heart somehow went out to them. When I unexpectedly became a mountain rustic and looked over the profound heart of sea to the four corners, although I would even have gone to the shadowless reaches unapproached in thought, there are limits to the motions of the brush, and I felt that matters had not gone

from the heart; since it would not do to have shown them to you out of the blue, I may be ill spoke of by later generations, in so far as they have received so much acclaim in this way.[18]

Aesthetic judgment of brushwork in such passages concerns itself with many of the same issues raised around Shōryōshū or Saiyōshū. Brushwork—in this case a mix of drawing, calligraphy, and poetry—evokes the heart-mind in relation to natural movements and operations. It is not enough to carefully copy characters. "There are limits to the motions of the brush," says Genji, "I felt matters had not gone from the heart." It is the heart-mind that allows the artist to echo or mime the operations of nature. There is a call for spontaneity. Nonetheless, it is the composure of the heart-mind that affects the viewers in "The Picture Competition." Likewise, in the "Plum Branch," the ideal of calligraphy is directed toward spontaneity or channeled nature. The notion of heart-mind as an aperture helps explain such ideals for brushwork.

We tend to think of emotional expression in opposition to regulation or organization. Yet, in the Heian world described in tales, because the heart-mind aperture is at once the site of dilations and contractions, emotional expression arises from the tension between them. It involves the tension of coagulation versus dispersion, or old models versus new expressions, or proportion and motion. It is as if the calligrapher must tune the strings of the heart-mind, make them perfectly taut so that they might respond to the vibrations of the world. Nativists like Motoori Norinaga were surely right to think of Heian Japan in terms of a world of emotion and sensation, but they were wrong to posit emotion in opposition to organization or regulation, as it so often is now. This is a structure of feeling, one that channels affect in the arena of political contest.

Discussions of calligraphy in The Tale of Genji describe a range of quite heterogeneous styles and judgments without attempting to develop a single, consistent thesis. Still, there emerges a grid of intelligibility for aesthetic judgment based on a loose competition between specific pairs. In "A Branch of Plum," Genji calls upon members of his entourage, his various wives and concubines, and his son, to fabricate perfumes and manuscripts for the presentation of his daughter at court. Judgments swing between specific pairs (which turn up throughout the tale).

— New versus old
— Kana versus mana

— Grass style versus stiff style
— Feminine style versus masculine style
— Yamato versus T'ang

The new often battles the old at aesthetic competitions. Genji himself, ever the renewer of order, often comments that this is a degenerate age in which people have drifted from the true models of the past. Overall, the tale follows the historical paradigm in which the high ages of the past supply the patterns and models for the present. The tension between old and new is loosely but not strictly aligned with a tension between mana and kana, and with T'ang styles versus Yamato styles (sometimes *kara* versus *wa*). A similar attitude prevails throughout. Even when victorious, kana and Yamato styles do not oust T'ang styles. Concern is expressed for how the old or the T'ang can be evoked, followed, renewed. Likewise with the stylistic differentiation of *kai* (stiff or regular style) and *sō* (grass or cursive style): able calligraphers like Genji have the capacity to shift from style to style. At different junctures, favor may fall to one style over the other, yet the logic of *awase* is one of permanent provocation or oscillation (not negation or absorption). Heian tales delight in the ways in which the mime plays with the model and allows for zones of autonomy (individuation). Yet mimicry is always related to authority, and even the call for mimicry itself is grounded in the T'ang legacy. Ultimately, when authority is situated, it is positioned squarely in the past; it is clear that the high ages and standards related to the emergence of the T'ang dynasty furnish the models for performative variations. The continued authority of T'ang styles might seem odd in so far as the T'ang dynasty fell in the early tenth century, and the Sung dynasty rose and splintered by the mid-twelfth century. It would seem then the T'ang model for dynastic emergence retained its hold on the courtly imagination, with the continued possibility for re-emergence and demand for renewal (and the inevitability of decline).

The Feminine Hand

In Heian texts, mana and kana seem to be generally associated with *wotokode* (masculine hand) and *wonnade* (feminine hand). Thus, the differentiation of feminine and masculine calligraphic styles roughly corresponds to a distinction between Yamato and Han/T'ang styles. The differentiation of gender in Heian styles is a complex issue, one that goes far beyond the boundaries of this study. Although I cannot address the issue fully in this context, it merits a brief discussion because it is such an important feature of calligraphic styles. In keeping with earlier arguments, I situate the question of gender in relation to calligraphic modes of differentiation and the cosmological imagination of community.

What does it mean to differentiate genders, or courts, or communities on the basis of styles? Commonly, the question is answered, as Suzuki does in *Kodaiwakashiron*, by replacing stylistic differences with ethnolinguistic divisions: Yamato forms are called Japanese language, and Han/T'ang forms are called Chinese language. In his discussion of the autonomy of kana culture, the feminine hand invariably comes into play:

> The stages toward the formation of the "feminine hand" (*hiragana* or *sōgana*)—a simplification of the "masculine hand" (so-called *man'yō-gana* in the stiff style)—were stages that steadily purified the *man'yō-gana* phonetics that employed Chinese and Japanese pronunciations for Chinese characters, and in so far as it became difficult to restore the original Chinese character, these stages also established the autonomy of the phonetic characters unique to our country.[19]

This is the reigning wisdom about the emergence of kana. There are three components—purity, autonomy, and femininity. A series of generalizations then mobilizes a discourse on the mother tongue. First, the feminine hand is collapsed onto the female sex—regardless of the fact that male poets also used it. Second, inscription is treated as purely phonographic. Third, Yamato styles are equated with Japanese ethnicity. As a consequence of these three reductions, the feminine hand is ultimately conflated with an unadulterated mother tongue. The alleged purity (or chastity) of Heian women becomes the site of Japanese autonomy. In the end, such reductions spin a dubious tale: that Japanese women remained pure and chaste, unadulterated by foreign forms.

Heian styles show, however, little interest in purity or chastity: forms entwine, couple, and interpenetrate. Recall too that Anderson suggests that classical sovereignty mobilized hybrids and hierarchies, rather than striving for purification or homogenization. Then, too, the lists of calligraphic styles in Heian texts are quite porous and heterogeneous.

The earliest extant usage of the terms wotokode (masculine hand) and wonnade (feminine hand) occurs in a passage from the *Utsuho monogatari* in which a number of stylistic designations are given: (1) the masculine hand, (2) the feminine hand, (3) a style that is neither masculine nor feminine,

(4) the reed hand and (5) katakana.[20] Kuboki Shōichi provides the standard interpretation: (1) the masculine hand corresponds to mana, (2) the neither-nor hand to sōgana or "grass characters"; (3) the feminine hand to hiragana; (4) katakana to katakana; and (5) the reed hand to reed hand.[21] Such an interpretation tends to organize the gender-labeled styles into a roughly developmental pattern; that is, as we are used to thinking that kana derive from a calligraphic cursification of Chinese characters, with a reduction in their number, the feminine hand is situated one stage beyond the grass style or sōgana.

Kuboki follows this line of stylistic derivation and claims that the gender-neutral hand corresponds to grass characters. In this way, the feminine hand is removed in advance from the realm of Chinese styles; he associates it with hiragana. But it should be pointed out that this association of kana with hiragana is completely anachronistic; the term itself does not appear until the Edo period. To introduce it is, in effect, to insinuate another level of difference into this list, because hiragana is more phonetic than sōgana. To support his separation of the feminine hand from grass characters, Kuboki turns to a passage from *The Tale of Genji* that mentions three styles: grass (sō), plain (tada), and feminine hand (wonnade). One could, of course, question the way in which Kuboki merges lists from different sources; but this is, after all, inevitable in a field in which documents are so scarce. I would simply like to suggest another reading of the same lists.

No less than five styles swarm onto the scene of writing, and in the *Utsuho* passage the implication is that one should become dexterous in all five styles. There is no simple sex or gender dimorphism; and it is particularly interesting that the passage evokes an intermediate, neither/nor style, a style that is seen as neither masculine nor feminine. The *Utsuho* list can be read alongside another source, *Saiyōshū*, the late Heian treatise on calligraphy mentioned earlier in this chapter. Apparently, education in calligraphy at the Heian court centered on *gyōsho* or current style. Students subsequently moved from this to the regular style or to the grass style, which are normally thought to correspond to masculine hand and feminine hand. In other words, one could view calligraphic styles in terms of masculine and feminine derivations from a "neuter" style rather than in terms of a movement from masculine Chinese forms to feminine native forms. This makes sense for a number of reasons.

— There arose a wealth of calligraphic styles, not reducible to a single-minded transformation.

—The formal and figural lability and permeability of Heian poetic texts suggests a zone of neither-nor.

—The terms *mana* and *kana* indicate formal or stylistic differences not linguistic ones.

Finally, if we think in terms of multiple derivations and transformations, it is possible to understand differently the Heian court's overlapping use of binaries like masculine/feminine and Yamato/Kara: not in terms of grammatical, racial, and sexual purity—that is, in terms of ethnolinguistic community—but, instead, in terms of the classical community. With its forms of regulated hybridity, the latter is geared not to strategies of exclusion, purification, or homogenization but to those of absorption, conversion, and hierarchicization.

This shift in emphasis helps us to understand certain aspects of the Heian imagination, in particular, (1) how it is that continental styles, however transformed or displaced, continue to be prevalent, even hegemonic, at court; (2) why gender mutability does not necessarily threaten the social order but, on the contrary, can confirm it; and (3) how femininity is dispersed and allocated across hierarchies and ranks in such a way as to foreclose the possibility of a feminine politics that is not consonant with court politics. These points demand further explanation.

Contemporary theory of sensory development tells us that, by and large, men and women are recognizable on the basis of their gait. This sexed gait, science submits, is not so much cultural as natural: women and men generally differ in the physical configuration of their center of gravity and their center of motion. Despite the claims for the naturalness of this difference, I would add that this difference never goes unconstructed. The case of Heian Japan, with its insistence on hobbling noble women with layers of robes and dresses, shows clearly how conventions contributed to a sexed dimorphism of movement and patterns of locomotion. Basically, feminine styles lower the center of gravity and raise the center of motion to such an extent that movement produces a wobbling, toppling, swaying, or swooning effect. I would like to suggest that the same dynamics—with a similar barbarous treatment of bodies—play into wonnade, with its emphasis on a similar tension between the coordinate center and the dynamic center. In other words, the Wang legacy, by opening the character to individuation, allows for mimicry with respect to gendered gaits or patterns of movement. The feminine hand, in brief, mimics a gait that is at once forcibly gendered yet apparently natural.

The dynamics of early Heian waka seem analogous. Tsurayuki's interpretation of the female poet Ono no Komachi makes sense in this light. He associates the Komachi style with a feminine weakness, like that of a noble woman who writhes in bed, devastated with illness and suffering. The poetic line turns and pivots too much for Tsurayuki: it fairly writhes and collapses. Indeed that is often said to be the hallmark of her poetry: a multiplication of pivotwords to the point of vertigo and collapse.

What does this shift in emphasis with respect to the feminine hand (and feminine poem) call attention to, other than a tendentious and even barbaric dimorphism of gender linked to an asymmetry of movement? First, it reminds us of the disciplinary apparatus that attends gendered styles, recalling that such differences draw out and implement physical differences, largely in the realm of movement, locomotion, and circulation. This is, in brief, an "overcoding" of bodies. The feminine hand, for instance, emerges in conjunction with the custom of cloistering noble women that developed in the course of the ninth century.[22] At Heijō-kyō in the Nara period, women frequently reigned (about half the sovereigns were female).[23] At the early Heian court, women apparently participated in the public composition of Chinese poetry. But, by the time of *Kokinwakashū*, one detects the woman deemed characteristic of court society: behind a series of screens, blinds, shutters, surrounded by female attendants, hobbled with layer upon layer of robes, the noble woman strategically conceals herself from the eyes of male courtiers, for seeing her was tantamount to knowing her sexually.[24] Men quite literally secured daughters, concubines, and wives within the wings and recesses of residences, constricting their movements with weighty attire and custom. Yet it was not a matter of purity and chastity but of strategic visibility and sexual alliance: the cloistered woman and her family could control how she was seen, and her future worth depended not only on the degree of her invisibility to male eyes but also on the quality of the poems that emerged from the darkness — the finesse of her hand as it yielded the brush, as it folded the paper. The wealth of her handicraft showed in the dyes and patterns of her papers, in the designs and textures of her robes, in the lure of her manufactured scents. Naturally, a noble woman did not make all these items with her own hands. Her hand, like her house, comprised a number of attendant hands and thus manifested both her skills and her resources, which would be integral in supplying the goods that served as items of exchange and that would assure the status of her man at the court. In this way, shifts in the woman's visibility located the feminine aura and authority in the dexterity of her hand; and for the noble woman, this aura enabled her to maintain a grasp on authority, though a tenuous one. After all, men not only could write in the feminine hand but could also assume ownership of the products of household manufacture.[25]

Of course, such an overcoding of bodies applied to men as well. It is hard to think of men's fashions, customs, and duties as any less restrictive. Nonetheless, there arose real differences with respect to the mobility of court women. Overall, the ability to move between styles and places belonged to male courtiers and coincided with a decrease in women's mobility and visibility. It is important to keep in mind that the authority of women depended on the aura of the feminine hand (in this enlarged sense), yet the feminine hand also exceeded them and thus "subjected" them. It is all too easy to repeat the Heian strictures around the feminine through a desire to see the feminine hand exclusively in terms of female autonomy.

Second, the shift in emphasis with respect to the feminine hand serves to undermine some of the assumptions of the discourse about the mother tongue, for it shows how that discourse works: it adopts the position of disciplinary power over court women, then extends that logic to the position of women in the modern nation; they are to be pure and virtuous bearers of the mother tongue. And so it is important to insist on this point: we simply cannot sustain an equation of kana, Japanese language, and women's purity.

Third, the "weakness" of the feminine hand derives from the play between coordinate and dynamic centers. As a result, calligraphic composition resorted to "contrapuntal" strategies of balance; that is, it made excessive dilations permissible and productive, provided they were balanced within an overall economy of interrelations. In Wang-derived styles, a very dynamic or even excessive character is brought into harmony with other styles. In sum, one would not expect to see such a thing as a feminine style in a purely autonomous state. And indeed, in the poetic anthologies for instance, we see either an alternation of styles or an emphasis on the relative proportion of characters and the rectitude of lines, as in figures 7 and 8. Appropriate then, to speak of the major kana texts in terms of a neither/nor space upon which stylistic differences—among them gendered differences—are brought into harmonious and productive relations of exchange and interchange (whence the alleged effectiveness of calligraphy and poetry).

Male courtiers wrote the feminine hand, as well as the feminine poem. A poet like Ki no Tsurayuki gained renown as a kind of female impersonator by writing poems in a feminine style.[26] Fathers who wished to promote their daughters at court found such skills of great use; not only could someone like Tsurayuki provide excellent calligraphic copybooks to instruct girls in various styles, including the feminine style, but a Tsurayuki could also compose poems in their names, helping to lure suitors. In other words, the increased mobility among styles belonged to men, first and foremost. This does not mean that court women had no access to power; in fact their activities and productivity (of paper, textiles, and so forth) were bound up in the political and economic exchanges of the court. It simply means that their role in the court hierarchies was not derived from a biological link to linguistic identity (that is, racially). It also means that the feminine hand cannot be equated with women's authority without some sense of mediation.

This gap between sex and gender opens up the possibility for gender mobility. That is, if a man like Tsurayuki could serve as a feminine impersonator of sorts, what was to prevent women from adopting masculine styles and serving in their stead?

It is not surprising that gender switches played a role in a number of Heian tales, most obviously in *Torikahebaya monogatari* and *Ariake no wakare*. In such tales, transformation and exchange are built into the interaction of gender, despite their apparent rootedness in physical or biological differences. Ultimately, in these stories, gender transformation is tolerated and even celebrated, provided it results in productive alliances. This is not a realm of anything goes, however, of free or random exchange or intercourse; it is ultimately an apparatus grounded in cosmological difference. It is cosmological in the sense that transformation is built into the conditions for binary operations and dichotomies. Transformation must, however, follow specific pathways and result in productive interpenetration. In brief, in the realm of social interactions, it would be easy to change styles or genders, but in the end, that exchange must result in productive intercourse — not to fulfill biological destiny but to satisfy the cosmological conditions for productive social transactions.

Conclusion

The calligraphy today deemed characteristic of the wa-style at the Heian court — that of poetry collections — is derived from the Wang styles of the T'ang dynasty, which both standardized styles and introduced an aesthetics of heart-mind reflected in an individuation of characters. This development can be thought of in terms of an introduction of smooth space into the character itself; that is, there is a potential for movement away from the strict striation of space within the inscription of individual characters. Instead of even rows of uniform characters, there are variations in size and speed that tend to differentiate characters, to impart individual signatures to different characters. Such a tendency is most fully actualized in the style known as "mad cursive" in which characters are of vastly different size and style and the overall composition is extremely heterogeneous.[27] Heian styles, however, never followed that route. The grass style of Heian manuscripts is quite regular: characters are fairly uniform in size (though initial characters in titles and topics tend to be somewhat broader and flatter), and columns introduce firm striations. The Heian style deploys the potential for introducing smooth space into characters in two ways: (1) columns tend to be irregularly indented and uneven in length, which creates diagonal patterns that cross through the composition (*chirashi gaki*, or "scattered writing"); (2) brushstrokes fluidly link two or four (and as many as six) characters in a single gesture.[28] See especially figure 7.

Such texts present styles that hover between smooth and striated tendencies. Inscription oscillates between two different formations, one that amplifies random fluctuations and modulations, one that imparts orientations and directions. Yet even the scattering of the grass style sustains distinct striations. It may push the Wang-derived potential to open characters to fluxes and variations, but it never allows inscription to lose its fundamental integrity and legibility. Calligraphy thus forms the basis for knowledge about the edge between randomness and order. Indeed, it seems to emerge out of natural forces as an expression of their implicit order. The Heian texts — that is, the poetic modes — play close to the boundary between smooth and striated space, in order to enact the potential of writing for ordering events.

In conclusion, although we can say that these features were, in some sense, specific to Heian calligraphy, they were also variations on the T'ang legacy — even grass-style kana texts. There is a nativist strain of history that would interpret these variations as signs of cultural autonomy or ethnic independence (and rationalist or evolutionist histories seem content to shore up the same national boundaries). Histories of Heian calligraphy occasionally signal the proximity of Heian styles to the T'ang tradition by dubbing them "styles of the ancient era" (*jodaiyō*), yet the goal for such histories remains the establishment of an autonomous Japanese tradition and sensibility, especially around the so-called wa-style of poetic texts. Heian texts, however, did not imagine stylistic variations as a basis for anything more than an awase-like contest. In fact, it is significant that Heian writers never equated stylistic differences with linguistic differences, though this is where modern accounts of Heian Japan ultimately strive to ground Japaneseness. Yet, as the operations of calligraphy attest, Heian Japan presents a mode of knowledge that did not ground itself in ethnolinguistic difference. Stylistic variations did contribute to the formation of boundaries but these differ profoundly from those suggested by the modern logic of ethnolinguistic territories. In fact, it is only when one moves beyond the Heian to the T'ang stylistic legacy that the functions and operations implicit to Heian calligraphy can be explored.

An additional feature characteristic of the Heian text is evident in the production of fantastical paperscapes: the tendency to layer different registers of expression. The poetic text deployed multiple registers of sensation—figural, musical, vocal, visual, verbal, pictorial—in order to compose a smooth or random interplay (modulations, alternations, juxtapositions, superpositions, oscillations). This is the topic of the next chapter, and it demands a kind of phenomenological attention to texts.

The "moment of the brush" brings with it enmeshed registers of expression. Its signs are at once visual and vocal; its art is intensely manual and gestural. Without some account of the interaction of vocal, visual, and manual registers, it is impossible to account for how the reader entered into these texts. It is not exactly a question of production and reception, for these notions ultimately relate to a closed economy of communication (sender, message, receiver), one that does not exactly obtain at the level of brushwork. With brushwork, it is a question of sensory interpellation—or, rather, embodiment. Calligraphy, which conjoins the visual/vocal matrix of the sign with the manual machine of the brush, is but the point of departure for vaster articulations and juxtapositions of the senses. In the next chapter, I will show that the Wang legacy not only opens the character to fluxes that align human hearts with the natural movements and operations but also enables the appearance of multisensible figures that embody the subject and the senses in a cosmological realm.

SIX. *The Multisensible Figure:*
Ashide Shita-e Wakanrōeishō

Moving down the page, the brush encounters an image, perhaps a riverbank or marsh, and at the point where the fluid line of characters meets the image, characters mutate into new forms. Some characters transform themselves into cranes, poised on one leg in the shallow waters of the strand; others sprout leaves, and their forms hover between the delicate blades of reeds and the forms of kana characters. This is the style known as *ashide* or the "reed hand." In some portions of the manuscript dubbed *Ashide shita-e Wakanrōeishō*—the "reed-hand under-picture rendition of the 'Collection of Yamato and Han Cantillations' "—there are also painted scenes behind the calligraphy, a *shita-e* or "under-picture" with images of horses, rustic huts, baskets, trees, flowers, and so forth. The combination of reed hand and under-picture enables any number of intersections between graphic and pictorial registers. For instance, in the segment of songs written for the new year, the lines of characters are superimposed on a picture of baskets, possibly for the collection of new herbs.[1] As the brush moves over the picture, the forms of characters and the leaves of plants overlap and twine, blurring the boundary between image and inscription, between seeing and writing, as in figure 9.

There are many registers and layers of expression to the "reed-hand under-picture Collection of Han and Yamato Cantillations." In addition to the calligraphic and pictorial registers, there are the vocal and musical registers implied in a collection of cantillations; and because the songs have words, there is a verbal register of expression as well. The modern standard editions of this poetic collection collapse these various registers onto the verbal register. (A glance at the standard edition of *Wakanrōeishū*, that is, the poetry collection without calligraphy or images, in the Shinchō series of

Japanese classics shows how transcription, annotation, and interpretation have congealed around the verbal register of Heian poetics at the expense of other registers.) There are a number of reasons for this insistence on the verbal register. First are the practical or empirical reasons: that is, there is precious little evidence about the vocal or musical register, and, what is more, it is difficult for modern readers to engage with the graphic and pictorial registers. Second are the ideological reasons, which are never entirely separable from the practical and empirical. I have already discussed in this regard how the insistence on the verbal register shores up the general emphasis on ethnolinguistic boundaries that characterizes so many studies of Heian Japan.

In addition to the various aesthetic registers of expression, there are diverse layers of expression involved in the production of this collection. One might speak of the calligrapher Fujiwara no Koreyuki (1149–1175) and the compiler Fujiwara no Kintō (966–1041) as well as the series of composers whose songs figure in this collection (not to mention the dyers and papermakers, who remain anonymous). To some extent, the names Kintō and Koreyuki correspond with the coordination of distinct registers of expression. That is to say, Kintō compiled the songs (vocal and verbal registers), while years later Koreyuki performed the brushwork (graphic and pictorial registers). How can we imagine this intersection of music and brushwork?

Around 1013, inspired in part by the Heian interest in the poetry of T'ang composer Po Chu-i, Kintō collected some 589 Han poems (kanshi) and 216 Yamato poems (waka). The resultant "Collection of Han and Yamato Cantillations" enjoyed great popularity at the Heian court. Among the extant manuscripts of Heian calligraphy, it ranks second only to Kokinwakashū, in the number of surviving copies and above Man'yōshū.[2] As suggested by the term rōei (here fancifully translated as "cantillation"), the rhythms of music, probably derived from T'ang styles, served as a format for conjoining Han and Yamato songs.

"The name rōei is of Chinese origin and is mentioned in the Wen-hsuan (Japanese, Monzen) and the Pai-shih Wen-chi (Japanese, Hakushi-monjū)," writes Eta Harich-Schneider in her study. "The meaning is: to sing joyfully with a loud voice. With reference to a specific type of literary and musical pastime in Japan the term seems to have been first used by Fujiwara Kintō. In contrast to waka, which are poems in Japanese style, rōei are exclusively vocal pieces on texts from the Chinese, or texts deliberately imitating the various Chinese literary styles.[3] The T'ang sources of this form of musical vocalization should raise some questions about how a collection of rōei came to include waka. Were both waka and kanshi considered material for rōei? A common musical form would seem to imply a fundamental equivalency of Han and Yamato modes.

Similarly, calligraphic performance can be imagined as a basis for the intersection of Han and Yamato forms. Indeed, in this context, music and calligraphy are analogous forms. There is a tendency, however, in current disciplines to establish boundaries between various arts, a tendency that covers over possible intersections. Harich-Schneider, for instance, moves back and forth between literature and music in her discussion; yet she avoids the possibility that the "Collection of Han and Yamato Cantillations" might serve multiple purposes, that it might provide a ground for the interpenetration of different registers. "The *Wakan-rōei-shū* was also a literary textbook," she writes. "It may even have served more as a pattern for calligraphy than as a 'musical score.' But one may have sung the rōei from these scrolls. It is the first collection in which the term rōei occurs, and this term, after all, is a musical and not a literary term." [4]

In a study of calligraphy inspired by the phenomenology of Merleau-Ponty, Jean-François Billeter takes a very different tack. He uses an extended comparison to musical performance in order to explain the dynamics of calligraphy: in calligraphy, strokes or traits, like notes, are attacked, drawn out, sustained, much in the manner of performance on a musical instrument. The qualities attached to a calligraphic performance of a text are analogous to those associated with a virtuoso rendition of a score.[5] Billeter's phenomenological discussion of calligraphy provides one way to imagine that brushwork and cantillation intersect at some level, in so far as both arise around a ground of rhythmic qualities and intensities. In the final analysis, Billeter champions a classic sense of control and discipline (as opposed to modernist and existentialist anxieties), linking qualities and intensities to the expression of an internal and ideal sense of the body (the body proper). He thus evokes ancient discipline as a balm for the anxiety of the modern era—a fairly common scenario yet a suspect one in that it exhorts us to overcome modern alienation with greater discipline and conformity. In this respect, his account reminds us that the contemporary evocation of qualities and intensities need not necessarily be liberating or progressive; it can involve an insistence on conventions and regulations with a call for the revival of ancient orders.

I nonetheless evoke Billeter's idea of a microaesthetic overlap of music and brushwork in order to shift analysis away from an insistence on grammars, genres, and languages as the grid of intelligibility for Heian poetics. Kintō's use of rōei-style cantillation points to a site where rhythmic qualities, not linguistic identities, provide the ground for poetic knowledge. Such a text demands that we begin not with distinct arts, genres, or languages but with aesthetic registers—different registers of perception, sensation, and expression. Unfortunately, there is little material available for even an imaginative construction of rōei-style performances at the Heian court.[6] The calligraphic record, despite its lacunae, provides greater latitude for the historical exploration of a-signifying or nonlinguistic forms of expression. For this reason, I tend to bypass the musical register and concentrate on the intersection of pictorial, graphic, and verbal registers. I will continue to use the term *layers of expression* to refer to the historico-communal dimension of the text—that is, such different layers of production as compilation, composition, and calligraphy. I use *registers of expression* to indicate the phenomenological dimension—that is, different sensory operations or potentials, such as seeing, speaking, and so on. I subsequently introduce the term *levels of expression* in relation to differences in magnitude—poems and images are larger than characters, yet smaller than scrolls, or seasonal cycles.

In 1160, when Koreyuki did the brushwork for *Wakanrōeishō*, the Heian court had reached a point of crisis. With the apocalyptic sense of entering the latter days of the law, and with power accruing on the eastern plains, the court devoted even closer attention to its realms of authority, especially its production of signs. There occurred an intensification of contests and expenditure, and apparently, an increased interest in the consolidating of calligraphic schools and lineages. Koreyuki himself wrote a treatise called *Yakaku teikinshō* in which he describes himself as the sixth descendant of the famous Yukinari, carrying on the styles consolidated into the Sesonji school.[7] Similarly, a text like *Ashide shita-e Wakanrōeishō* recalls the glories and lineages of the Heian court; and a resplendent performance of that text could serve as a sign that past fortunes might be recalled and sustained. With his performance of the graphic and pictorial registers, Koreyuki could evoke the prestige and authority of Kintō's famous compilation. In sum, we can situate the text in relation to a bid for authority. We should also recall that the text itself is a form of wealth; it is integral to the economic exchange. In this analysis I will try to deal with the questions: "What kind of authority?" and "How might it work?"

Initially, the pictorial register of Koreyuki's performance seems to consist of illustrations for the poems; or at least, the images seem appropriate to Kintō's layout of poetic topics in the two scrolls. The first scroll presents the cycle of seasons and unwinds from the first days of spring (from the new year) through the summer, autumn, and winter. The second scroll range across a series of topics: wind, clouds, dawn, pine, bamboo, grasses, monkeys, wine, mountain water, former capitals, mountain temples, Buddhist matters, princes, singing girls, intimate friends, love, impermanence, whiteness. The first scroll, with its seasonal cycles, might be said to concern celestial movements, while the second, with its loose series of things, places, and relations, might be said to concern terrestrial events. The under-pictures represent images that are, in some sense, germane to the topics, yet the link is not exactly that of illustration. Images are appropriate or auspicious but they do not really depict what the poems say. Then too, the scenes of the under-pictures are not framed. They have porous boundaries, and their lines are drawn out in such a way that they appear to form the contours of hills, shores, or riverbanks. Thus images emerge out of an expanse of unwinding paper, then dissolve into strokes and traits that return into the texture of tangled fibers. At the end of each scroll, images and poems both fade away, into a blankness that is not exactly a void (for it is replete with textures and nuances). In brief, the logic of the images is not that of illustration, any more than that of the poems and topics is narration. There are links and associations, cycles and series, that demand a rethinking of the relations of image and text.

The practical and analytical separation of image and text is often considered constitutive of modern modes of representation, particularly in the West. Foucault calls attention to the modern divide between image and text and approaches this problematic in a novel way—at once historically, aesthetically, and discursively. First, he locates a general historical moment in Western Europe: between the fifteenth and the twentieth centuries a separation arose between the plastic and the linguistic. "The two systems can neither merge nor intersect," he writes, signaling that plastic representation must bear a resemblance to what it shows, while linguistic representation must exclude resemblance between the sign and its referent. "What is essential is that verbal signs and visual representations are never given at once," he concludes. "An order always hierarchizes them, running from the figure to discourse or from discourse to the figure."[8]

Foucault is concerned with modernist modes that subvert the modern injunction to separate and hierarchize images and texts. His point of departure is Guillaume Apollonaire (1880–1918), whose calligrams let verbal signs and visual representations appear at once. Thus the calligram—in which the letters of a poem take on the shape of the something named in the poem, "aspires playfully to efface the oldest oppositions of our alphabetical civilization: to show and to name; to shape and to say; . . . to look and to read.[9] This is precisely the anomaly presented in a text like *Ashide shita-e Wakanrōeishō*, an anomaly that modern standard editions have done their best to suppress: the joint presentation of verbal and visual registers, which suggests a regime of reading profoundly different from those of modern studies.

Despite the cleverness of his calligrams, however, Apollonaire remains for Foucault thoroughly enmeshed in the modern order of representation. Rather than undermining modern notions of representation, calligrams, on the contrary, are deploying it in order to operate a "double capture." Cleverly arranged on a sheet of paper, signs invoke the very thing of which they speak, and in return, visible form is excavated by words that work at it from within, spinning a web of significations that fix it in the universe of discourse. "A double trap, an unavoidable snare: How henceforth would escape the flight of birds, the transitory form of flowers, the falling rain?"[10]

A look at the images drawn beneath the "Collection of Han and Yamato Cantillations" suggests something analogous to the double capture of the calligram. One series of poems, those that deal with the first days of the new year, seem to enact a kind of mutual snare of seeing and speaking. Beneath the lines of calligraphy looms the image of a woven basket, a basket in which one might collect the first sprouts of early spring. On the first day of the rat of the new year, emperor and courtiers would leave the capital for a designated site outside the capital. They would pull up pine saplings to plant in gardens in the capital—evergreens as a sign of longevity, of ten thousand years. They would pluck fresh sprouts of the seven auspicious herbs; and these herbs, brewed in a rice gruel, would impart good health to the emperor, as well as to members of other households that prepared the herbal gruel.[11] Superimposed on the scene of grasses and herb baskets, the lines of poem sing of the ten thousand years of the evergreen saplings, and of new herbs and eternal health. Because the poems seem to sing what the scenes depict, the intersection of poetic utterance and painted image seems to be one of mutual reinforcement: a double capture, an avoidable snare. Again, see figure 9.

Likewise with the reed hand: as the brush winds over the porous edges of the basket scene, characters mutate into shapes that recall grasses and birds. There arise relations that do not seem entirely arbitrary: as the line of characters crosses the drawn-out contours of the image, it transforms into sprouting grasses and cranes standing along what might be a riverine strand. For a series of poems on the new year, what could be more appropriate than characters that transform themselves into cranes (signs of longevity) or into herbs and grasses (brewed for vitality)? In sum, there are at least two levels at which something like a double capture seems to occur: images depict what poems sing, and then, the sound-forms of characters mutate into tiny images that reinforce the vitality and longevity praised in the songs. How henceforth to escape the longevity and vitality promised by saplings and sprouts?

In *Ashide shita-e Wakanrōeishō*, however, the relation between seeing and speaking is not exactly like that of the calligram. The calligram reinforces and relies on the authority of the proper name, because the poem says what the shape depicts, and vice versa. This is a modern logic of representation based on depiction and illustration—one that takes the amplified form of pictography, as in Apollonaire. It is not surprising then that, for Foucault, it is René Magritte's "unraveled calligrams" that take the honors. The unraveled calligram perverts or subverts pictography. Magritte disturbs all our seemingly stable bonds between language and the image, with figures like "this is not a pipe," in which the authority of the proper name (and its image) is challenged.

Ashide shita-e Wakanrōeishō, like the calligram, affords an intersection between seeing and speaking, or singing and looking, one that is not arbitrary. There are modes of resonance among sounds, figures, images, and songs; yet these do not function like depiction, illustration, or representation; they are not pictography. For this reason, analysis of *Ashide shita-e Wakanrōeishō* might easily slide into a modernist or even postmodernist space—that is, a space that challenges the modern order of representation—alongside commentary on the work of Magritte, or Klee, or Kandinsky. In fact, I turned to Foucault as a point of departure for *Ashide shita-e Wakanrōeishō* in order to highlight the problematic situation of the nonmodern or premodern in contemporary analysis.

On the one hand, with its insistence on the verbal register, our current standard editions (as well as disciplinary divisions) strive to situate *Ashide shita-e Wakanrōeishō* within the modern order of representation: poems designate, and images illustrate or embellish. On the other hand, a counter insistence on styles and figures tends to align it with the modernist challenge (and the critique of modernity)—a counterstrategy that always runs the risk of a simple appropriation of historical otherness. In order to navigate these difficult currents, I retain the critique of modernity in order to gain insight into the otherness of the Heian text. I also insist on the authorities implicit in the premodern or nonmodern text, in order to avoid a facile sense of liberation from all orders.

Even though, like the calligram, *Ashide shita-e Wakanrōeishō* involves a kind of double capture, I have already suggested some fundamental differences. (1) Its images are not framed in distinction to inscription; it also allows for minute interpenetrations of sounds and shapes, as with the reed hand. This implies that its double capture crosses various levels of magnitude, whereas the so-called modern order of representation insists on convergence only at the (pictographic) level of designation and illustration (the brushstrokes of a painted illustration, for instance, need not depict the story; only the overall image does so). In short, the scope or range of double capture is greater, at once vast and intricate. (2) The *Wakanrōeishū* does not congeal around one author or artist but comprises various layers of expression. (3) Its zones of microaesthetic intersection, in conjunction with the porous boundaries of picture and song, imply very different qualities, which are related to rhythms and intensities rather than image and proper name. If these differences—related to levels, layers, and registers of expression—can be summed in a single word, it would be *resonance*.

To explore the logic of resonance, I begin with an extended analysis of a series of poems from *Ashide shita-e Wakanrōeishō*, a segment from the first day of rat of the new year, when courtiers gathered evergreens and sprouts from the fields around the capital. I look first at a poem by Songiyau (or Songyō), a Buddhist name adopted by Tachibana no Aritsura when he took his vows in 944 (he is also known posthumously by the Buddhist name Zairetsu; his birth and death dates are unknown). But I shall preface my transcriptions, translations, and interpretations of his poem with some comments about centering the analysis on a poet versus paying attention to a chorus of expressions.

It is common in waka studies to organize analysis around the composer.

For instance, one could trace all poems attributed to Songyō in various anthologies and then search for mentions of him in diaries, records, and so forth. Yet there remains the question of whether, in a text like *Ashide shita-e Wakanrōeishō*, expression centers on, and originates with, the composer. What of Kintō the compiler? What of Koreyuki the calligrapher, who actually signs the poem? Too often the proper name of the poet forecloses discussion of the multiple layers of expression. In fact, the insistence on centering analysis on proper names and poets ensures that the art of compilation and inscription will be treated as supplements to the verbal register of the poem. It presupposes that these other modes of expression have no significant effect on, or interaction with, the verbal register.

Aesthetic judgments in *The Tale of Genji*, for example, attend to a number of layers simultaneously, mentioning the calligrapher, the illustrator, the composer, the paper, the spindles of the scroll, the stand on which it lay, or any number of combinations of effects. Similarly, at poem contests, courtiers fashioned elaborate miniatures of gardens in which to present the poem, in which case, visual presentation could be said to precede its inscription, and its inscription to precede its recitation. Heian aesthetics did not dwell on the verbal register. In different circumstances, it may be that composition or recitation came to the fore, but even then it was not a matter of signification pure and simple. Overall, Heian aesthetic judgment remained unconcerned with isolating registers of expression. What counted was the "chorus" or "choreography" of expressions—the ways in which courtiers differentiated and coordinated inscription, recitation, and composition with other modes of production. Traditionally, of course, the Confucian legacy ranked poetry above calligraphy, and calligraphy above painting, and this legacy formed the general background for Heian arts. If poetry ranks highest, however, it is not because it purifies the verbal register. The traditional privilege accorded to poetry does not mean that the verbal register rates higher than the graphic or pictorial register. Poetry ranks highest because it comprises image, word, music, and gesture; it incorporates or synthesizes various modes of expression. Its virtues thus lie in its synthetic potential (not in linguistic purification).

Scholarly apparatus is heavily invested in philology, linguistics, and the isolation of the verbal register, and such an apparatus is inextricable from assumptions about the isolation, homogenization, and purification of national cultures and languages.[12] That I turn to transcription and translation of a segment from *Ashide shita-e Wakanrōeishō* attests to the hold of that legacy. My analysis, however, calls on figural registers of this text—under-pictures, calligraphy, poetic imagery—in order to decenter the usual emphasis on the verbal register. (Of course, as Foucault cautions, not all modes of visuality decenter our traditions.) Layers of expression—Songyō, Kintō, Koreyuki—suggest that we need to think in terms of a chorus and choreography. The poem then is already a hybrid affair, a site of synthesis of levels and layers of expression.

The first song in the sequence, the Songyō entry, is a Han-style song written in the *gyō* or current style with a fluidity that borders on *sō* or grass style. The poem sings of courtiers who grasp pine saplings and branches of flowering plum trees and carry these signs of vitality and longevity back to the capital to harness the forces of the new year. (See also figure 9.)

倚松根摩腰　千年之翠満手　折梅花挿頭　二月之雪落衣　　尊敬
Against pines we recline, our hips at their roots rub;
evergreen fill our hands with one thousand years;
branches of plum flowers, plucked, adorn our hair;
spring snows fall on our robes.　　Songiyau[13]

The body of the courtiers fairly merge with the pines and plums—roots on hips, pine boughs in hands, plum flowers brandished aloft with petals fluttering down on patterned robes. The forms of human bodies—like the patterns of robes—conjoin with the forms of spring growth deemed so auspicious in the first days of the new year. In the domain of poetic imagery, courtiers overlap with pines and plums. In addition, there is the visual confusion of seasons. Those white petals that scatter from above, falling on patterned robes, are they the snows of spring? Has winter lingered to scatter its snow petals on the first days of spring?

Those who hold branches of plum flowers overhead hover between two seasons. They pause at the moment of the new year when winter becomes spring, and falling snows give way to falling petals. This becomes an eternal moment: with evergreens and plum blossoms in hand, the courtiers grasp not only two seasons but also the longevity of one thousand years. The courtly body becomes an eternal, renewable body, akin to that of trees and flowers. The visual merging of courtiers with roots, boughs, and petals is reinforced in the vocal register: the rhythms of characters form two couplets that resonate in almost perfect parallels; pines merge with humans, imparting one thousand years; flowers merge with humans, imparting an eternal spring. Within the song itself there is a kind of double capture between speaking and seeing: vocal rhythms and visual images together conspire to conjoin two patterns—the cycles of the seasons with the actions of humans. Thus the song deftly twines the courtly body with cosmological patterns.

Even in the space of the poem, without reference to calligraphy or compilation, there is a double capture of seeing and speaking. Without speaking or intoning in a certain way, one would not arrive at the visual conjunction of humans and seasons—or, at least, one would not arrive at a dexterously punctuated and rhythmically aligned conjunction. In this respect, vocal rhythm is a way of marking off space as well as of keeping time. For instance, this Han-style poem uses vocal rhythms (and tonal sonorities) in order to arrive at a kind of spatial delineation of parallel lines that reinforce a superimposition or fusion of two forms: trees and humans. Following standard practice, I have transcribed and translated the poem in accordance with such vocal patterns. It is significant, however, that calligraphy unfurls its vertical columns without concern for a scriptural replication of vocal patterns. It does not even break its lines in accordance to the couplets. This is significant because it shows that the spatial logic of calligraphy differs greatly from Western poetics, which, with its logic of the frame, demands a digression.

If one thinks of poetic meters and feet in a literal way, then poetry is a way of delineating space by pacing and measuring with the voice-foot. Without the leaps, skips, and bounds of spondee and trochee and such, the poetic foot would be a plodding step, the left-right-left of a tired shuffle or a steep military march. By the twentieth century, the walk-and-talk of poetic meter came to imply a kind of stiff, dimwitted marching, even with its variations in gait and bounce. Successive generations of poets tried different ways of organizing poetic space, inventing new rhythms—changeable rhythms, arhythmic rhythms—in an attempt to alter the rigid pace of the French alexandrine or English iambic pentameter; or, in Japan, to break the march of alternating fives and sevens inherited from the court tradition. Yet this sense that the old rhythms had become restrictive and senseless is more complex than a simple desire for vocal or rhythmic novelties. It also relates to transformations in the graphic and visual presentation of poetry.

Modern typography lends itself to a consolidation of the quadrate effect of poetry: the straight margin holds the left edge of the poem in place, and on the right, the line breaks, typically in conjunction with meters and rhymes. Thus visual and vocal patterns were made completely complicitous. Likewise with the pictography of the calligram: for all its playfulness, when it converts typography into pictography, the calligram simply augments and encrypts the logic of the frame. Michael Butor, for instance, complains that calligrams "have the major drawback of being, for the most part, nothing but texts laid out according to the lines of a drawing that is very poorly executed typographically.[14] Typography shores up a convergence of visual and vocal registers, which ensures the inevitability of the frame, in the poem as in the calligram. This system is no stranger to modern Japanese poetics, either.[15] The framing of poetry (as a kind of quadrate space of resemblance) is characteristic of *modern* poetics, in which visual patterns and vocal patterns converge to define and delineate poetic space.

Modern poetics has come to rely heavily on the frame in order to render art; words are graphically, visually framed in order to render them poetic. For all its sonorities, we might not read "April is the cruellest month, breeding lilacs out of the dead land, mixing memory and desire, stirring dull roots with spring rain" as a line of poetry. But T. S. Eliot opens *The Waste Land* with

> April is the cruellest month, breeding
> Lilacs out of the dead land, mixing
> Memory and desire, stirring
> Dull roots with spring rain.

The visual breaks give a different cadence to his sentence; the gerunds become appoggiatura leaning into, and generating, the expectation of resolution. The words are now a poem. The graphic breaks of the line form the outline of a rhythm that became Eliot's hallmark: a line with beats that mimic and purify the rhythms of colloquial English, banishing the singsong walk of iambic pentameter without resorting to free verse. Of course, even as Eliot relies on the poetic frame in order to establish his poem, he challenges this legacy in other ways.

Within the poetic frame, correspondences could spring up between painting and poetry. Throughout the nineteenth century, as art objects moved into galleries and museums, the poem often modeled itself on the objet d'art; poems painted pictures, drew symbols, sculpted objects. Then, as images within the frame began to waver and were sublimated under the close empirical eye of the Impressionists, French symbolist poets likewise framed an aesthetics of glimpses in poetry, using dark-voweled rhymes and fleeting symbols. By the end of the nineteenth century, poets had identified the frame as a form of aesthetic closure, and they began to rupture the frame, strategically. The poetic frame had become both a boundary and a site of transgression.

When Pound, Eliot, and other artists of their generation turned to the museum with its isolated objects and framed pictures, they lauded the fragment, the incomplete portion of history that opened uncertainly into the present. Pound arrives at visual patterns or figures that isolate and fragment the voice in an attempt to fracture the frame of the poem and set it in motion.

> Spring . . . .
> Too long . . . .
> Gongula . . . .

So speaks a fragment of Sappho in Pound's dialect. The rest of the poem does not survive, and yet . . . . Well, that is Pound's point. A papyrus fragment appears as if in a frame, yet in a frame that remains eerily incomplete, a frame that can no longer quite contain or complete the past that it resurrects in isolation.[16]

Now the mainstream of academic accounts of Heian poetry avoid the modernist raid on the frame. This is especially true of Anglo-American scholarship, with the exception of Mark Morris, who has consistently raised the question of whether waka is poetry at all.[17] In particular, Morris challenges the ways in which translators impose quadrate space on waka, such as I have done with the above Han-style poem. This is an engrained practice, one that entails a number of stages and assumptions. The modern Japanese editions too strip away the graphic and pictorial registers in order to isolate the verbal register. They frequently alter the usage of characters, for the ease of the reader and often introduce typographic breaks to indicate the grammatical emphasis of the poem. Still, in the modern Japanese edition, the waka poem retains a sense, albeit greatly diminished, that it is a line. Anglo-American translations, however, break the waka pattern of 5-7-5-7-7 syllables into five lines, and array them in a quadrate space (or, as in the above Han-style poem, make the syllabic breaks 5-6-5-6). This is to ensure that the reader will see waka (or kanshi) as poetry. To counter this domestication, Morris suggests that we think of the waka in terms of a line—which point becomes important in the discussion below.

There is another aspect to the domestication of Heian poetry: the imposition of quadrate space is a continuation of the practice of isolating and privileging the verbal register, which grounds us in a form of ethnolinguistic interpretation. For instance, the Han-style poem above might be transcribed into classical Japanese, to suggest (as Karaki Junzō does) that Heian courtiers couldn't possibly have understood or performed it as classical Chinese. It may be that Heian Chinese was quite idiosyncratic, but it cannot thus be collapsed into Japanese. In fact, as *Ashide shita-e Wakanrōeishō* shows, the Heian differentiation of terms like "Chinese" (*kan*) and "Japanese" (*wa*) do not correspond to modern linguistic boundaries. Nevertheless, our ethnocentric insistence on the poetic frame tends to shore up the assumptions of ethnolinguistic analysis. Indeed, it is not unusual for Anglo-American translations of Heian poetry to transcribe the poems in modern Japanese, as in the two translations of *Kokinwakashū*. All in all, Japanese and Euro-American practices of transliteration and translation are thoroughly complicitous in the imposition of the frame of modern Japaneseness on Heian poetry.

The modernist raid on the poetic frame does not really deal with such engrained practices and the assumptions that surround transcription and translation. But then, it would be unrealistic to expect translations to unravel an entire discipline and methodology. That is the goal of analysis and interpretation. Moreover, there are all manner of problems that attend the modernist emphasis on difference, not least of which is its potential for complicity with nativism and orientalism. At present, I wish to explore how modernist poetics nonetheless makes possible a different encounter with nonmodern forms like Heian poetry, one that highlights the possibility of their aesthetic differences. For Pound in particular, the encounter with traditional Japanese and Chinese poetry suggested a poetics that defied the modern logic of sound and image.[18] First and foremost, these other poetics suggested to Pound another mode of visuality in relation to poetic imagery—as in his famous haiku.

> In a Station of the Metro
> The apparition of these faces in the crowd;
> Petals on a wet, black bough.

In this poem, a suppressed simile juxtaposes or "superposes" two images (faces and petals)—images or ideas. "The 'one image poem' " Pound wrote, "is a form of super-position, that is to say, it is one idea set on top of another.[19] His take on poetic imagery, now almost a commonplace, lays the ground for understanding such poetry in terms of visual overlap or "superposition" rather than depiction, illustration, on representation.

In the wake of Pound, it is hard not to see Songyō's poem in terms of superposition. The Songyō poem deftly evokes human forms and tree forms, and without any indication of comparison or simile, poses one on the other, to the extent that humans and spring trees entwine inextricably. Of course, there are some important differences between Pound and Heian poetics. First, there is the Heian insistence on conventional expression. Second, Heian poetics evokes a kind of visuality that might be called "pattern recognition"—as with patterns of fluttering blossoms and those of falling snowflakes; or, the forms of trees (roots, boughs, etc.) and the forms of human bodies (hips, hands, etc.)—and these are often patterns of motion.

Third, the act of pattern recognition crosses levels of expression. In Songyō's song, characters themselves show a certain visual affiliation with poetic imagery. The poem selects characters whose left side (the radical or signific) repeats trees and hand. Of course, Pound too evoked the visual qualities of Chinese characters, particularly in his "Cantos"; and yet, for all his rhetoric of energies and mimicry, his imagination of characters remains close to pictography. It seems that, regardless of the modernist effort to break the poetic frame, modern typography consistently reintroduces effects of resemblance into its matrix. It is in this way, in particular, that a poetic form that derives its sense of line, center, and boundary from calligraphy differs profoundly from modern or modernist poetics. The movements of the brush itself mime the movements of things. Yet, rather than depict things or reproduce their semblance, calligraphy follows and makes manifest the mobile patterns of phenomena. Its use of dynamic centers evokes a sense of animated bodies. In this respect, resonance differs from superposition (as well as pictography), and this digression into modernism helps us to elucidate some of its qualities. Whereas superposition works to introduce play between vocal and visual registers in order to break the poetic frame, resonance begins with unframed interactions among sensory registers in order to locate centers of motion. By locating centers of motion and establishing patterns of resonance among them, Heian poetics lays claim to a vast project of synthesis. Calligraphy is integral to this project.

The synthetic potential of calligraphy is nowhere more obvious than in the stylistic shifts that attend the transition from Han to Yamato song in *Ashide shita-e Wakanrōeishō*. Songyō's song is a Han-style song, and Koreyuki renders it in the "current style" or "running style" (*gyōsho*). The current style is sometimes construed as the cursive intermediate between the "stiff style" (*kaisho*) and the "grass style" (*sōsho*). Billeter however argues convincingly that the current style is extremely close to the stiff style, while the grass style is significantly different from both. His remarks make sense in this context for two reasons. First, *Saiyōshō* indicates that Heian instruction in calligraphy began with the current style, substituting it for the stiff or standard style. Second, the distinction of stiff/current style versus grass style corresponds nicely to the Heian differentiation of mana and kana. (Recall that the Heian differentiation of mana and kana corresponds generally to Han/T'ang versus Yamato styles.) This is precisely what occurs in *Ashide shita-e Wakanrōeishō*: the brush shifts deftly from Han to Yamato song, from current to grass style, or from mana to kana. (See figure 9.) If this shift is parsed only in terms of the verbal register, the result is incommensurable grammars and genres. If it is read calligraphically, then it can be read for its stylistic resonance and synthesis. As we see below, other features support the notion of stylistic synthesis.

For example, Mibu no Tadamine, who flourished around 920, composes:

子の日する野辺に小松のなかりせば
千年のためしになにをひかまし　　　忠岑

Were there no evergreen saplings in the fields of this new-year day,
what would we draw forth in anticipation of one thousand
generations?　　　Tadamine

Tadamine poses a riddle about the signs of spring. His question, thoroughly disingenuous, follows directly from the imagery of the preceding song. If there were no pines rooted in the fields, he asks, what would courtiers pull up and take back to the capital as signs of longevity?

Note that Tadamine's song question captures the event through the repetition of its gestures. Its query does not challenge the act of drawing forth evergreens. It takes that gesture and mimes it in a riddlelike query. The rhetorical twist of the poetic line constitutes a gesture. The verb for "drawing forth" (*hiku*) resonates with gestures, even that of the act of writing: drawing out lines. Thus the poem replicates and amplifies the ritual act. It says nothing, it shows nothing. It simply turns and gestures. Rhetorical questions, suppositions, and riddles, so common to Heian poetry (whether Han or Yamato style) conjure up a sense of doubleness, yet the outcome is already captured. "Were there no evergreens in the field," he poses. Of course, there are evergreens, and in this sense, such queries always effect a capture—not of resemblance but of gesture.

The gestural twist of poetic queries recalls the analyses of Tokieda Motoki in the context of pivotwords and other aesthetic twists in ancient poetry. Tokieda sees the structure of the Japanese sentence in terms of boxes within boxes (irekokata kōzō). Rather than subjects and predicates, with subjection and predication, he finds nested or embedded structures; grammatical operations seem to gather around a kernel. Tokieda himself focuses on structure and signification, but his analyses can support a-signifying or nonlinguistic structures as well. In his account of the aesthetic turns of ancient verse, for instance, he no longer draws boxes *within* boxes; there boxes overlap boxes. If we override his rectilineal emphasis and replace boxes with circles, his diagrams would ressemble those of mathematical sets and subsets, in which shared elements generate circles within circles, and circles that overlap other circles.[20] It is interesting that Tokieda arrives at interlinked and overlapped boxes (or circles), for this metaphor allows for a concentric model of resonance that is not unlike the structure of the calligraphic line with its interlinked centers. Of course, this is to push Tokieda beyond the realm of Japanese grammar (where he apparently wishes to dwell), into an analytics of lines and centers. Nonetheless, his diagrams of the aesthetic turns of court poetry aptly sketch its logic of gesture and capture. It is as if Tokieda, in his exploration of court poetry, discovers an a-signifying or nonlinguistic structure related to the intersection of poetry and calligraphy. Just as the brush turns around the center of a character, the rhetoric of the poem twists, queries, and gestures around an event. In this sense, like the character in the Wang legacy with its dynamic center, the poem unfurls a mobile pattern.

When Mark Morris challenges the imposition of the quadrate frame on waka, he asserts that the waka is, first and foremost, a line. If waka is a line, phrase, or sentence, he suggests, then waka poetics comprises various ways of slowing, turning, shifting, elaborating the movement of a line. We can think about this in relation to the calligraphic line. The waka line meanders on a sinuous path, weaving and pivoting. Its visual consistency comes from the rhythmic falling and centering of the brush. As the brush moves down the page, it oscillates laterally through the strokes of each character: to each character it imparts a center of motion (which is not a center of gravity). As the brush moves fluidly into the flexible strokes of the grass style of kana, it moves from center of motion to center of motion; each character is the site of an emergence of a pattern in an open series of patterns with centers of motions.

The brush falls as a leaf falls, turning, wheeling, pivoting around a center, now lifted in another gust only to flutter down again. A line of calligraphy is analogous in its movements to the falling and fluttering of an object (a leaf, a petal, a feather) that turns and pivots on the currents of the air, buoyed by the friction that defies gravity. The delight expressed in seasonal poems for showers of leaves or petals or snowflakes recalls the dance of the brush: a falling motion that hovers, oscillates, whirls and turns around a center. The songs that speak of love often tell of waters that rush and flow, flames that flicker, dyes that seep and run. The movements of the brush recall these movements, too. It is a liquid writing with ink that flows, flickers, seeps, runs. The movements of the brush seek the center of these movements. The brush, in this sense, does not simply fall down or seep across the page: it hovers in the way that petals trace the currents of air, it flows in the way that waters trace the contours of the land, shot through with potential and kinetic energies.

So often poetic treatises speak of the ways in which writing and singing soothe lands, humans, human relations, but this activity does not follow from the logic of the frame (which constructs a bounded space in which contradictions come into harmony). Clearly, calligraphic activity can produce boundaries, lines, and spaces, yet these are not those of typography, or even of Roman letters. Roman letters sit upon a line (petals on a wet, black bough), and modern typography furthers their aura of gravity. Roman letters lope across the horizontal, feet on the ground, measuring the line. Chinese calligraphy, however, centers each glyph, locating a center of motion that makes the character appear to hover in its own space. The calligraphy of characters delineates space in ways that call attention always to various centers of motion, and to the resonance that arises between centers of motion. Topologically, calligraphy aims to align centers of motion in harmonic patterns so that new centers of motion, arising between other centers, also enter into resonance. When poetic treatises directly relate writing to ruling, it is not surprising that the ideology in question is one of concentric centers, of relations between centers, and of motions toward and away from centers. This is what Deleuze and Guattari describe as a major type of imperial line (that is, a line that rends the abstract line from smooth space, converts it and accords it values). For them, the Chinese imperial line entails a supraphenomenal encompassing.[21]

In terms of a supraphenomenal encompassing, one can imagine how song strives to capture dynamic forces. For instance, Tadamine's poem associates its quizzical gesture with regenerative forces — the return of spring and the eternal green of the pine. It is as if the poem had replicated or harnessed these generative forces, channeling them into the gesture of drawing forth the lines of poetry like the evergreen needles of the pine. The riddle or rhetorical question introduces a gap, without which there could be no motion or generation. Without the gap, there would be only static depictions and resemblances. Heian poetry and calligraphy are, above all, mobile, replete with forces. They do not attempt to fix occasions but to regenerate events in a bid to ensure the movement of things and humans (albeit in accordance with orderly patterns).

Almost predictably, then, the next song poses a kind of rhetorical query. It too moves with the rhythms of grass-style kana, cantillating a Yamato song.

> 千歳までちきりし松も今日よりは君にひかれてよろづ代や経む
> 能宣
>
> Might the evergreens with their promise of one thousand years,
> from this day drawn forth by you, lord,
> pass ten thousand generations, too.　　　Yoshinobu

Ōnakatomi no Yoshinobu (921–991) adopts a pose that flatters the emperor. If pines are said to live one thousand years, and if emperors are said to live ten thousand generations, will a pine drawn forth by the emperor live ten thousand years?

This rhetorical query, too, is disingenuous, with its naive juxtaposition of two temporal sequences. What happens, Yoshinobu asks, when two different temporalities meet? Would the greater span act on the lesser? In Heian poetics, the greater frequently affects the lesser — as seasons affect humans — and yet only through mutual affinity. In this respect, the lesser affects the greater as well, and their interaction is a matter of resonance. If the emperor lends his auspicious longevity to the long-lived pine, it is because the pine is already a sign of longevity. Of course, poems never pose these interactions in terms of facts; poems spin out queries, doubts, riddles, and hints. This is because song aims to keep open the space of encounter, however disingenuously. Song aims to navigate in the space of an interval: not quite a gap, not quite an overlap.

Each of the poems cited thus far introduces a space of encounter between two levels, and frequently these doubles exist embedded or superimposed within other doubles. Songyō's song juxtaposes human forms and spring forms—an encounter of two realms or two times: that of the earth and that of the heaven. The two coincide, for an interval. In Tadamine's song, the evergreen of this earth promises to pass into eternity. His song, too, poses the encounter in the mode of supposition and anticipation. Then Yoshi-nobu stages an encounter of the evergreen and emperor, but now the pine stands as the terrestrial form (only one thousand years), while the emperor stands as the celestial form (ten thousand generations, or eternity). In sum, each song poses an encounter of greater and lesser (so to speak), and these are directly related to terrestrial and celestial phenomena: humans and sea-sons, evergreens and longevity, evergreens and imperial generations.

The encounter of terrestrial and celestial forms is integral to Heian poet-ics. Indeed the "Collection of Yamato and Han Cantillations" poses an analogous logic at the level of its two scrolls. The first scroll coordinates songs on the cycles of the seasons, while the second scroll unwinds a series of topics, events, places, and so on. Each scroll is, in effect, one movement, opening with a header and closing with a stretch of paper. These parallels enable a juxtaposition or superposition of the scrolls, one that involves an encounter of terrestrial series (scroll two) and celestial cycles (scroll one). Of course, the topics are not strictly regulated and aligned, and many of the poems seem equally suited to one scroll as to the other. The encounter of terrestrial and celestial phenomena is not confined to a single level of expression: it arises within poems, between poems, and between scrolls.

This is part of the art of compilation: in the encounter between terrestrial and celestial forms, song locates and captures the affinity between them. This capture is not static but dynamic. Song harnesses the forces that move between terrestrial and celestial realms. It strives for poetic linkages, not to contain and possess but to channel and direct affinities. Each song entails internal operations of overlap (figural, rhythmic, thematic, and imagistic forms of superposition, juxtaposition, apposition, etc.), and these internal overlaps mesh with external operations of overlap between songs, and even between scrolls. Fields of different dimension (dynamic boxes or circles) coincide, intertwine, or overlap, forming a concentric order in which there always occurs an opening that enables the interpenetration of fields. Thus, poetry and calligraphy, with their formation of centers of motion and con-centric resonance, make possible a dynamic alignment of earthly signs, human emotions and actions, and heavenly forms.[22]

The hints and feints of riddle, however disingenuous, sustain the dynamism of encounter. Fujiwara no Kiyotada (d. 958), in the next Yamato-style song of the sequence, introduces an erotic charge into the play of affinities.

子の日にしめつる野辺の姫小松ひかでや千代のかげを待たまし
　　清正

Slender and lovely the evergreen in the fields designated for this day of new-year rites: if I do not pull it up, will I pine one thousand years in its shade?　　Kiyotada

The slender and lovely pine directly introduces the feminine figure (himeko-matsu), and the poet wonders if he ought to draw her forth (pull the pine up). If he does not, will he wait for her eternally? Will he wait for her as long as he would wait for the young pine to mature into shady boughs? Kiyotada deploys a common vocal play on the word matsu, which designates both the verb to wait and the noun pine. In this way, he conjoins the time of lovers and the time of ages. Naturally, there is a discrepancy between the time of humans and that of the pine's thousand years, but the song links them. The human time of erotic longing joins the cosmological time of generation in the dynamics of the word itself (matsu).

The dynamics of a pivotword like matsu often encourages commentators to linger in the verbal register. As discussed in Part one, scholars like Akiyama Ken have tried to associate pivotwords with kana, and kana with phonetic inscription; thus they conclude that the pivotword is the hallmark of the Japanese language and a sign of Heian independence. There are, however, a number of reasons to challenge this ethnolinguistic reduction of pivotwords. Not only are similar operations found in Han poetics, but they are also entwined with visual resonance. As in Kiyotada's poem, in which patterns pivot and double: himekomatsu twines the slight stature of the pine (hime) with the elegant slightness of the noble lady (hime). Both sounds and images double, and there is always a resonance between the doubled speech of pivotwords and the doubled vision of mitate. Finally, as Yoshino suggests, the aesthetics of the pivotword relates to the figurality of inscription. At this level, it is Koreyuki's reed hand that comes to the fore. The style of the last three Yamato-style songs, with their queries, turns, and doubles, is the grass style. Then, as the brush crosses the drawn-out traits of the basket scene, kana characters seem to sprout leaves or change into cranes. Moreover, within many of the images are forms that seem to be characters. Ashide shita-e Wakanrōeishō is full of zones where there is no hierarchy or division between image and text—or rather, zones in which visual and vocal registers are not differentiated—again, as in figure 9.

The intersection of visual and vocal registers imparts a synthetic power to the Heian text. This is most evident in the shift between Han and Yamato styles. For instance, the new-year sequence moves from Kiyotada's query about the slender pine to a Han-style song by Kan (Han abbreviation for Sugawara no Michizane, 845–903). There occurs a figural shift from the grass-style variations of kana to the current-style variations of mana as well as a rhythmic shift from the 5-7-5-7-7 of Yamato-style song to the 4-6-4-6 of Han-style song. The theme shifts from transplanting pines to gathering new herbs (*wakana*).

> To nip sprouts in the fields—
> common wisdom recommends to women of verdant heart;
> to blend fresh broths upon the fire—
> by custom men entrust to her pliant fingers.   Kan

Images of grasses sprout alongside these poetic words of wisdom. In addition, Kan, or Michizane, deploys Chinese characters that replicate these grasses. He selects characters that bear the radical (or signific) for grass, amplifying his diction with images of grasslike nipping, grasslike heart, grasslike fingers.[23] The space of the under-picture and the space of the character interpenetrate. Figures of grass run through and within the lines of song. And the lines of song that speak of collecting new herbs run alongside the picture of a basket for collecting new herbs. On so many levels, sounds and images resonate, capturing the vitality of new herbs, a vitality become as irrefutable and irrevocable as a draught of new-year brew.

Michizane's poem exploits the visual potential of those characters that Hsu Shen classified under "sound and form" (形声文字), which category actually comprises the largest number of characters. In such characters, one element presents the sound of the character, and the other element (the radical or signific) furnishes a figural clue about the character's classification (related to stone, bird, water, fire, horse, cart, or any number of objects). The dynamics of sound-and-form characters makes possible Michizane's repetition of grass significs. It introduces microaesthetic intersections of visual and vocal registers at the level of the character, intersections that proliferate into the space of poetry and picture. This is what the reed hand, with its emphasis on grassy forms and traits, does. The visual registers of *Ashide shita-e Wakanrōeishō* thus show that it is impossible to reduce songs to the verbal register and thereby divide Han and Yamato into incommensurable genres or grammars.

In this text, both are stylistic variations on an aesthetics of what could be called a multisensible figure, which is the basis for the synthetic potential of the Heian text. In a phenomenological hypothesis about the art of Francis Bacon, Deleuze describes the multisensible figure. In such a figure, he writes, every level or domain of sensation would have a way to refer to the others; there would be an existential communication between color, texture, tone, gesture, verb, image—akin to the communication of each of the senses with the others. This kind of originary unity (of the senses) would be in direct contact with a vital power, a power that is rhythm, a force that is more profound than seeing, feeling, hearing, and so forth.[24] There is something like this at work in the Heian text. At some fundamental level there is an intersection of various registers of sensation, as if seeing, sounding, and feeling were somehow interchangeable, as if there existed a primordial rhythm or multisensible figure beneath and beyond human acts.

Yet the Heian text is unlike modern or modernist art. Where a painter like Bacon could be said to make rhythm visible, or a composer to make rhythm audible, the Heian text does not evoke a metaphysical or practical separation of senses around different arts. A poetry collection like *Ashide shita-e Wakanrōeishō* directs attention to a chorus of compilers, composers, calligraphers—not to mention to dyes, papers, scrolls, spindles, cases, tables, and so forth. Although each layer imparts an individuated style, there are no originary signatures. The Heian artist enters into a vast signature that is rhythm; he or she is embodied in the multisensible figure in the act of making it legible. For the modern artist, Deleuze implies, such a stance would entail certain dangers, not least because of the way in which it associates community, vitality, and cosmology and locates its order in nature. The modern artist inevitably looks into the abyss but must not leap over it too lightly or quickly.

The Heian artist, it might be said, looks away from the abyss. Heian courtiers frequently represented the regions outside the capital as realms of darkness, full of unintelligible squawks, an unsettling babble of forms; and these realms of darkness threatened to overwhelm the radiance of the capital. Chaos looms on the edge of the Heian order, and inside it as well: parts of the projected capital remained unfinished or fell into ruin, and tales warn of thieves and vagabond on the prowl there. Only close attention to the rendering legible of rhythm assured the proximity and continuity of radiance, a radiance that shone from the multisensible Figure to be actualized in the rhythms, figures, and gestures of calligraphy and poetry. Still, the contemporary appeal of Heian probably lies in its concern for walking the boundary between order and chaos, for entering into zones where it no longer seems possible to extract an intelligible order from chirps, sighs, and stomps, and for rendering those sensations legible.

PART III. THE SONG MACHINE

SEVEN. *Two Prefaces, Two Modes*
of Appearance

Two prefaces flank the twenty scrolls of poetry in modern editions of *Kokin-wakashū*. At the opening appears the *kanajo* or "kana preface" attributed to Ki no Tsurayuki, principal compiler of the anthology. At the close appears the *manajo* or "mana preface," attributed to Ki no Yoshimochi (866–919). The final phrase of the mana preface seems to attribute it to Tsurayuki too (臣紀貫之筆謹序), but the reference is to Tsurayuki as either the principal compiler or the calligrapher. Other manuscripts of the mana preface attribute it to Yoshimochi, as do subsequent commentaries.[1]

The differences between the two prefaces are largely stylistic. Although they present differences in tone and inflection, and elaborate on different topics to a greater or lesser extent, on the whole, they present two versions of the same materials.[2] Because the kana preface can be linguistically related to classical Japanese, and the mana preface is closer to classical Chinese, the tendency has been to explain the discrepancies between the two prefaces in linguistic terms and, by way of language, to treat the linguistic differences between them as evidence of cultural or mental differences.[3] In this way, linguistic considerations permeate stylistic differences with the problematic of Japanese versus Chinese. Commentators with a nativist agenda say that the prefaces glorify Yamato song over Han poetics, that it establishs the primacy of waka over Chinese modes. The two prefaces do indeed sing the praises of Yamato song. Even so, their praise always passes through the categories and ideologies of Han poetics and situates Yamato song alongside Han song. Accounts that parse the prefaces into two distinct languages, cultures, or sensibilities cannot begin to explore such mediation.

The prefaces use the terms *Han* and *Yamato*, but the two terms interact stylistically in ways that preclude any neat separation of cultural or linguistic identities. The stylistic differentiations in the prefaces involve a very different political project. The prefaces never say, "Waka are better than Han poems"; they say, "Waka are wonderfully efficacious." The prefaces never say, "Han poetics perverted or distorted our language and culture"; they say, "Yamato song is efficacious in the same way that Han song is." An evaluation of qualities lurks in the defense of waka, but, while the prefaces eloquently plead the case of waka, their defense of waka does not exclude Han poetics. Thus the praise of waka does not construct an ethnocentric identity—a particular (Japan) against a universal (China). If there is a universal at work, it belongs to the realm of cosmological patterns and directional forces.

That both prefaces have survived is indication enough that Yamato and Han styles entail a permanent provocation, a specific type of "agonism" akin to the agonist movement that surrounds poetry competitions. The existence of a "Japanese" preface and "Chinese" preface issues a challenge to those who would equate a proclamation of poetic efficacy with a statement of ethnic or linguistic identity. A number of questions arise, however. Why are there two prefaces? Which one comes first? Which one is of greater importance? If one is of greater importance, why are there still two?

At Heijō-kyō and Heian-kyō, before the writing of the kana preface to *Kokinwakashū*, prefaces to anthologies and chronicles were in mana, that is, in various configurations of classical Chinese. The kana preface was indeed novel in its way. Yet it arose alongside the mana preface, and their simultaneity has provoked commentary about which was primary. As E. B. Ceadel notes, arguments can be made both ways. Some early editions of *Kokinwakashū* used only the kana preface, and some late-Heian commentaries already treated the kana preface as the only preface. What is more, with respect to later poetics, the kana preface became one of the most important poetic formulations, probably the poetic formulation for subsequent generations. And yet, it did not supplant the mana preface. A number of early editions used only the mana preface. In addition, prefaces to subsequent anthologies were often written in mana (like those for Tsurayuki's *Shinsenwakashū* and Kinto's *Wakanrōeishū*). Ceadel concludes that it is impossible to know from external criteria which preface came first. The kana preface dominates our sense of *Kokinwakashū* only because, in recent times, the tendency was to ignore or disparage the mana preface.[4]

Ceadel's goal is to call attention to this overlooked or disparaged document. Although he makes no mention of the political motive implicit in the suppression of the mana preface, it is apparent enough: to suppress the mana preface is to affirm the Japaneseness of waka by undermining its links to Chinese poetics. Ceadel, following the lead of certain postwar scholars (e.g., Ozawa Masao, Ōta Hyōzaburō, and Konishi Jin'ichi), spells out the strong links between the two prefaces and Chinese poetic theory. His argument is basically this: the mana preface is a solid restatement of poetic principles and ideas found in prefaces to Chinese collections such as Wei Hung's Major Preface to *Shih Ching*, Hsiao T'ung's preface to *Wen hsüan* and Chung Hung's preface to *Shih p'in*. Ceadel concludes that the mana preface was the original version because its rhetoric is closer to these sources than Tsurayuki's. In addition he feels that the mana preface, in layout and sequence, is more logical and complete than Tsurayuki's kana preface. The latter derives from and elaborates on the mana preface, not always lucidly; it "stands revealed as possessing little real originality in its subject-matter and as having a number of defects in its structure." [5]

John Timothy Wixted, in his article on the two prefaces, interprets the *Kokin* prefaces in relation to various Chinese prefaces and challenges some of Ceadel's statements about Tsurayuki's lapses. He finds that the passages in Tsurayuki's preface that deviate from the mana preface can also be traced to Chinese sources. Tsurayuki need not have derived the kana preface entirely from the mana preface; there are signs that he borrowed from Chinese sources independently. That Tsurayuki later wrote a mana preface to *Shinsenwakashū* demonstrates his capabilities in classical Chinese poetics. [6]

As Wixted demonstrates, it is impossible to use internal or external criteria to establish the primacy of one preface over the other at the time of compilation. The historical record points inexorably to the prefaces' parity, disrupting attempts to prioritize their order of emergence, even though the kana preface subsequently played the greater role in the court legacy. Following the line of inquiry established in previous chapters, I would like to suggest that, in the context of early Heian poetics, the significance of the two prefaces lies in their parity and conformability to each other. Their existence, I believe, is part of an imperial project that sought to coordinate two modes of poetic composition and exchange—attributed to Han and Yamato—but without having recourse to an ethnolinguistic apparatus.

Wixted follows a common line of argument when he writes that Yoshimochi tends to stress the pragmatic and didactic functions of poetry, while Tsurayuki tends to emphasize its expressive orientations. Yet a word of caution is in order with respect to the use of such terms as *expressive* and *lyrical* to describe the poetic formulations of these prefaces. Such terms often evoke ideas of Romantic self-expression and underemphasize the role of formal regulation in organizing poetic expression. In his discussion of expressive functions, Wixted cites a phrase from the Major Preface to the *Shih Ching*: "Emotion stirs within and forms into words. As the words are inadequate, one sighs them. As the sighing is inadequate, one sings aloud. As the singing is inadequate, without knowing it, the hands start to dance, and the feet to beat in time."[7] In this passage, a range of forms give order to emotion or intent, and the emphasis falls not on emotion (as mental expression or interiority) but on the mechanics of vocalization, gesticulation, and rhythm. In the legacy of Romantic poetry that informs modern notions of lyric, the emphasis falls on the expression of the poet's inner emotions overflowing, exceeding, and transcending forms.[8] In the poetics outlined in the *Kokinwakashū* prefaces, however, as in their Chinese sources, the emphasis falls on regulating and fixing forms in order to organize and channel emotions in the proper paths. Which is to say, it is not so easy to separate Yoshimochi and Tsurayuki on the basis of expressive/lyrical versus pragmatic/didactic. The two prefaces announce the same goal for waka poetry, one not unlike that of the Major Preface: their goal is not self-expression but self-cultivation through forms; and self-cultivation aims to align human emotions with the designs of the imperial court by way of a cultivation of "natural" forms (celestial patterns, directional forces, seasonal rhythms, etc.).

Wixted understandably vacillates on the question of how the two prefaces differ from one another, and how they differ from Chinese prefaces. In such a poetics, the combination of individualizing and totalizing procedures (to borrow Foucault's phrase) is extremely tricky. Wixted concludes that "there is no new critical theory in the *Kokinshū* prefaces; it is all based on Chinese models." But then, from situational differences in diction, he submits that "the concrete vocabulary of the applied criticism in prefaces evidences a sensibility that is not subject to Chinese models."[9] Despite his cogent genealogy of the prefaces in relation to Chinese poetics, Wixted seems unwilling to forsake the ethnolinguistic framework. It may very well be that, from our perspective, a difference in sensibility by way of vocabulary is detectable; and yet the prefaces to *Kokinwakashū* have an entirely different project than the enunciation of an "un-Chinese" sensibility. Chinese or Japanese identity is an artifact of ethnolinguistic interrogation; the two prefaces do not seem to have that kind of (linguistic) consistency. Nor do they inscribe a conflict between China or Japan, or between different linguistic sensibilities. Yet they do inscribe some specific conflicts, which tend to inscribe cultural difference in the space between different circuits of poetic production and circulation—and it is these, I would argue, that are often confused with ethnolinguistic difference.

Houses and the Court

Historians usually discuss the differences between the imperial order of the Nara court and that of the Heian court in terms of ritsuryō kokka and ōchō kokka. These two terms do not translate particularly well. Bruce Batten suggests "code-based state" and "imperial court state," respectively.[10] The ritsuryo state or code-based state refers to the imperial order that emerged after the Great Reforms of the eighth century, first exemplified in the edicts of 646, which abolished private title to land, established an inner realm for the empire with a capital city, registered the population, and introduced a new system of taxation. These codes followed the principles of land tenure that emerged around the imperial courts in China and were finally codified in the T'ang Dynasty. Such measures aimed to make all lands and movements (production, distribution, reproduction, migration) accountable to the throne. Japanese and Anglo-American scholars, with the wealth of recent archaeological discoveries, presently agree that the ritsuryo state flourished in the early eighth century, and that the Yōrō Code of 718, the last and best known of the ritsuryo compilations, reflects the actual organization and operation of the Yamato state, with its ideal of absolute imperial authority.[11]

The ōchō kokka (imperial court state) involved a regency system in which a regent, frequently the emperor's maternal grandfather, advised the young emperor. In the late ninth and early tenth centuries, the northern branch of the Fujiwara family succeeded in marrying a series of daughters to a series of emperors, thus exerting great influence over enthronements and abdications. By encouraging emperors to abdicate at a young age, the Fujiwara regents could continue to advise and dominate a succession of young emperors. Because this regency order coalesced around the time of Kokinwakashū, historians see the early tenth century as the time when the imperial court state (ōchō kokka) that defines the political organization of the Heian period emerged.

Institutional historians have long broached the question of whether the order of the Heian court represents a decline of the ritsuryo model or its continuation. Bruce Batten, in his overview of Anglo-American scholarship, takes issue with its emphasis on continuity from the ritsuryo state to the imperial court, arguing, on the contrary, that the image of a breakdown of the ritsuryo order better suits the administrative changes instituted. Behind these debates over the continuation or dissipation of the ritsuryo ideal lies a search for the emergence of Japan as a nation. They follow a logic similar to the histories of Heian calligraphy: the dissolution of the T'ang ideal of regulation signals the emergence of properly Japanese forms. This is because the historical understanding of Heian Japan has also been based on an opposition between the native and foreign. This view becomes all the more entrenched when scholarship is organized around the nation, for scholars begin their analyses with the national territory. And so the nation inexorably emerges as the end of analysis. When Batten argues for the dissolution of the T'ang ideal, he glimpses Japan on the horizon: "Although gradual in nature, the shift toward decentralization had a profound impact on the later development of the Japanese state." [12]

I propose a somewhat different image of the Heian court, one less easily situated within a developmental model, one that does not demand a choice between centralization and decentralization, or consolidation and dissipation—or ultimately, foreign versus native. I primarily derive this other image from literary histories rather than institutional histories, but there are some important overlaps in the realm of *hare* and *ke*.

The terms *hare* and *ke* first appeared in late Heian and early Kamakura discussions of poetry, but it is generally acknowledged they provided an important methodological framework for earlier poetics. The distinction between them was applied to a number of different realms—clothing, architecture, topology, styles, and so forth—and one can tentatively think of them as analogous to formal versus informal.[13] In *Kokin* prefaces, the series of associations with hare and ke might be thus tabulated:

Hare	*Ke*
Han/T'ang poetics	Yamato poetics
court ceremonies	amorous exchanges
imperial collections	house collections
day, clarity	night, obscurity

In addition, scholars usually associate ke exchanges with an unofficial, oral line of transmission (versus official, written records of the hare line). I will return to this distinction.

In the *Kokin* prefaces, the ke mode roughly corresponds to poetic exchanges that take place around "houses" (*ie*). Historians trace these houses back to the *uji* (often translated as "clan") that existed at the time of the formation of the imperial system. Apparently, the existence of autonomous clans or families presented a constant threat to the centrality of the imperial court, for clans had their own leaders and hereditary priorities not readily subordinated to the court.[14] Frequently, the erosion of the ritsuryo model is attributed to the continued authority of clan genealogies and properties. Sometimes clans are said to predate the Chinese imperial system and are therefore sometimes construed as an indigenous social stratum. Amino Yoshihiko, however, has done a great deal to combat the notion that uji are clans (in the sense of families), or that they are indigenous formations based on ethnic affiliation: uji, he insists, are political assemblages.[15]

In accordance with Amino's definition, the houses could be said to be political coalitions based on marriage alliances and principles of heredity that remained in tension with the imperial ideal of governance. Yet it is not a matter of native families versus foreign bureaucracies (as Saigo Nobutsuna, for instance, claimed). One can think of the ke mode in terms of poetic exchanges related to a political assemblage that exerts its authority in the realm of marriage alliances among courtiers.

On the other hand, the hare mode was related to court functions and to the poetic exchanges that took place around court ceremonies, and it was primarily these exchanges that were recorded in imperial anthologies. The first imperial collections in the early ninth century were anthologies of Han forms like *shih*: *Ryōunshinshū* (814), *Bunkashūreishū* (818) and *Keikokushū* (827), which take the collective appellation *Sandaishū*, in reference to the three generations of imperial authority that reached its apex around the emperor Saga (reign 809–823). The prevalence and prestige of anthologies of Han-style poems at the court linked the hare mode to continental-style imperial practices associated with the ritsuryo ideal.

At the time of *Kokinwakashū* in the early tenth century, the hare mode was associated with Han poetics and T'ang ideals, but it was a stylistic distinction, much like mana. Just as mana came to refer to a certain style of writing (rather than a grammar or language), so hare referred to a mode, style, or site of composition. For instance, in Suzuki Hideo's description of the ideal of Chinese poetry of the Saga generations, shih poetry constructed an idealized, unchanging site around the emperor occupied by court and courtiers. And, as he notes, in the *Kokin* prefaces it is the imperial poetics of *Sandaishū* that informed the imagination of court song. Even when the kana preface makes reference to *Man'yōshū* poets or Yamato poets of earlier eras, it confuses *Man'yōshū* with *Sandaishū* and the hare practices in vogue in the early to mid-ninth century. Similarly, in the mana preface, Yoshimochi declares that the emperor Heizei (806–809) ordered the compilation of *Man'yōshū*; yet there is no evidence that *Man'yōshū* had any status as an imperial anthology. Nonetheless, both the *Kokin* prefaces associate *Man'yōshū* with *Sandaishū* (just as the *Man'yō* script was associated with mana). In sum, for all their associations with Han/T'ang versus Yamato, the terms hare and ke did not involve distinctions between Chinese and Japanese, or between foreign and native.

Instead, hare and ke involved stylistic distinctions closely associated with competing political assemblages, and it is a commonplace of waka scholarship that the *Kokinwakashū* was the moment of reconciliation or combination of ke and hare modes—of the court and the houses, which were clearly not trivial in political terms. Generally, the reconciliation of the two modes is described as a kind of fusion or unification and is usually related to the rise of the emperor-regent system. Suzuki, for instance, associates *Kokinwakashū* with the rise of the regency, because the regency moved into the space between the marriage alliances of houses and the authority of the imperial lineage. And when he discusses the transmission of song between *Man'yōshū* and *Kokinwakashū*, he writes, "In the reception of old poems, I think that, although there are differences between oral transmission and the medium of written records, we should think of them in terms of one world, one space of transmission." [16]

In his discussion of hare and ke, Naitō Akira traces them back to *Man'yōshū* and also speaks of fusion around the time of *Kokinwakashū*:

> When we look at the state of *Man'yōshū* songs, the source of waka, we have the impression that there are two different currents to it. First, there is the current of songs produced with an awareness of large audiences at public sites like court ceremonies, imperial progressions and banquets; the classic form can be seen in the poems produced by poetic experts (the so-called palace poets) like Hitomaro and Akahito. Second, there is the current of everyday poems exchanged at private

sites between men and women; a wide range of poems, beginning with anonymous poems, are included. We cannot, of course, draw a distinct line between the two, but the differences between these two currents of poetry that vary with respect to site afford one important perspective from which to consider the history of waka.[17]

In *Man'yōshū* the poetic modes of hare and ke imply some rhetorical differences, and Naitō asks whether the same is true of *Kokinwakashū*. Looking at "congratulatory poems" (*gaka*) versus "love poems" (*kohi no uta*), he finds that there is no way to distinguish hare and ke currents rhetorically or situationally. He thus concludes that the two currents fused in the generation of poets immediately before *Kokinwakashū* (i.e., the Six Immortals).

Like Suzuki, Naitō locates hare and ke within *Man'yōshū* and sees it concluding with fusion around the time of *Kokinwakashū*. But I would like to challenge their notion of poetic fusion and unification. The image of *Kokinwakashū* as a site of fusion serves to contain poetic diversity within waka poetry: the troublesome diversity of earlier poetics enters into a single space, a single world. Theirs is a rather impressionist model of development that culminates in Japanese purity and autonomy (to use Suzuki's words).[18] I would propose, on the contrary, that the reconciliation of hare and ke is not as absolute as fusion or unification. Again, *awase* provides a good model for mediation between doubles: a permanent contest, an incessant oscillation between poles that does not attempt to erase difference (to fuse or eradicate elements) but rather to mobilize a ground of difference. Moreover, because difference exists prior to, and outside of, human mediation, one can think of this process as a cosmological mode of differentiation. Through the *Kokin* prefaces, I argue below that the result is not an autonomous Japan, or even a unified court, but rather a diurnal coordination of daytime and nighttime activities at the court that accommodates and directs cosmological difference.

One aim announced in the prefaces was to combine house collections with old poems. The kana preface says that the emperor ordered the compilers to offer up a collection that would include old poems not found in *Man'yōshū* as well as their own poems. The mana preface is more explicit: it puts the compilers' poems under the rubric of "house collections."[19] As we have seen, these two lineages, "old poems" and "house poems," roughly correspond to hare and ke. The prefaces posit houses as sites of romantic traffic and marriage alliances, which result in flowers without fruit. "In the world now," writes Tsurayuki, "in so far as the human heart flowers with the hues of passion, aimless songs put forth nothing but fruitless words, generating unintelligible words, with branches submerged in the houses of passion, and thus they have become incapable of producing ears of grain, in proper places." [20] The mana preface uses a similar analogy to expose the dangers of prolixity: "The fruits all fall, the flowers alone flourish." [21] The poem-flowers of the houses are not suited to proper places (the imperial court) because their mode of generation tends to unchecked or unwarranted proliferation: flowers not seeds or fruits.

Old poems, on the other hand, are credited (in the mana preface) with the ability to generate in accordance with proper patterns. And in the kana preface, Tsurayuki presents this image of the days when old poems flourished:

> The sovereigns of the high ages, at dawns of spring flowers and on evenings of autumn moon, summoned their people in attendance and had them offer up poems on a series of matters. The sovereign looked over the thoughts and feelings of those who wandered into uncertain places speaking of following flowers, of those who sought paths through the unmarked gloom speaking of longing after the moon; he would rule on their aptness and error. [22]

Tsurayuki writes here of two modes of movement: to and from the emperor. There are the movements into uncertain places and unmarked gloom—to places beyond the purview of the emperor, by way of poetic movements that pursue flowers and the moon (flower and moon being indicators of travel in accordance with distinct signs or designs). Then these obscure yet intelligible movements return to the eyes of emperor, where his judgments provide the guarantee of their intelligibility: some are wise, some foolish, some apt, some improper. While poems of houses tend to wander into darkness, producing flowers without fruit, the poems of antiquity tend to arrive at the emperor, producing ears of grain.

Tsurayuki's distinguishes ke and hare in terms of excessive generation (prolixity) versus proper generation (cultivation) and introduces the rhetoric of obscurity versus clarity. Such distinctions recall the association of hare and ke with textile patterns: hare refers to the patterns on robes to be worn for court appearance, while ke alludes to those worn on excursions or at home in informal circumstances—again, hare matches with the court and ke the houses. The court is specifically the "dawn court" (朝), where male courtiers meet each morning at dawn in proper attire. At night, however, male courtiers might don ke robes and travel to houses in order to attend to the business of their alliances with women.

The polygamous practices of the court meant that men could have any number of wives or concubines, and their wealth and position at court tended to depend on the quality of their marriage alliances. A male courtier would establish his position by marrying into a certain rank or family. His success depended on his ability to sustain and hierarchize his alliances in accordance with their quality. Because the courtly emphasis fell on quality rather than quantity, a great deal of attention was paid to the texture and intensity of romantic dalliances and alliances. It should also be recalled that messengers who delivered poems and letters received recompense for their services, usually in the form of textiles; in an economy based on rice and land, certain commodities often deemed ornamental in a modern context (e.g., cloth, paper, boxes, scrolls, and such) provided a format for the exchange of wealth. Thus alliances formed around poetic exchanges, and wealth shifted hands. Under the cover of night, important transactions took place between houses, transactions that could affect the authority of the emperor and the configuration of the court. Because these transactions involved an exchange of poems and generated poetic correspondence, the poetic record of houses traced the formation of these nighttime alliances and transactions.

Hare and ke also came to refer to the organization of the Heian residence. Hare designates the main entrance and the quarters where visitors were received. The practice of cloistering noble women confined women to the wings of the residence, far from the eyes of suitors or interlopers, and the wings were designated as ke. The elaborate, choreographed stealth of courtship brought men to the ke wings of residences under the cover of night, where they would attempt to woe their way past a series of barriers (screens, blinds, ladies-in-waiting); they would attempt to prove themselves with a series of poetic performances and encounters, the success of which depended on the quality and intensity of their music, dress, calligraphy, perfumes, poems, and passions. Similarly, men attempted to gauge the quality of a woman's affection and position through these exchanges. The tales of the Heian monogatari recount innumerable examples of such encounters.

When Tsurayuki writes that the houses of passion engender unintelligible poems that are like flowers without fruits, he proposes that the emperor should be the judge of the quality of these poems—an act that would assure the visibility and propriety of ke exchanges. He speaks of "those who wandered into uncertain places speaking of following flowers, of those who sought paths through the unmarked gloom speaking of longing after the moon"; such poetic movements are those of men on nighttime quests for attractive ladies (flowers and moon were not so much symbols for women as indicators of motivated travel). In the high ages, Tsurayuki states, the emperor would judge the aptness and error of the poems. They came into the light of the court, under the emperor's eyes, thus bringing order to the proliferation of love exchanges and marriage alliances beyond the immediate purview of the dawn court.

It is easy to see why this reconciliation of hare and ke modes suggests the rise of the regency system to many commentators. Of course, in the regency system, the substance of this reconciliation is not the elimination of one mode by the other, or their fusion. Two power formations are brought into alignment, an alignment that entails an eternal intimacy and perpetual provocation between two forms of movement and exchange—an endless tension between the power of the regent's house and the power of the emperor.

Tsurayuki's kana preface drew its models of sovereignty in part from the imperial banquets and court ceremonies of *Sandaishū*. There was another source, too: Tsurayuki's model of a sovereign who deliberates over poetic matters also points to contemporary poetic practices around awase or contest. The sovereign who judges wise and foolish compositions is much like the arbiter who presides over a competition. In historical terms, waka, awase, house collections, and the regency came to the fore at about the same time.[23] And so, in many ways, awase provide an appropriate format for thinking about how *Kokinwakashū* reconciled or combined hare and ke modes of poetic production and circulation.

Topologically, the initial sites for awase came between hare and ke. Contests first took place in the residences of retired emperors or dowagers— figures related to yet removed from the throne; figures who retained an authority and mobility within the court without ruling; figures who occupied a site related at once to houses and to the court. Poem contests, modeled on imperial banquets in the style of *Sandaishū*, constituted ceremonial occasions but not imperial ceremonies. What is more, it was through the persons and residences of these mediators that imperial authority found itself challenged and legitimated—for in them, imperial authority was doubled and multiplied. Architecturally, the residences of retired emperors or dowagers also came between court and houses: retired emperors built lavish residences in a style that combined monastic modes with those of residences and palaces.[24] Stylistically, poems exchanged at houses or collected in house anthologies became visible in new ways through poem contests. The compilers of *Kokinwakashū* included a large number of awase poems. In sum, awase enabled a poetics that coordinated hare and ke modes of poetic production and circulation to emerge.

This awase-style mediation of two different circuits of exchange helps explain why historians continue to debate the overall development of Heian institutions. Just as Heian texts open into contests between old and new, or between T'ang and Yamato, so it would seem that two different circuits of exchange (of poems, goods, alliances) were also combined in such a way that neither one could overturn the other. They remained juxtaposed or counterposed, their permanent agonism grounded in diurnal cycles of activities. Naturally, because hare was associated with formal, Chinese-style events, and ke with Yamato forms, there is a temptation to recast Heian modes of mediation (juxtaposition, superposition, resonance) into teleological histories. This temptation brings with it a number of impossible choices: Did Heian Japan fulfill the T'ang ideal, or did it dissolve it? Should the emergence of indigenous institutions and styles be situated at the Heian court or in its dissolution? In this context, Thomas Keirstead's discussions of "medievality" provide an important reminder that Heian Japan, like medieval Japan, cannot really serve as an origin or a source of identity for modern Japan.[25] Its institutions were simply too heterogeneous and too loosely coordinated to result in anything like a modern nation. In the case of awase-style mediation of hare and ke, the competition between different circuits cannot be resolved, it can only be directed; and, because difference ultimately arose from without, it always returned to a cosmological ground.

Coda: Diurnal Modes of Appearance

I mentioned above that hare and ke are often associated with a written line of poetic transmission and an oral line, respectively. For this reason most scholars see a fusion of the two lines when kana and waka emerge around the time of *Kokinwakashū*: because the standard notion is that kana unified speech and writing, it follows that written and oral forms of poetry combined. They conclude, therefore, that inscription became transparent to (Japanese) speech. In an earlier chapter I argued, from a number of different angles, that Heian poetics opened a space of interplay between visual and vocal elements—not least of which was a loose interchange between speech and writing (although bound by rules and conventions). In the final chapter, I characterize the way in which Heian waka combined speech and writing as a mode of disjunctive synthesis. This mode of synthesis relied on the rhythmic, musical qualities of calligraphy rather than on the phonetic potential of kana. As a transition to that discussion, I explore how Heian poetics avoided any imputation of priority to speech, and how the tension between hare and ke opened up the tension between recitation and inscription into diurnal cycles.

At poem contests, the competitors read and wrote poems, but there was no priority given to these acts. Far too often we take the spontaneity of recitation to signal an original act related to the spontaneity of speech. Yet, given the intense preparation demanded of competitors, it is difficult to imagine any poem appearing de novo, if only because the conventionality of poetry demanded such intense discipline and memorization of models. Poems were always, in effect, inscribed in advance onto the courtier's body. Moreover, there is evidence that, in some instances at least, poems were written first then recited, and what is more, competitors sometimes recited or reworked poems written for other occasions, or written in preparation for the contest.[26] Then, once it was recited at a contest, a poem might be recorded. In other words, poems traveled through several circuits of vocalization and inscription, resulting in any number of variations and revisions.

Poem contests allowed for a format in which various combinations of recitation and inscription were possible. Competitors drew on already written poems, responded to topics, and generally exhaustively searched the written record in preparing their recitations, in the hope of having their poems recorded. The vagaries of the verb *yomu* (recite, read, count, compose) point to this vocal and visual nexus, and so, even more so, does the use of the word *ji* or "character" (字) to describe poetic count (of syllables). Is the act of counting a poem an act of speaking or writing?

In his "Tosa Journal," Tsurayuki makes a number of connections between inscription and recitation that reinforce many of the claims made in this study.[27] First he begins with the strange, now famous comments about journals being something that men usually write, but here a woman will try her hand at it. Then, in one instance, when someone recites a muddled poem, he says that, even if it were written down, it would not make sense.

Similarly when a message comes from the imperial court, it sounds like a poem, but only when someone writes it down is it clear that, indeed, it is like a poem (having thirty-one syllables). In both instances, Tsurayuki stresses the importance of the brush in establishing the number of syllables (fixed at thirty plus one, as he notes in his *Kokin* preface). In addition, there are encounters between Yamato and Han song in which the Yamato courtier writes his song in characters in order to make it intelligible to the courtiers of T'ang (*morotosi* or "Kara-land"). In this instance it is clear that it is not a question of the translation of signification, particularly with respect to the relations evoked between the moon—that is, the relations between celestial configurations and inscriptions. It seems, rather, to be a matter of an ontological mediator that bypasses and transcends speech. Similarly, Tsurayuki's many remarks about the spontaneity of song from children or from grief attest to the prior ontological status of song. What seemed to count were the rhythms imparted by inscription. And so, empirically and subjectively, it is not possible to give priority to speech simply because waka involved vocalization. Which is to say, it is impossible to make a de jure argument of a de facto situation.

If we return to the idea of poetic composition as a differentiation-coordination of vocal and visual elements, we see that the stylistic dimensions of hare and ke expand this coordination of elements beyond the boundaries of the poetic text. It is often remarked that the hare mode concerned those poems that entered the official written record. Hare poems were poems to be seen, not only at the court under the eyes of the emperor, but also by way of the brush. Hare existed within an integration of visibilities—visibility at the court, visual proximity to the sovereign, and the visual authority of written records—whence its association with court attire, dawn court, and formal modes of reception. Ke, on the other hand, was found in the context of nighttime travels and trysts, generating darkling vocal patterns akin to the robes worn in the cloistered wings of residences or under the cover of night. Ke patterns never quite became visible the way hare patterns did. This does not mean, however, that they had no relationship with writing, that is, with pattern and design. Both were modes of appearance—whence their association with dress, architecture, travel, and so forth.

Because hare squares nicely with the written record and with the imperial anthologies of Han-style poems, it is tempting to equate ke with an oral line of poetic transmission, one that follows the contours of speech—poems spoken but never recorded—an invisible line of oral transmission.

Indeed, waka scholars continually make the leap from visibility and vocality to a distinction between script and speech and, by extension, from native speech to foreign script.

Suzuki provides a good example. He posits the existence of two lines of poetic transmission from *Man'yōshū*—one oral, one written—but feels that *Kokinwakashū* marks the fusion of oral and written lines of transmission. This is because he takes kana to be a phonetic marking in which sound and mark fuse: one world, one language, one mind—pure Japanese, so to speak. The problems with this position have already been discussed at various junctures. (1) Such an interpretation provides no account of Chinese-style vocalities; even if we claim that Heian courtiers pronounced Chinese poorly or inadequately, we must admit that Chinese poems and scripts entailed some level of vocalization. (2) It includes no account of the vocal transformations and deviations of so-called Japanese speech. (3) The figural usage of kana, so integral to Heian poetry and calligraphy, is omitted. Finally, (4) poetry is equated with native speech and ethnic identity, and the translinguistic or nonlinguistic use of figures, rhythms, and gestures is wholly suppressed. In sum, Suzuki assumes that Chinese script was pure seeing and that Japanese speech was pure speaking until, subsequently, the kana of *Kokinwakashū* fused pure vision and pure speech into purely Japanese phonetics. The logic of hare and ke, however, do not sustain a logic of speech without visibility or of script without vocality. The two categories suggest topologies, styles, patterns, and modes of movement and appearance.

Hare, as I said, is related to the imperial court, the dawn court, sovereignty, and visibility, and ke to the houses, night excursions, alliances, and vocality. This manner of seeing and speaking recalls Maurice Blanchot's dialogue in a chapter of *Infinite Conversation* entitled "Speaking Is Not Seeing."[28] On the one hand, he says, seeing involves centripetal forces that use the wisdom of land together with the tyranny of sun and light in order to measure distances and fix scales; on the other hand, speaking summons centripetal forces that wander under the stars at night, disrupting and uprooting the reign of day. Similarly, around the Heian court, the wandering of courtiers among dark houses disrupted the visible authority of the emperor; and poem exchanges in the dark interstices among houses threatened to vitiate the rule of the imperial court. These two poles of poetic activity generated a range of intermediate styles, varieties, and forms. The goal of *Kokin* poetics was to posit the court as the general site of exchange, not to fuse the two or eradicate one mode in favor of the other.

For Blanchot, the desire to fuse these two forces (centripetal seeing and centrifugal speaking) is a distinctly modern perversion, in which the gaze prohibits differentiation between the modalities of seeing and speaking. This is precisely what Suzuki does: he fuses hare and ke into a single entity, and unifies seeing and speaking within a phonetic gaze. Blanchot, on the contrary, follows the disorientation and disruption of speaking in order to break the fusion of speaking and seeing. He tends to refuse any amalgamation of the two.

The logic of *Kokinwakashū* is neither Suzuki's fusion and unification nor Blanchot's disorientation and disruption. It sought to coordinate seeing and speaking and was a logic of oscillation that derived its authority from natural cycles. That is, it entailed a logic of appearances and disappearances: the night wandering balances the dawn returning: the male courtiers who traveled in the dark seeking the moon, who wandered to strange unknown places following flowers, returned to the court at dawn with the traces of their excursions and encounters in the form of poems exchanged on slips of paper. At the court, in its radiance, the traces of their amorous adventures came to light, whether shown to companions or furtively glimpsed. Thus the sovereign eyes of the court—the ubiquitous "eyes of people" (hitome)—judged the error and aptness of their movements. The daytime and nighttime activities of courtiers were coordinated into diurnal and nocturnal patterns like the cycles of dawn and dusk, as natural as the oscillation of day and night; and such day/night alternations linked with the broader, longer cycles, of months, seasons, years, and reigns.

The two prefaces, which are consonant with Han/T'ang poetics, presented a politico-aesthetic ideal for Yamato song. It is possible to read the specific ideal of the two prefaces in terms of the interaction of hare and ke—that is, in terms of the coordination of these two modes of appearance, each related to a nexus of activities around the Heian court and having, always, political consequences. In aesthetic terms, hare and ke implicated a differentiation between the modalities of seeing and speaking—or more precisely between two modes of appearance and disappearance. By extension, this affords us another way to think about the interaction of mana and kana—as well as about the interaction of the documents labeled "mana preface" and "kana preface."

The mana style, it is assumed, was one of greater visual complexity with respect to characters. It used a greater number of characters, probably in the stiff or current style. The kana style, derived from the grass style, used fewer characters, possibly rendering vocal elements in more obvious ways. Yet mana were not silent figures; nor did kana usage present a transparent transcription of sound. Each presented a different configuration of sound and mark and a different stylistic tendency. It is useful to recall the earlier discussion of smooth and striated space in Chapter 5. The calligraphic and compositional layouts associated with mana tend to introduce orientation and direction, while those associated with kana allow greater latitude for divagation. What emerged from the graphic interplay of divagation and orientation were styles of inscription that followed the edge between smooth space and striated space. These styles situated inscription in a zone where order arose. It is as if inscription at once traced nature and introduced culture—as if there were no distinction between nature and culture.

The interplay of the two *Kokin* prefaces can be seen in analogous terms but at another level of organization. Their simultaneity situated poetics between divagation and orientation in order to assure its resonance with court activities and appearances. Poetry and calligraphy emerge as the mediator, exchanger, or calibrator in political interactions related to a diurnal, cosmologically grounded order.

I conclude, therefore, that the parity of the two prefaces pointed, first and foremost, to the stylistic oscillation between two politico-aesthetic configurations. The same process of oscillation/coordination occurred in the rhetoric of the prefaces: Yamato song was parsed in accordance with the six principles of Chinese poetry, the performance of Yamato song was linked to the performance of Chinese poetry, and the history of Yamato song was intertwined with the history of Chinese poetry. Such a poetic project had very little to do with the linguistic, grammatical, essentialist genres that the modern criticism continually proposes for it. The two prefaces turned to a poetics of rhythm, figure, and gesture precisely because these poetic elements provided a way to coordinate diverse patterns and designs by deftly bypassing differences that would emerge at the level of speech or grammar. By way of rhythms and figures, Heian poetics sought ways to bring patterns into resonance, to coordinate two configurations. Like the politico-aesthetic mode of Chinese poetics, but in a specifically political space, this Heian project entailed oscillation not fusion, coordination not unification, expansion not consolidation, empire not nation, rhythms and figures not grammar and speech; concentric cycles rather than lines of development, and centers of motion rather than boundaries.

EIGHT. *Tsurayuki's Song Machine*

Generation, Emotion, Motion

In the kana preface, Tsurayuki criticizes the songs exchanged amorously in houses: they are unproductive and unintelligible; their patterns make no sense and produce nothing but flowers of passion ("fruits all fall, flowers alone flourish," chimes the mana preface). Tsurayuki proposes to make these passions and exchanges productive and intelligible, and his model for a productive organization suggests to him the ears of grain of flowering grasses (*hanasusuki ho ni idasu beki koto*).[1] Such organic analogies—or, more precisely, generative analogies—give shape to the rhetoric of the prefaces. From the outset, the prefaces join seeds, roots, hearts, poems, and leaves. Tsurayuki opens with these remarks: "Yamato song, with seeds in the human heart, generates myriad leaves of words. Because humans in this world are things grown thickly over with countless acts, they make utterances that link words felt in the heart to things they see and hear."[2]

Frequently this passage is taken as evidence of a close link to the natural world among the early Japanese—an alleged love of nature that adheres in the Japanese spirit. The Heian link of humans and nature, however, is not one of Romantic appreciation or passion for an untouched, untrammeled nature. The Heian link between humans and nature produces a specific organization related to the cultivation and domestication of wild growth.

The opening lines of the preface establish the paradigm for a nature that entails generative force. Seeds, writes Tsurayuki, generate myriad leaves of words in the human heart, and people tend to become overgrown with acts. With these brief phrases, Tsurayuki yokes natural generation, poetic production, and human action and emotion: words germinate, poems proliferate, and humans are "grown thickly" with acts. To bring order to these potentially prolix generative forces, Tsurayuki will evoke a kind of cultivation. People link the seeds germinating in the heart to things that they see and hear—"percepts" (sights and sounds)—which he later associates with the forms, rhythms, and patterns of an order at once terrestrial and celestial.

According to Tsurayuki, heart-seeds germinate into word-leaves in accordance with sensations or percepts: humans "make utterances that link words felt in the heart to things they see and hear." The realm of percepts plays such an important role because they emerge through pattern, rhythm, or form. Thus when humans sense things, they perceive orderly and intelligible patterns. In effect, Tsurayuki places sensory patterns prior to perception: the patterns that humans perceive belong at once to the realm of human sensation and to the cosmos (there is no prior interior space that looks out on the world). Neither nature nor human, in this logic, are inherently wild; nor are human pulsions and drives articulated against an exterior. The term *nature*, therefore, is misleading in this context; for, in effect, Tsurayuki relies on patterns that are prior to a division of interior and exterior and different from a modern distinction between nature and culture. Cosmological patterns, celestial rhythms, and terrestrial forms belong to a realm of sensation that precedes perception. For lack of a better word, however, I use the term nature, with these qualifications.

Because Tsurayuki wishes to call attention to a nature that is already replete with forms and patterns, he follows his account of heart-seeds germinating into word-leaves with a passage on the songs of birds and bugs (frogs being in the general category of 虫 or "bugs"). "When they hear the calls of warblers singing in the flowers, of frogs dwelling in the waters, is it not that all living things count/compose songs? Song is what moves heavens and earth without applying force, draws out the feelings of unseen dead spirits, soothes between man and woman, and calms the heart of fierce warriors." [3] In the calls of warblers, in the chirps of frogs, a form or pattern emerges—that of a song or poem (*uta*). Tsurayuki tells us that birds and bugs sing songs; or rather he says *uta wo yomu*: they count, recite or compose songs or poems. When birds and bugs chirp and warble, their act is both composition and recitation. Which is to say, the cries and calls of birds and bugs emerges from a realm of patterns, rhythms, and forms, and so, their cries and calls emerge with a count, beat, rhythm, or pattern. Tsurayuki places the emphasis on forms that need not be invented, that emerge spontaneously. These forms and patterns are prior to humans, prior to human perception or cognition of them. Forms emerge and impart pattern to things seen and heard; and at the sites where forms and patterns appear, nature cultivates itself, domesticating its own proliferation, spontaneously manifesting order. Since rhythms and patterns emerge naturally and spontaneously, the role of humans is to follow patterns and mimic natural forms—this does not mean that they are to copy the songs of bugs and birds but that they are, by their nature, able to sense the celestial and terrestrial patterns that inform chirps and whistles. To recite/compose song or poetry is to locate the site where forms emerge; it is to pursue and continue those forms. Thus song produces effects: it weeds and tames the wild proliferation of nature into cultivated growth by following nature's own spontaneous organization.

In this vision of nature's spontaneous order, song is a kind of assemblage, an interface between the human and natural orders that is at once organic and machinic.[4] The song machine is a mediator or exchanger between humans and nature (nature here comprises celestial rhythms and terrestrial forms). It moves heaven and earth; it calms warriors, dead spirits, lovers. In all those activities that tend to wildness and imbalance, song provides a pattern, a rhythmic count, a form, through which these human actions (and emotions) become cultivated and domesticated. As sites for cultivation, Tsurayuki provides a list of asymmetries: between heaven and earth, between warrior and opponent, between living and dead, between man and woman. Song moves between these asymmetrical pairs, taming the potential energies that arise through their kilter. The song machine both follows and organizes the potential forces that arise across these apparently natural asymmetries.

It is important to understand that natural asymmetries and cultural asymmetries are one and the same thing in this poetic mode. It is not possible to question whether certain asymmetries (say, between man and woman) are not in some sense cultural and artificial, for artifice (human act) and nature coincide in the song machine. That is the function of the song machine: to coordinate human actions or emotions with the movements and forms of nature. Of course, this utopian machine relies on certain hierarchies: from the start, Tsurayuki writes of seed and generation, implying seminal, masculine forces of cultivation at work in nature. Moreover, his organic rhetoric is never far from a Confucian paradigm of self-cultivation: where and how to sow seed; how to cultivate and expend one's generative forces. Just as one sings in measured beats and counts, so one sows seeds in even rows with measured intervals.

Tsurayuki proposes to bring cultivation to human hearts at the site where nature already appears organized: in the rhythms and patterns that pervade sounds and sights (in sensation). "Because humans in this world are things grown thickly over with countless acts," he writes, "they make utterances that link words felt in the heart (*kokoro ni omohu koto*) to things they see and hear (*mirumono kikumono*)." I translate *nareba* as "because," which might suggest a causal relationship between the two phrases; but its meaning lies somewhere amidst *when, as,* and *because;* it implies a relation of continuity and simultaneity (efficient rather than formal or final causality). In other words, Tsurayuki says that the heart/percept link occurs in conjunction with the prolixity of human acts. The emotive movement from heart-seeds to word-leaves occurs in efficient conjunction with visual and acoustic patterns.

I translate *omohu* as *feeling* or *to feel* because it implies an outward movement of the heart and senses (emotions or out-motions). And yet, since these emotions are to follow natural or cosmic patterns, they are not without order or logic. It is possible to translate omohu as "thinking" as well as feeling, yearning, longing, or emoting. Then, too, with its association with the beats and rhythms of songs, omohu implies "counting" as well. In fact, counting provides a good analogy for omohu, for counting implies both a mental act of ordering and a physical state of corporeal rhythm. Generally, I render omohu as "emotion," with the qualification that emotion in this context indicates an outward movement, a form of mimicry in which acting, feeling, and thinking are nearly simultaneous.

Tsurayuki aligns human emotions with percepts, because these percepts —sounds and sights (mirumono kikumono)—emerge in alignment with nature's forms. There are three levels, as it were: (1) prior forms; (2) sensation or percepts, or what humans see and hear, such as the cries of birds and bugs; and (3) human emotions, or what emerges from the heart and moves humans into action. The level of prior forms (rhythm, pattern, figure, etc.) becomes coincident with sensation, and the realm of emotion, by following sensation, comes into alignment with nature. The emotive movement from heart to word parallels the generative movement from seed to leaf. Words are leaves, as in leaves of words (*kotoba* or *koto no ha*), and hearts are the site of seeds. Because (or as) Yamato song couples the movement from heart to words with the movement from seed to leaves, it couples generation and emotion. Thus different levels align, but their alignment must remain active and mobile. The goal is to align and direct motions or forces, not to arrest or contain them.

There is, in this poetics, a profound dislike of disorder, wildness, or untamed nature. Or maybe it is a poetics that simply does not countenance the abyss or catastrophe. In any event, Tsurayuki's poetics equates spontaneity with order and always forces spontaneity into order; it abhors decadence and unproductive or unmanaged movements. Ultimately, it is a normative model (not motivational or psychological). Tsurayuki aims to ensure that heart-seeds not only flower but develop fruit (or grain), coming full cycle to seed. So it is that Tsurayuki pays particular attention to the movement between heart and words, looking for signs of generative deviance—degeneration, which results from prolixity—the rot that occurs where growth becomes thick and rank.

Tsurayuki's poetics constitutes a kind of normative order in which the expression of human feelings are directed and delimited, not liberated. Of course, the same might be said of any form of expression: it gives form. But Tsurayuki's poetics are particularly adamant on this point: emotive forces are to be patterned in accordance with celestial rhythms or terrestrial forms; and when he uses song to engage the realm of sensation, he does not aim to liberate emotion from forms. On the contrary, his goal is to make sensation coincide with the cosmos in such a way that perception becomes a mediator and so serves to channel emotive forces into their proper circuits. Heian poetics refuses a human-centered expression even as it makes a beauteous call to the senses. Indeed, Tsurayuki aims to prevent the emergence of a human-centered subjectivity.

Frequently, Tsurayuki's emphasis on pattern and figure is overlooked in order to make his account more compatible to modern notions of lyric expression and description. The Rodd and Henkenius translation of the passage quoted above has it that "many things happen to the people of this world, and all that they think and feel is given expression in description of things they see and hear." And, in a footnote, they remark: "The majority of Japanese poems, no matter what the topic, rely heavily on images from nature."[5] Such notes, comments, and translations are perfectly consonant with the modern Japanese translations and commentaries, which resort to a vague Romanticism in order to wrench a "Japanese" sensibility from Heian poetics. But Tsurayuki has different aims, about which he is exceedingly clear: humans do not use images or descriptions to convey prior emotions; sensible forms come first, and emotions must follow their patterns and rhythms, for sensation provides the link to extrahuman forms.

The heart-word paradigm is essential to understanding how Tsurayuki envisages poetic composition. To understand his analysis of heart (kokoro) and words (kotoba), it is important to keep in mind that the emotive space between heart and words is always analogous to the generative space between seeds and leaves. Because generation is the operative analogy for Tsurayuki, it is not surprising that his examples so readily evoke male-female relationships: the logic that couples emotion and generation evokes procreation and reproduction. Thus the proper interaction of word and heart extends to proper interactions between man and woman and incorporates a range of human actions and relations. "Among those whose names resound in recent times, namely, the rector of monasteries Henzeu, the patterns of his songs excel yet bear little truth (or fruit: *makoto sukunasi*). It is as if one sees a woman drawn in a painting and feels one's heart move in vain." [6] Tsurayuki thus submits that Henjō (Henzeu) produces patterns (*sama*) of words that are unproductive and untrue. The heart moves yet goes astray. It aims at false, fruitless targets. It recalls a man who pursues a drawing of a woman rather than the woman herself: the union will have no productive outcome in the proper sense. Words move and beguile in vain; hearts emote in fruitless, truthless directions.

As the example of Henjō demonstrates, Tsurayuki directs his criticism at famous poets of the generation preceding his own. He discusses six poets, the Six Poetic Immortals (六歌仙) who flourished around the mid-ninth century. It is no accident that he chooses six poets, to match the six principles or designs of Han poetics (六儀). They suggest the *ke* circuit of Yamato songs—the houses of passions with night excursions and alliances. However, the six designs belong to the *hare* mode, because they, being derived from Han poetics, produce poems suited for the imperial record. The Six Immortals only enter the imperial record with some effort on behalf of the chief compiler: Tsurayuki must first apprise the reader of the design flaws inherent in the poems of the Six Immortals. He lets us know that their poetic patterns would have to be adapted to, or aligned with, the hare mode of high antiquity. That is the art of his anthology, announced so clearly in the preface: to situate one form or pattern with respect to other patterns such that no array of forces dissipates or goes astray, so that all movements harmonize resonantly and productively.

In the poems of the Six Immortals, Tsurayuki submits, there is a noticeable lack of alignment between heart and words. Generative and emotive forces, as a result, tend to form improper patterns. Seeds (in the heart) generate luxurious, prolix, yet fruitless growth (flowery leaves of words). This analogy continues in his criticism of another of the Six Immortals, Ariwara no Narihira: "As for Ariwara no Narihira, heart abounds, and words lack. It is as if scent lingers while the wilted flower loses its passion colors."[7] Tsurayuki declares that in Narihira's poems the generative movements of the heart exceed its leaves of words. At that moment when the plant wilts and fades, when leaves of words lose their vigor—even then the heart persists. Emotions exceed words in the way fragrance lingers on a bloom past its prime.

At issue for Tsurayuki are the emotive forces of omohu that move between heart and word (kokoro ni omohu koto). Emotions—outward motions of the senses—threaten to go astray, to wander far afield, to deviate from the paths that Tsurayuki wants to establish for imperial poetry.

In his third example of heart-word imbalance from the Six Immortals, Tsurayuki calls attention to the patterns of robes. Recall that patterns on robes in the context of Kokinwakashū relate to modes of movement and exchange. "As for Funya no Yasuhide, words are skilled, but the design does not suit the status," he writes. "It is as if a traveling merchant wore fine robes."[8] In other words, robes suited to courtly appearances appear in the wandering mode of merchants in the realm of ke movements. It is as if the ke mode, in its outward motions, carried off courtly status with it, removing it from the imperial palace. With this example, it becomes evident that emotive forces do not reside exclusively in the realm of heart-seeds and word-leaves. They extend to movements of people in and around the court. The emotive forces of omohu implicate not only a psychic dimension but a physical and political dimension as well. For Tsurayuki, the figural dimensions of poems suggest configurations related to the movements and appearance of courtiers. To regulate the movement between heart-seeds and word-leaves is also to regulate the actions of courtiers. The poetic rectification of patterns extends to courtiers' dress, rank, position, and mobility.

The Yasuhide poem cited by Tsurayuki (KKS 4:249) is the acrostic poem in which the poet asks, "Is it because 'tempest' (嵐) consists of 'wind' (風) and 'mountain' (山) that we call the tempest a wind from the mountains?" This visual play on Chinese characters receives Tsurayuki's approval for its skilled words: its words are like fine robes. The character play, evoking Han styles, gives the poem a touch of courtly splendor. (Recall that the Heian court adopted the styles of T'ang dress worn at Ch'ang-an.) Tsurayuki approves of Kara-style finery but, he warns, it must not be used indiscriminantly, without regard for rank and status. The status of Yasuhide's poem does not merit T'ang finery. It is not clear whether Tsurayuki's comments on status mean that the poem is too fine for the occasion of its composition, or whether he refers to Yasuhide's own position or rank. Or maybe he means that the fancy character play is too fine for the sentiment of the poem: the poem's message is rhetorically and rhythmically banal and evokes raging winds and violent weather for no particular purpose. In any event, it is as if a merchant wandered away from the Heian court sporting precious Chinese robes. Tsurayuki aims to prevent this type of poetic movement in which a resplendent visual usage of word-leaves allows the heart to range freely; a kind of poetic mode that plays loosely with prestigious finery.

With the example of Otomo no Kuronushi, Tsurayuki resorts to similar objections about position and pattern. "His designs are lowly," he writes. "It is as if a mountain man rested in the shade of a flowering tree with a bundle of firewood on his back." [9] In this example too, he addresses those whose trades lead them out of the reach of the capital, and establish their position vis-à-vis the finery of the capital: no fine robes for merchants, no fine flowers for rustics. The ke mode, in order to coordinate with hare activities, must be delimited in its divagations and peregrinations. Poems and people must depart and arrive at court in the proper dress with the proper patterns of movement.

The Heian court relied on a number of ways to delimit movements and exchanges in and around the court. Male courtiers had a rank or position within the court bureaucracies that expressed itself not only in terms of duty but also in terms of mobility around, and proximity to, the emperor. What is more, the design of the capital followed geomantic forces, mimicking directional and calendric designs in the layout of its avenues, residences, temples, and palaces. Courtiers checked their movements against astrological configurations, which resulted in "directional taboos": on certain days a person could not move in certain directions, according to the particular configuration of signs at his or her birth. All in all, movements in the capital emerged from the complex interaction of bureaucratic positions and directional configurations. In 894 and 895 two important restrictions appear: first, the abolition of official missions to the T'ang court; and second, the limitation of movement outside the capital to courtiers below the fifth rank. These measures were not simply part of an attempt to assert an autonomous identity for the court (as one often reads) but of an effort to regulate the movements of courtiers outside the capital, lest they form alliances with estates or other courts or accrue continental wealth and knowledge in unpredictable ways. The profound unrest of the T'ang court at this time surely increased the worries of the Heian court.

These restrictions did not, however, bring an end to traffic between the Heian court and the continent; in fact, traffic continued to increase and multiply. The goal of such restrictions was to direct exchanges and movements into specific channels, channels that bypassed high-ranking courtiers in order to reduce the possibility of seditious exchanges around the palace. Unfortunately, there is precious little documentation on this topic, and the field is open to speculation. In his study of the links between "non-agricultural peoples" (hinōgyōmin) and the medieval emperors, Amino Yoshihiko presents a provocative hypothesis that provides another way to think about Tsurayuki's interest in the appearance and movement of woodsmen and merchants.

Amino argues that the Kamakura period brought about more than a new geopolitical division of power between the Heian court and the Kamakura bakufu. In addition, as the samurai government strove to bring agricultural production and farmers under its sway, court elites moved to tighten their hold on the nonagricultural peoples who traditionally exploited nonagricultural lands and took charge of commercial exchanges, transportations, and craftwork. This effort was the source of the special relationships of the emperor with loggers, fishermen, hunters, artisans, itinerant merchants, and other workers whose travel ensured the distribution of goods and services. Amino traces such connections to those responsible for stocking the emperor's table (kugonin), who obtained special privileges from the emperor, such as safe-passage guarantees and tax exemptions.[10] Although thorough genealogical studies of these associations have yet to be written for the Heian period, Amino's work puts Tsurayuki's efforts to link emperor and nonagricultural modes in a new light. It would seem that the modes of appearance and circulation associated with the division between hare and ke echo Amino's descriptions of agricultural versus nonagricultural circuits of production and exchange.

Tsurayuki's poetic criticism draws explicitly on the regulation of courtier's movements. If his continual superposition of figural and political topologies can be read with any confidence, the channeling of emotive forces in his poetics has a direct effect on courtiers' movements within two inter-related dimensions: (1) in the realm of alliances and lineages (houses of passion); and (2) in the realm of exchanges and excursions within, around, and beyond the capital. As Tsurayuki's examples illustrate, this traffic control entails strict hierarchies based on rank, position, residence, and gender. Its utopian moment, however, lies in the maintenance of hierarchies not their elimination because, if hierarchies are sustained, then no mode of movement need be eradicated: all modes of movement will resonate in productive, natural synchronies. If movements are properly hierarchized, then they are perfectly coordinated: patterns of movement become as resonant and synchronous as the movements of asterisms.

Thus the normative force of Heian poetics and politics resided in the maintenance of hierarchies (enforced with promotion, demotion, banishment, corporeal punishment, and execution). Yet, in another sense, the Heian order encompassed so many interstices and so much movement that it looks far less disciplinary than the modern nation. In this respect, it is a telling point that modern commentaries rarely mention such interstices and movements but almost exclusively speak of linguistic and cultural consolidation. That is how our modern disciplines have tended to interact with normative hierarchies: they frequently make Heian hierarchies appear ideologically familiar, rational, and friendly, as if to say, "This is just a process of cultural consolidation and national emergence!" Historians discuss the Heian court in terms of a series of rational bureaucratic measures: how did bureaucrats attempt to consolidate the court, its centrality and prosperity, and how successfully? Never is it imagined that the emergence of states entails violent or drastic measures; one of the great myths about early Japan is the relatively benign development of a rational and contractual form of imperial federation. Rarely is it acknowledged that the logic of political representation may entail quite a different mode of emergence. Maybe this is why institutional histories of early Japan so studiously avoid poetics, despite the ubiquitous role of poetry in the conduct of imperial and personal transactions: poetic discipline demonstrates an order of political representation at odds with simple narratives of bureaucratic trials and errors, contracts, and breeches.

Tsurayuki's song machine makes statements about the social or political effectiveness of poetry; it claims that waka will bring a stable order to the imperial realm. The effectiveness of poetry derives from its ability to function as an exchanger or mediator between natural forms and human actions, and only the correct use of patterns can align them. At the level of pattern, form, rhythm, and so forth, the song machine proposes to work on the human directly, to operate at a level of sensation prior to perception, emotion, cognition, and action to bring about a specific alignment to those realms. In sum, Tsurayuki's song machine would exert its effects through an ordering of the senses.

Visuality

In his account of the Six Immortals, Tsurayuki places particular emphasis on seeing. Of the monk Kisen of Uji, Tsurayuki writes that his "words are faint, and starts and stops are indistinct. It is as if dawn clouds obscured the autumn moon as one gazed at it." [11] He admonishes the monk that what should be sharp and clear (autumn moon at dawn) appears obscurely and faintly (moon through clouds). Where there is no distinct pattern of words, how can the heart be properly directed?

Tsurayuki resorts to visuality in discussing the other Immortals. Henjō draws alluring yet false pictures; Narihira's words are like fragrant yet color-drained flowers; Yasuhide's words present robes too elegant for his emotive position; Kuronushi's words draw an incongruous picture: a woodsman beneath cherry blooms. In sum, Tsurayuki often describes these discrepancies between heart-seeds and word-leaves in terms of visual incongruities. And yet, in his own poems, how often he resorts to visual confusion and double vision; in fact, the superposition of two images or patterns is one of the hallmarks of his style. How do Tsurayuki's poems differ visually from the ones he takes issue with?

"Heart abounds, and words lack," Tsurayuki writes of Narihira. "It is as if scent lingers while the wilted flower loses its passion colors." Tsurayuki seems to dislike the juxtaposition of scent and sight in which the senses give us two different moments of the flower: one smells a flower in its prime yet sees a flower that is past its prime. Such a discrepancy, for Tsurayuki, presents an unstable allure: just as scent lingers beyond sight, so the heart tends to move beyond words. And so, when Tsurayuki himself plays with the movement between scent and sight, he assures us that there is a harmonious coincidence of the two senses (as in KKS 1:39).

くらふ山にてよめる　つらゆき

梅の花にほふ春べはくらふ山闇にこゆれどしるくぞありける

Composed about Dark Pass—Tsurayuki:

Cross the cusp of spring
waft scents of plums' flowers;
though I cross the Dark Pass
in darkness, signs appear!

The topic itself—Kurahu Mountain or, as I have rendered it, Dark Pass—suggests obscurity, and Tsurayuki writes a poem about crossing Dark Pass in the darkness. Yet, through the darkness comes the fragrance of plum trees in bloom. By identifying that fragrance, the poet locates himself: since plums are harbingers of spring, he knows that he is on the cusp of spring. And so he concludes that, even in the darkness, he has signs. He knows his position in the cycle of things, for scent tells him exactly what sight would tell. Scent and sight become analogous modes of perception, but only insofar as both modalities entail orderly patterns. What does it matter if he cannot see so long as he can smell patterns and locate himself? As always, Tsurayuki locates himself within a nature that is calendrical or cosmological, within the celestial rhythm (the turning of seasons). And the use of Kurahu Mountain, a sort of pivotword, gives further indication that Tsurayuki's nature does not consist of landscapes but of rhythms and patterns: the name of the mountain turns and pivots between being a place name and verb, imparting an active, mobile pattern rather than describing or representing a static site.

Many of Tsurayuki's poems play with the obstruction of seeing or the confusion of images. For instance, scattering petals evoke falling snows in the familiar mode of "visual overlap" or *mitate*. But Tsurayuki does not complicate vision simply to play an elegant game. It is the complication of vision that enables patterns and rhythms to emerge, which enable us to sense resonance between terrestrial and celestial forms. In order to achieve this mode of visuality, Tsurayuki's poetics develops a logic in which poet and reader do see not directly but obliquely.

Konishi Jin'ichi enumerates the ways in which the "oblique style" (倚傍) characteristic of the Six Dynasties in China (ca. 222–589) informs the poetics of *Kokinwakashū*, in particular that of Tsurayuki. "The oblique style," Konishi writes, "is one in which the poet 'approaches from the side,' taking a roundabout way instead of proceeding straight toward his objective." [12]

Characteristic of poetic obliquity, Konishi explains, is a tendency to describe things not in the language of the moment of perception but in different, highly contrived terms. And so the oblique style appears clever and precious, almost specious in its logic, for it calls attention to perceptual and intellectual processes, lingering over fine points of logic, and employing extended comparisons, antitheses, cause-and-effect speculation, and numerical conceits. This obliquity has given *Kokinwakashū* its modern reputation for preciousness, contrivance, and ratiocination. At the turn of the century, Konishi notes, Masaoka Shiki described it as "boring and witless; a bad joke; a pointless grinding away at logic," and Basil Chamberlain followed suite, calling it "a substitution of hairsplitting puerilities for the true spirit of poetry." Konishi aims to disarm such criticisms when he concludes, "Instead of applying modern value judgment to this phenomenon and dismissing it as conventionalization, we should concern ourselves with its significance, recognizing that the poets of the *Kokinshū* age followed preexisting literary models in preference to saturating their poems with the 'truth' of immediate experience, and that poems like Tsurayuki's are manifestations of the fondness for obliquity that he and his contemporaries shared with Six Dynasties poets." [13]

Konishi vacillates on the issue of why Heian poetics and Six Dynasties share a fondness for obliquity, and chooses to explain their similarity in terms of influence. "I believe there can be no doubt of the existence of direct Six Dynasties influence on the Heian *shih*, and through it on the *Kokinshū* style," he writes. "Cultural similarities between the two societies may be presumed to have played a significant facilitating role." [14] But Konishi disavows any direct political similarities between the "social instability" of the post-Han era in China and the "security and stability" of early-Heian Japan, although he acknowledges a cultural similarity in the aristocratic classes' adoption of a conservative stance toward lineage and precedent. Yet he insists on their political differences; this is rather mysterious as he also claims that the oblique style reflects the spirit and social conditions of the age. [15]

For Konishi, social conditions apparently do not extend to political stability or instability, which seems a bit hard to sustain. Moreover, it is hard not to see his apparent contradiction as a projection of postwar Japan's perplexed relations with Communist China. Ivan Morris confidently projected Japan's postwar order onto Heian Japan and described the court as a brilliant light that shone in splendid isolation on a dark sea of barbarity—signaling that Japan had its (aesthetic) place in the civilized world (the Anglo-

American order). Konishi for the most part follows suit. Yet his efforts to separate the cultural and political become quite perplexed, and in the end he questions the purity of Japanese beauty.[16]

Rather than resort to a separation of cultural and political realms of activity (which Heian poetics tends to conflate), we could look at waka poetics as a form of knowledge. It does not limit itself to a reflection of existing conditions, but proposes to act on the human body and the social order; in this respect, it constitutes an active and productive discourse.

Moreover, it is not sufficient to say that the courtiers who use the oblique style betray an international sensibility. In *The History of Japanese Literature*, Konishi speaks of international relations between Korea, Japan, and China in the ninth century. But again, there are so many contradictions. Strictly speaking, the history of the ninth century does not allow us to draw national distinctions in the modern sense. When Heian courtiers use the oblique style, they partake of an "interimperial" order, using forms, scripts, languages, and styles that do not belong exclusively to any one court. This order is reminiscent of Anderson's notion of "classical community."

Tsurayuki's use of the oblique style avoids direct vision or apprehension, but the indirectness of poetic obliquity is not a mere game; it is a way to get at patterns and rhythms. The oblique style involves pattern recognition rather than a direct apprehension of objects. (Of course, there is never any truly direct apprehension of objects, if we acknowledge that the organization of perception involves mediation and hierarchies.) In effect, pattern recognition provides a way to move to the level of sensation and to bypass perception (with its subjection of the object). A poetics of pattern recognition opens a specific way of knowing, based on rhythm, figure, form, and so forth. It takes place on a level that avoids the exterior-interior divisions of perception. It takes place on a level where different senses intertwine. In this sense too, this poetics implies an imagination that differs profoundly from the notion of nationness, for it deals with sensory operations in a way that transcends or avoids an opposition between the universal and the particular.

In Tsurayuki's poem about crossing Dark Pass, he shows us that olfaction can serve as well as vision in the recognition of patterns. The poem simply says, "I know how to recognize rhythms, forms, and patterns, and so I know how to compose them, properly and auspiciously." Pattern recognition also opens the poem outward: however personal or individual Tsurayuki's style may be, it aligns itself with external patterns, and these are cosmological as well as social: they include seasons, dress and rank, rules of courtship, and so forth.

Presumably, unlike those of the Six Immortals, Tsurayuki's own poems produce patterns that open properly into external patterns, precisely because rhythmic or patterned sensation opens out into natural rhythms. When the emperor ordered Tsurayuki to present a poem (KKS 1:59), the poet responded in this manner.

> 桜花咲きけらしなあしひきの山の峡より見ゆる白雲
> There have flowered cherries! There in
> A gorge in the footlorn hills billows
> Show whitely.

By convention, white clouds—the billows that show whitely—point to the emperor, to the august palace resplendently concealed high in the clouds. The complication of vision, in the style of mitate, confuses banks of flowering trees and banks of white clouds, but this superposition of images does not aim at sheer confusion; it culminates in the emergence of a visual pattern that opens into the imperial order. Spring cherries in full bloom, without a hint of fading or scattering, dissolve into white clouds, which serve as a sign of imperial splendor. (The imperial palace and person are conventionally said to be hidden in the clouds, exalted on high.) In this way, Tsurayuki relates the patterns of the seasons to imperial magnificence. Note that the hills or mountains bear a makurakotoba—a "pillow-word" or a kind of epithet—asibiki yama, which imparts rhythm and pattern to this manner of seeing; yet, strictly speaking, asibiki has no identifiable meaning—"footlorn" or "leg-tiring" are mere speculations. This is a rhythmic, patterned nature, and Tsurayuki refuses a realistic mode of vision in order to open the vision into a recognition of pattern to ensure that the peak of spring aligns with full bloom, which in turn aligns with white clouds (or emperor).

As this example suggests, the oblique style of poetics comprises modes of perceptual confusions similar to the visual confusions of mitate.[17] The oblique style also recalls Joshua Mostow's account of the interaction of poem and image in Heian aesthetics for which he coined the term *visual pivot*.[18] Through poetic obliquity, particularly in Tsurayuki's work, vision oscillates, doubles, and pivots. The poems excel at a kind of double vision that generates patterns that capture the potentially vagrant forces of emotion. But then "capture" may be the wrong term in so far as it implies containment and boundaries.

In Tsurayuki's poetics, even as vision doubles and pivots, its oscillations create a center of motion. The emergence of a center of motion ensures that the visual pattern has a kind of consistency; that is, the visual pattern turns around a center, hovering between two moments without dispersing into multiple moments. Tsurayuki's poem (KKS 2:89) is a good example.

> 亭子院歌合の歌　つらゆき
> さくら花散りぬる風のなごりに水なき空に波ぞ立ちける
> A poem for the Teijiin poem contest—Tsurayuki,
> On the crest of a gust
> scattering cherry petals linger as
> on waterless skies
> furls a wave.

The poem comes from a poem contest held in 913 at the residence and under the auspices of former emperor Uda.[19] Although retired and tonsured, Uda nonetheless exerted an authority at once nonimperial and quasi-imperial—an important reminder that poem contests mediated between ke and hare in terms of sites of composition.

The image of petals gathered on the wind doubles with the image of a wave that gathers. Just as the flower petals pause in the air, held on the wind's currents, so the wave remains poised at its crest, furled. Movements halt at the point of transformation. The scattering of blossoms marks the turning point of spring, and yet the petals linger aloft, not yet falling. It is as if the wave of spring pauses at its peak, unwilling to break. The flowers will not fall, not yet; they linger as a reminder (nagori) of the peak of spring. The superposition—or more precisely, resonance—of two images lets spring hover at its point of disappearance without disappearing.

Where images overlap, knowledge emerges: the currents of the wind recall the motion of waves on water, and yet the skies are waterless. Why are the movements of flowers on the wind like the movements of waves? Because the movements of days and seasons follow cosmological patterns, patterns that courtiers must observe and know. The world is a world of movements, movements of days, seasons, tides, waves, winds, flowers; so many movements that it would seem impossible to juxtapose any two in a coordinated manner. Yet Tsurayuki effects precisely that coordination. He uses the two images simultaneously in such a way that the two oscillate around a center of motion. In this way, rhetorically and imagistically, the poem literally brings composure to images, emotions, and events. Ideally, each poem would inscribe such a center of motion, and a balance between heart and word would make it distinct and intelligible.

But then, some poems, like those of the Six Immortals, present patterns that are not quite properly centered. When poems do not balance and direct the movement between heart and words correctly, an overly dissipating or constricting pattern results; the poem is without a distinct movement between word or heart, that is, without distinct center of motion. This is precisely his criticism of Ono no Komachi (in chapter 5), the only woman poet he discusses. He complains that her style is full of pathos and weak, like a noble woman fallen ill; but then in women's songs, a lack of strength is appropriate. Since the style deemed characteristic of Komachi is exemplified by the use of pivotwords and kinwords, it would seem that Tsurayuki sees the abundance of pivotwords she uses as a kind of weakness. The line twists and turns, and the song fairly writhes with emotion, but there is no strong binary structure to direct emotion in predictable ways. For Tsurayuki, this is an illness, a kind of dissipation of emotive energies.

An imbalance of heart and words results in a dissipative pattern in which emotion overruns words—or in a constrictive pattern in which words overwhelm emotion. Tsurayuki's preface generally shows the greatest concern for the potential for dissipation and degeneration. To compensate for and balance such dissipative patterns, he aims as a compiler to situate indistinct or decadent patterns in relations to other poems in such a way that generative forces are not dispersed but enter into other centers of motion. Each poem, with its own center of motion, acts as a minor gravitational field pulling energies into it. Some poems have less attractive force and must therefore be situated in juxtaposition to poems with greater attraction in order to keep energies moving without dissipating. It is in this sense that Tsurayuki's imperial anthology directs and channels movements more than it bounds or contains them. The seasonal scrolls, with their cyclic economy, are the most obvious manifestation of this impulse, but it extends to other scrolls and to relations among scrolls.

Inscription and Compilation

Tsurayuki, at the outset of his preface, establishes the simultaneity of emotive forces and generative forces. Ideally, the movement from heart to words parallels the movement from seed to leaves. And so, natural generative patterns supply the patterns for human emotion: the movement from seed to flower to fruit to seed; or, in the seasonal scrolls, the movement from spring to summer to fall and winter; or, in the love scrolls, the movement from rumor to glimpse to letters to trysts to separations. "Generative pattern" comprises all manner of forms, rhythms, motions and cycles in the terrestrial and celestial realms—whence the importance of getting them right.

Tsurayuki's discussion of poetic count is a case in point. Once he has established the link between uta wo yomu (composing/counting) and the calls of birds and bugs, he discusses the celestial and terrestrial efficacy of poetics to introduce the subject of characters and rhythmic count: "In the age of the gods when things cut to the quick, the characters (moji) for songs were unfixed and direct, and the heart of words was indeed not distinct. With the age of humans, ever since Susanowo, [humans] have counted (yo-mikeru) thirty characters with one additional character." [20] Usually, the word moji in this passage is translated as syllables or otherwise related to poetic speaking rather than writing, which forces vocal figures into a very narrow sense of language. Yet, although it relates to poetic vocality, moji (文字) also implies figure, pattern, and the designs of script. Tsurayuki's interest in vocal figures and patterns has absolutely nothing to do with a realistic transcription of speech. Direct pronunciation or realistic depiction of speech are precisely what his poetics shuns. Just as in this passage he strings an epithet (tihayahuru) upon "age of the gods" (kami no yo) in a way that disrupts reference, so he lets us know that direct, unfixed usage of characters results in indistinct, hard-to-understand patterns. Tsurayuki wants forms that are fixed and indirect. His moji may also be thought of as figures, that is, as an abstract counting machine. And, to define waka, Tsurayuki arrives at an abstract figure: "thirty characters with one additional character."

Inscription dominates Tsurayuki's sense of poetry. In the Tosa nikki, when he hears a potentially poetic phrase, he writes it in order to see whether it indeed follows a pattern of thirty-one syllables. But this sense of writing is not phonetic, even if it involves vocality. It is not an attempt to make writing adequate to speech but to make vocality fit the patterns of writing. Writing does not transmit or transcribe speech; on the contrary, speech must be refigured to align with figures. Speech then becomes more like music or math, for it is figures and rhythms that bring order to the heart. The linguistic message occupies no more than a corner of this poetics, and even when that message is harkened to, it is attended to obliquely, on the level of convention and allusions to earlier patterns. It is an effect not a cause or source of poetry. Tsurayuki's poetics reaches for figural space. For this reason, it is absurd to see him as a defender of the Japanese language or even as a bearer of a Japanese sensibility. Those concerns could not be farther from his project—which is to combine singing or composing (uta wo yomu) and counting or figuring (moji wo yomu).[21]

Tsurayuki's sense of figures or characters is consonant with notions common to Chinese inscription. Chang Huai-kuan, in the *Shu tuan* (early eighth century T'ang), writes of the mythic inventor of writing, Ts'ang Chieh, that he could simultaneously observe the celestial meanders of the constellations and the terrestrial marks and tracks of turtles and birds.[22] Ts'ang Chieh, legend has it, possessed four eyes, two to watch the heavens and two to observe the earth. With his double vision, he invented characters, a mode of writing that draws from celestial and terrestrial patterns. Similarly, with his double vision, Tsurayuki sees both flowers and clouds, or a gust of scattering petals doubled with a furling wave in the heavens, or the white hair of age doubled with the snows of winter. Double vision combines terrestrial patterns with celestial patterns.

As the legend of Ts'ang Chieh suggests, it is the nature of characters to partake simultaneously of both realms. For this reason, the use of characters demands a great deal of attention and regulation: at stake is the alignment of terrestrial and celestial patterns. These notions provide the background for Tsurayuki's comments about song patterns in the kana preface: "Song is what moves heavens and earth without applying force, draws out the feelings of unseen dead spirits, soothes between man and woman, and calms the heart of fierce warriors." Tsurayuki writes of song (uta) as if it were characters (moji); he sees no difference between singing poems (uta wo yomu) and counting characters (moji wo yomu). Songs and characters compose patterns that move between the two realms, heavenly and earthly. Such patterns, of course, are not static but mobile: song moves, draws out, soothes between, calms. Like characters, songs are active and generative; they don't contain or represent the signs of earth and heavens; they move between, functioning as potential sites of orderly generation and alignment. "In this way," Tsurayuki writes in a style that mimics Chinese parallel prose, "poems have generated many and multiform heart-word-leaves (kokorokotoha) that esteem flowers and admire birds, that lament mist and pity dew."[23]

Fenellosa and Pound's account of the Chinese character, which drew broadly on this notion of characters as generative forces, tended to a certain reification of the Chinese character, making individual characters into self-sufficient generators. Tsurayuki's sense of song and character, however, relates directly to the motions of calligraphy, to the act and art of writing with a brush, to the continuous, coordinated movement from pattern to pattern, character to character. He deals not with the written character but with the writing character, for it is in the movements of the brush that the acts of composing song and counting characters coincide. This is why Tsurayuki must write a phrase before he decides whether it is poetry or not. If characters and songs may come between heavens and earth, it is because the brush moves between, draws out, soothes.

As the brush moves through a character, it imparts not just a pattern but a center of motion as well. The center of motion organizes the gestural energies of the character, drawing strokes around it. The character appears to float and hover, for its center of motion defies gravity. Yet the brush continues down the page; the gestural energies of a character pivot around a center of motion but never come to a standstill: the brush passes into other configurations, locating the centers of motion for a series of characters. Characters differ in their configurations and energies; some tend to disperse or tilt, to lose their distinctness of pattern or their consistency of motion. Such is the Wang legacy. And then the art of the brush is to work in the interstices, coordinating the various patterns and centers into a continuous open series. There are starts and stops in the series but no closure; the brush channels and directs energies into patterns, it prevents dispersion and dissipation by way of centers of motion, but it never attempts to contain or close their series.

Tsurayuki uses the same mode in the composition and compilation of poems. *Kokinwakashū* does not eliminate such allegedly weak or unbalanced song patterns as those of the Six Immortals. On the contrary, in a way analogous to the calligraphic coordination between characters, *Kokinwakashū* calibrates the movement between poems by situating a poem or groups of poems vis-à-vis other poems and groups: poems emerge in sequences. One part of the art of *Kokinwakashū* is to situate poems with respect to topic in various scrolls: seasons, travels, grief, congratulations, love, names of things, and so forth. The twenty scrolls are almost a symmetrical pairing of ten and ten, reminiscent of the strong parallels and antitheses of Tsurayuki's poetic compositions.

1. Spring (1)   11. Love (1)
2. Spring (2)   12. Love (2)
3. Summer   13. Love (3)
4. Fall (1)   14. Love (4)
5. Fall (2)   15. Love (5)
6. Winter   16. Grief
7. Congratulations 17. Miscellaneous (1)
8. Partings   18. Miscellaneous (2)
9. Travels   19. Miscellaneous Styles
10. Names of Things 20. Court Songs, etc.

The two-column list of scrolls enjoins us to make symmetrical pairings, the most evident being the pairings of the seasons and love; but there is always a lag or shift: there are six seasonal scrolls but five love scrolls. But then winter matches grief, and symmetry returns, only to have another lag or gap appear. The procedure recalls that used in Tsurayuki's poetic compositions: the production of doubles with a slight lag or gap, which spurs a perpetual agonism. Some editions do not contain the twentieth scroll, yet the patterns still hold; with nineteen scrolls, the tension between symmetries and asymmetries works just as well. With twenty scrolls, significantly, the total number of poems is 1,111. The emphasis thus falls on the interval of one, on the act of counting in integers. The integer 1 imparts orderly intervals and asymmetry in an assemblage that permits an endless interpenetration of elements.

The sequences within and across scrolls impart a cyclic movement. The first ten scrolls begin with the first day of spring of the new year. They move to the last day of winter; and on the last day of winter, just before the new year, songs open into congratulations—reminiscent of the new year. After congratulations, there occurs a gradual dispersal of auspicious unions—into the scrolls on partings and travels—then an unwinding into the names of things in which the sequences open into names and categories. This unwinding of the seasonal cycle into congratulations and separations and then into names prepares for the scrolls of love poems, for these emerge out of an almost patternless space, providing the barest rumors and glimpses between future lovers. The love scrolls move gradually from glimpses to exchanges to trysts, but always with a lag or gap between the two lovers: encounters are always glancing hits, and, inevitably and variously, the bond dissolves, opening into poems of grief and lamentation, after which the cyclical momentum disperses into miscellaneous poems and styles to prepare for the emergence of the first day of spring.

Overall, the twenty scrolls (or nineteen) delineate two cycles of emergence and disappearance, one dominated by the seasons, one by loves, each cycle emerging from and dissolving into the other. The symmetry between the two parallel cycles is strategically not exact. *Kokinwakashū* symmetries are overbearingly strict and deliberate yet calculated to generate patterns in an open series. Always the interval of one intervenes to displace symmetries, to propel cyclical movement, to open an infinite series. In this way, Tsurayuki's poetics attempts to construct a perpetual motion machine with an infinite open series, and at three levels simultaneously: character, song and scroll. And surely it is for this reason that Tsurayuki declares the primacy of "thirty characters with one additional character." In the space of the waka, the additional one assures a slight yet distinct asymmetry; it ensures that the waka line never breaks into thoroughly symmetrical and, therefore, potentially closed or immobile patterns.

As with the brushwork of Koreyuki's rendition of *Wakanrōeishū*, Tsurayuki arrives at a form of disjunctive synthesis. In *Ashide shita-e Wakanrōeishō*, the art lay in the strategic production and regulation of disjunctures in various layers (figure, color, and pattern of paper, illustration, calligraphy, composition, compilation), in order to induce resonance between elements within and among registers (of expression). In *Kokinwakashū*, the art of disjunctive synthesis involves resonance among centers of motion in open series. The interval of one allows for a calibration of disjunctive synthesis: the disjuncture could be described as an aperture, one that must be strictly regulated in its degree of contraction and dilation. The interaction of heart and words is precisely such an aperture, to be held at the dilation/contraction setting of one.

Tsurayuki's asymmetrical count of "plus one" is also consonant with ninth-century transformations in waka prosody or rhythm. The general prosody of the thirty-plus-one line involves a rhythm of 5-7-5-7-7. The long poems (*chōka*) of Man'yōshū, whatever their original rhythms, came to be read in a pattern of alternating fives and sevens, with strong symmetrical pairings of 5-7 and 5-7. The envoi (*hanka*) to the long poem rounded off the sequence with 5-7-5-7-7, from which the short poem (*tanka*) is said to derive its syllabic count. In the course of the ninth century, and particularly in *Kokinwakashū*, the appellation *waka* was attached to the short poem, and the latter was referred to as a "Yamato song."[24] In the period from the late *Man'yōshū* to that of the Six Immortals, it seems that the symmetrical rhythms of the long poem lingered in the short poem. In brief, the count of thirty-one tended to break into 5-7/5-7-7. The waka rhythms of *Kokinwakashū*, particularly those of the compilers' generation, transform those rhythms, maximizing asymmetries in the line. Clifton Royston (working from the analyses of Iwatsu Motoo) summarizes what is surmised about waka rhythms.

> We do not have musical notation for Heian and Kamakura period recitation, of course, but we can infer something of it. . . . The last syllable of the first line was drawn out, and followed by a pause of about three beats. . . . A similar pause followed the second line (. . . but this may have been a lesser musical break). Again the final syllable of the third line was drawn out and followed by a three-beat pause. The end of the fourth line is drawn out but there is little or no pause between it and the final line.[25]

The *Kokin* waka tend to form a pattern of 5-7/5/7-7, with the ghost of a break remaining from the pattern 5-7/5-7. In his poems, Tsurayuki often runs the rhythmic and grammatical links across the first 5-7-5 syllables and binds the final 7-7 together, as in the poem cited above (KKS 2:89): *sakura hana tirinuru kaze no nagori ni ha mizu naki sora ni nami zo tatikeru* ("On the crest of a gust scattering cherry petals linger as on waterless skies furls a wave"). The first seventeen syllables conveys one phrase, image, or idea: as a reminder or keepsake, the wind that scatters the petals of cherry blooms. In the following fourteen, another phrase, image, or idea emerges: on the waterless sky, a wave rises or furls. Because Tsurayuki gives the opening five syllables the customary solidity of a topic (*sakura hana*, cherry flowers), the prosody of his line neatly follows the prosody described by Royston: 5/5-7/7-7.

What is the upshot of the 5/5-7/7 prosody of thirty-plus-one syllables? It is mobile patterns and open series: Tsurayuki's preface announces the numerical asymmetry of the line, and his poems echo and elaborate it in their rhythms. Analogously, Tsurayuki, the principal compiler of *Kokinwakashū*, compiles sequences of poems into mobile patterns by way of doubles that never quite match (to a count of 1,111). And if the calligraphy attributed to him is any indication, the rhythms of the brush are at odds with 5-7-5-7-7: in the brushwork of his own house collection (*jikashū*), the starts and stops of the brush have nothing to do with vocal rhythms of fives and sevens.[26] Calligraphy imparts its own rhythms and styles to poems, almost irrespective of the vocal register of rhythm. In short, in, around, and through the poem, the registers of rhythm, image, brushwork, and compilation result in anexact layers and asymmetrical doubles. But the logic of the intervals, patterns, and centers of motion ensures the consistency of this poetic assemblage. And it is the art of the brush that best explains how Tsurayuki attempts to coordinate the various registers.

Like the act of compilation, calligraphy does not linger on the individual poem but passes through poems, inventing an open series of mobile patterns. The brush individuates yet does not frame or isolate characters. And it is the same with compilation: it attends to patterns and centers of motion, looking for the mobile, energized passage from poem to poem, topic to topic, character to character. The movements of the brush are able to open poetic forms into terrestrial and celestial realms because the discipline of writing with the brush entails an education in pattern recognition and rhythmic sensation. Brushwork entails a learning with the body that operates at, or provides access to, a mode of sensation (sensible and abstract forms) that is not yet perception, emotion, or cognition. Of course, brushwork itself is not the ground for the emergence of forms of representation, perception, and cognition, for it is itself a form. There is a logic and procedure common to calligraphy and compilation that makes visible for us the discursive ground of Heian poetics.

Modern editions eradicate that logic, treating calligraphy and compilation as transparent or neutral modes of representation. For modern commentaries, brushwork and scrolls amount to no more than a featureless plane from which the individual voices of poets emerge to express themselves. The modern emphasis falls entirely on individual composition. Modern editions join poem and proper name and frame them; and modern criticism tends to treat each poem or author in isolation; the name attributed to the poem supplies the source and limit for its content. As for the act of compilation, it is assumed that the anthology presents another level of containment, one whose principles do not disrupt the authority and authenticity of the individual poem but only place it in a prestigious context: an imperial anthology like Kokinwakashū simply increases the prestige of the author; the author or poem gains the imperial stamp of approval. This is one treatment of poetry, which modern editions and commentaries attempt to raise to the status of science. Tsurayuki, however, works from a very different set of principles.

For Tsurayuki, rhythms and patterns are not neutral or transparent modes of representation, whether they are imparted at the level of calligraphy, composition, or compilation. In an anthology like *Kokinwakashū* the importance of all three registers raises questions about the ways in which we think about authority and expression. Which level of expression should we attend to? Modern editions and commentaries remove this uncertainty by centering expression on the individual poet, by insisting on the lyric voice, and by eradicating modes of expression that decenter or dissolve the modern poetic frame. Yet even a cursory glance at the various registers of expression in *Kokinwakashū* serves to deconstruct the designs of modern editions. Yet alongside this deconstruction, it is important to heed the construction enabled by calligraphy, scrolls, composition, and so forth.

As the prefaces make abundantly clear, the aim of *Kokinwakashū* is not deconstruction but a direction of emotive forces and generative forces by way of patterns and centers of motion, in ways directly related to the logic of Han poetry, calligraphy, and cosmology. Han modes lie at the heart of Tsurayuki's ability to move across the registers of calligraphy, composition, and compilation—three activities for which he was renowned—by way of a politico-poetic cosmology. Therefore what we today name Tsurayuki is a conglomeration of activities, many of which are simply attributed to the name Tsurayuki. In Heian poetics, the proper name indicates a prestigious nexus of activities or styles associated with an individual in the way a robe is associated with a body: pattern, weave and color indicate a rank, position, and occasion, but that nexus can be replicated or entered into by others. Like characters and poems, names are individuated, but incorporation proceeds apace, directing, channeling, and overcoding subjects.

There are a number of reasons why modern accounts of Heian poetics have so much trouble with the figural dimensions of the *Kokin* project. First, it makes no attempt to inscribe linguistic or cultural boundaries but operates at the level of rhythm and figure in a way that confounds the notion of waka poetry as a particularly Japanese form. Two, it raises difficult questions about the relations of the Heian court with courts across East Asia, since the lines of conflict and exchange among courts do not correspond to modern nations: it is impossible to speak of Japan, Korea, or China as bounded, homogeneous entities in this context. Three, the *Kokinwakashū* makes difficult the separation of aesthetics and politics that is necessary to the modern vision of waka as lyric poetry: for all the beauty to be teased out of its rhythms and figures, the *Kokin* project is imminently rational and frankly ideological.

Around the turn of the century, Masaoka Shiki, the inventor of the modern haiku, launched one of the most enduring attacks ever directed at *Kokinwakashū*. In one critique, he takes issue with the first poem of the anthology, a waka that plays with the confusion which arises when the first day of spring (the new year) arrives before the end of the twelfth month. In the lunar calendar, the first day of spring and the first day of the first month of the new year coincided; but in intercalary years, a certain month was repeated in the year and the progression of months were delayed—with the result that spring arrived in the twelfth month. Tsurayuki and company open the anthology with a poem about this slippage between solar and lunar schedules (KKS 1:1).

> ふる年に春たちける日よめる　在原元方
> 年のうちに春は来にけりひととせを去年とやいはむ今年とやいはむ
> Recounted on a day when spring arrived within the old year—
> Arihara no Motokata,
> Within the year spring has come,
> another year shall we say,
> or shall we call it this year?

This example, for Shiki, symbolizes all that is aberrant and abhorrent about *Kokinwakashū* and Tsurayuki. Of this poem Shiki writes that it is boring and witless, a bad joke—rather like joking that the child of a mixed marriage is neither Japanese or foreign. There is nothing clever about it at all.[27]

It is in some sense appropriate for Shiki to use this strange analogy to a child of mixed race, for in doing so he signals, maybe unintentionally, that the *Kokin* project concerns itself with reproduction and with doubles, mixtures, and hybrids. It applies extremely rational criteria to the production of antitheses, parallels, symmetries, and such in order to bring order to the space between two terms, which space comprises all manner of asymmetries, including male-female interactions and procreation. Ultimately, however, because Tsurayuki's assemblage operates at the level of sensation, these patterns are not so much a form of mediation as they are mediators; that is, waka constitute mediators, exchangers, or transformers—in short, a song machine.

For Shiki, needless to say, this is not poetry at all. And in many ways, his judgment is apt. Shiki sought a modern space for poetics, and his is a poetics with a radically experiential and objectivist vision that allows intensive hybridization within a bounded, purified space. Because he is intent on a certain kind of interior poetic space, he rejects the song machine; it is too rational and mechanical. But, then, as Yoshimoto Taka'aki points out, Shiki overlooks the fantastical and metaphysical aspects of *Kokinwakashū*.[28] Yoshimoto's remarks could be taken a step further: *Kokinwakashū* is not so much about metaphysical or fantastical poetry as it is about the ordering of the senses, about the ways in which rhythmic, patterned sensation can open out into celestial rhythms and terrestrial forms. Its poetry does not merely represent and reproduce these forms and rhythms, it opens into them and follows from them. It is every bit as logical and mechanical as Shiki says, and every bit as metaphysical and fantastical as Yoshimoto says: *Kokinwakashū* is a song machine that calibrates heart and words to the proper intervals.

As Shiki suggests, Tsurayuki is the mechanic of the Heian politico-poetic order (rather than a great author or poet). Tsurayuki tinkers with songs, calibrating their centers of motion and gauging their patterns in order to align them in cycles, like so many gears and wheels in a great machine. It is a fantastical machine insofar as its mediators and transformers act alone and in tandem within an open series. And the operative analogy would again be to characters and calligraphy: the character as a figure that partakes of celestial rhythm and natural forms but that links resonantly in an open series. It is on this note that Tsurayuki closes the kana preface— with a statement about figures or characters (moji), natural forms (willow threads, bird tracks, pine needles), human emotions and actions (deeds, eras, desires) and celestial rhythms (the moon in the great heavens). Writing moji with the brush produces eternal, perpetual patterns of song.

> Although Hitomaro has gone, the acts of songs have remained. Even though eras shift and deeds pass, and delights and sorrows come and go, the characters (moji) of songs continue. Should they be retained as changeless as birdtracks and transmitted as long as rampant vines, just as the evergreen needles never scatter and vanish, just as the threads of green willow always trail, then people who know the designs of songs and obtain the heart of words surely will look up to the high ages and yearn for this day, just as we look to the moon in the great heavens.[29]

Tsurayuki's poetics are numerical, logical, and mechanical, but the levers and wheels of his machine are not those of the modern era, of, say, the printing press. In the song machine, the brush is his lever and the heavens his wheel. The tip of the brush is like the eccentric that transforms lateral or reciprocal motion into cyclical motion (or the reverse).[30] With the brush, reciprocation or oscillation is transformed into cycles, and back again, and at any number of different levels. Waka are machines that make lines hesitate and break, oscillate and resonate, in order to open into natural rhythms, patterns, and cycles. With his seminal brush, Tsurayuki calibrates these waka machines in time to the motor of the heavens, laying down the seeds of song in perfect intervals, harnessing the emotive forces of the human heart. And so, even as their eyes trail after the moon, even as they cast their words to the winds, even as their bodies, like robes, become as porous and patterned as a starry sky, courtiers enter into a realm of sensation that can be calibrated with the brush and that the empire can count on in its dawn order.

NOTES

Introduction: Unstating Heian Japan

1 Benedict Anderson, *Imagined Communities: Reflections on the Origin and Spread of Nationalism* (London: Verso, 1983), 14, 19.

2 Ibid., 20, 22, 26, 26–27.

3 See Stefan Tanaka's study of the formation of tōyōshi (Oriental history) in Japan. *Japan's Orient: Rendering Pasts into History* (University of California Press, 1994).

4 "Of course, there was no national language equivalent to today's *hyōjun kogo* (standard spoken Japanese, or NHK Japanese)," Naoki Sakai writes. "Motoori translated the *Ko-kinshū* into a dialect probably unintelligible to Japanese living in other remote regions." *Voices of the Past: The Status of Language in Eighteenth-Century Japanese Discourse* (Ithaca: Cornell University Press, 1991), 264, n. 27.

5 See "Archaeology and Identity." In *Multicultural Japan: Palaeolithic to Postmodern*, ed. Donald Devon, Mark Hudson, Gavan McCormack, and Tessa Morris-Suzuki (Cambridge: Cambridge University Press, 1996).

6 In his introduction to *Text: The Genealogy of an Antidisciplinary Object* (Durham: Duke University Press, 1992), John Mowitt gives an excellent overview of the stakes and differences of the philological and semiological text.

7 In English, the best overview of the introduction and usage of "calendrics" (such as the sexagenary cycle) appears in Masayoshi Sugimoto and David L. Swain's *Science and Culture in Traditional Japan A.D. 600–1854* (Cambridge: MIT Press, 1978), especially "Science in Chinese Wave I" on calendar cycles and the five phases (56–63). In Japanese, the understanding of calendrics is so central (though untheorized in poetry studies) that classical dictionaries supply the fundamental information in charts and appendices.

8 This point often crops up in Francine Hérail's study of the Heian court: *La Cour du Japon à l'époque de Heian aux Xe et XI^{ie} siècles* (Paris: Hachette, 1995).

One. Revising the Rebus

1   The mana preface to *Kokinwakashū* mentions 905 (the fifth year of the Engi era); but because songs in the anthology can be traced to poetry contests that took place after 905, scholars presume that the date mentioned in the two prefaces is that of the edict for compilation; the presentation would have taken place some time after the date of the latest poem, around 920. As for the practice of collecting waka, *Kokinwakashū* has the prestige of being the first imperial anthology of waka. Masada Shigeo, however, in "Tennōsei to waka: chokusenshū o megutte," *Kokubungaku: kaishaku to kyōzai no kenkyū* 34:13 (November 1989), 54–60, suggests that a number of previous emperors attempted collections of waka, although, for various reasons (primarily length of reign), these collections were never completed.

2   It is common to differentiate among three eras. In the first are the songs of poets from the compilers' own generation, from roughly the late-ninth and early-tenth centuries. In the second, the poets of the mid-ninth century are represented by the Six Poetic Immortals. The third, or earliest, era contributes songs that seem to be from the late eighth and early ninth century, though these are hard to pin down historically. They are often marked "anonymous," and are said to derive from a line of oral transmission. Many of them overlap in time with the songs of the late *Man'yōshū*.

3   Kojima Noriyuki, in *Kokinshū izen: shi to waka no kōryū* (Tokyo: Hanawa shobō, 1976), looks at the legacy of Han song at the early Heian court in terms of an "age of adulation of Han styles" (115) and sets the stage for a "bicultural" approach to *Kokin* waka.

4   Wada Atsumu, "Shinhakken no moji shiryō: sono kakkitekina yakuwari," in *Kotoba to moji*, ed. Kishi Toshio, Nihon no kodai 14 (Tokyo: Chūōkōronsha, 1988), 32–33. I translate the passage from the book of charms (*Jakyōjugonhossoku*) in order to render the complexity of its divagations: *ware omohu, kimi no kokoro ha hanaretsuru, kimi mo omowaji, ware mo omowaji.*

5   Sigmund Freud, *The Interpretation of Dreams*, cited in Slavoj Žižek, *Looking Awry: An Introduction to Jacques Lacan through Popular Culture* (Cambridge: MIT Press, 1991), 51–52.

6   Ibid., 52.

7   Félix Guattari, *Chaosmose* (Paris: Galilée, 1992), 17–18.

8   Karatani Kōjin, *Origins of Modern Japanese Literature*, trans. ed. Brett de Bary (Durham: Duke University Press, 1993).

9   *Man'yōshū* 4:707. Because these are ancient characters, some are unavailable on Japanese software. I therefore use the character 椀 for もひ, which would normally appear with the hen 土 and the tsukuri 完.

10 There is nothing new about this notion that the inscription of early Japanese poetry entails rebuses. I simply have chosen to make it the point of departure for analysis, rather than viewing it as an obstacle or a conclusion. J. Marshall Unger writes, "Not uncommonly, combinations of Chinese graphs were used to form rebuses, the correct 'reading' of which depended only in a circuitous way on the semantics of the corresponding Chinese morpheme." "The Etymology of the Japanese word /kana/," *Papers in Japanese Linguistics* 7 (1980), 174–75. He cites the account of Roy Andrew Miller in *The Japanese Language*

(Chicago: University of Chicago, 1967), 96, which is a good introduction to the difficulties of Man'yō inscription.

Two. Kana Inscription and Stylistic Differentiation

1   Komatsu Shigemi, Kana, Iwanami shinsho 679 (Tokyo: Iwanami shoten, 1968), 64–65.

2   Unger, "The Etymology of the Japanese Word /kana/", 173–84.

3   Kūkai, "Sangō shiiki," ed. Yamamoto Chikyō, Kōbōdaishi Kūkai zenshū 6 (Tokyo: Chikuma shobō, 1984), 5. Since my translation deliberately, and perhaps idiosyncratically, expunges all traces of an overriding "consciousness," I give Hakeda's translation too: "For any natural phenomenon or literary work there exists a cause. The sun, the moon, and the stars appear when the sky is clear. A man writes when moved. So the Eight Trigrams of Fu Hsi, the Tao-te Ching, the Book of Odes, the Elegies of Ch'u were written down by men who were inspired from within. Of course, there can be no comparison between these sages of the past and a common man of the present such as I, yet somehow I feel compelled to express my inner-most feelings." In Kūkai: Major Works, trans. Yoshita S. Hakeda (New York: Columbia University Press, 1972), 101–2. The attribution of this text to Kūkai is somewhat apocryphal, yet it is not at odds with his general theories of writing. Hirayama Mitsuki, Eien no sho: Kūkai hen (Tokyo: Yūhōdō, 1969) is the general source for my interpretation. I use Hirayama's interpretation in greater detail in chapter 5.

4   Robert Treat Paine and Alexander Soper, in The Art and Architecture of Japan 3d. ed. (New Haven: Yale University Press, 1981), discuss the excavation of P'o-hai (Palhae), a court allied with the Tang from the eighth through the tenth centuries, suggesting its similarities with the Heian capital (343; 361–62). In addition, Konishi Jin'ichi, in "The Genesis of the Kokinshū style," finds the same varieties in the waka of Kokinwakashū as in the song of the Six Dynasties and the Sui Dynasty (as well as the early T'ang).

5   Kaneko Shūichi, "Sui tō kōtai to higashi ajia," in Tō to Nihon, ed. Ikeda On (Tokyo: Yoshikawa Hirobumi kan, 1992).

6   Amino Yoshihiko, in Umi to rettō no chūsei (Tokyo: Nihon editaaskuuru shuppanbu, 1992), challenges the notion of the closure or isolation of Japan. He has written a great deal that undermines the notion of a pure and homogeneous ancient society; see, for example, Nihon shakai to tennōsei, Iwanami bukkuretto 108 (Tokyo: Iwanami, 1988).

7   In this study, I deliberately downplay discussions of rhetorical devices in the interpretation of waka poetry because of the way they delimit the Japaneseness of waka in advance. In addition, although the rhetorical categories stem largely from the late medieval and early modern periods, the emphasis on them has created the impression that Heian poets actually thought and composed in such terms. Generally, the following kinds of devices are distinguished in early-modern commentaries: makurakotoba or "pillow-word," utamakura or "poem-pillow," jo or "preface," kakekotoba or "pivotword," and engo or "kinword." The first three are deemed characteristic of Man'yōshū. Then, in the mid-ninth century, with the Six Poetic Immortals, the latter two come to the fore. Finally, the poets of the generation of the Kokin compilers tend to "revive" the pillow-word and the preface, often in conjunction with pivotwords and kinwords.

8   Saigo Nobutsuna, *Nihon kodai bungakushi*, Iwanami zensho 149 (Tokyo: Iwanami shoten, 1951), 116–17. The chapter cited here is entitled "Waka to kanshi" in a section on the age of lyric poetry (Jojōshi no jidai).

9   Ibid.

10 Ibid., 117–18. I render *minzoku* as "folk," though "people" is also appropriate, in order to highlight the problematic convergence of lyric modes and folklore studies (*minzoku-gaku*).

11 Ibid., 118. Kitayama Shigeo, in *Nihon no rekishi 4: Heian-kyō* (Tokyo: Chūōkōronsha, 1973), discusses the political battle for the throne in which Yakamochi took part unsuccessfully (25–27). His account clarifies why Saigo is so invested in this conflict, for Kitayama continually evokes the battle between clans (*uji*) in terms of bloodline (much as Saigo evokes womb and blood). Amino Yoshihiko, however, in *Umi to rettō no chūseio* 23, reminds us that uji was a political assemblage, not a clan in the sense of family lineage.

12 Saigo, *Nihon kodai bungakushi*, 118–20.

13 Suzuki Hideo, *Kodaiwakashiron* (Tokyo: Tōkyō daigaku shuppankai, 1990), 395.

14 Ibid.

15 Ibid., 397–98.

16 Ibid., 394.

17 Ibid., 401.

18 Karaki, *Nihon no kokoro no rekishi* (Tokyo: Chikuma shodō, 1976), 1:63. I have rendered *kunten* and *kaeriten* as "diacritic marks," *okurigana* as "inflections," and *kundoku* as "Japanese reading."

19 Wallace Stevens, "The Creations of Sound," in *The Collected Poems of Wallace Stevens* (New York: Random House, 1990), 310–11.

20 E. J. Hobsbawm, *Nations and Nationalism since 1780: Programme, Myth, Reality* (Cambridge: Cambridge University Press, 1990), 133.

21 Robert Borgen, *Sugawara Michizane and the Early Heian Court* (Cambridge: Harvard University Press, 1986), 221–22.

22 Fujiwara Katsumi, in "Ōchō bungaku wa naze kanshibun no seisei ni hajimaru no ka," *Kokubungaku* 29:14 (November 1984), 18–24, suggests that Sugawara no Michizane played an important role in the ninth-century construction of new spatial and intellectual relations to nature (and property). Oosone Shōsuke, in "Shijin Sugawara no Michizane wa naze ippō de kajin datta no ka," ibid., 25–31, questions whether one should see Michizane primarily as a kanshi poet; he maintains that Michizane's kanshi expression is waka-like in its personal lyricism.

23 Unger, "The Etymology of the Japanese word /kana/," 175.

24 The figural overlap of *Man'yōshū* with Han forms is striking in calligraphic manuscripts; the manuscripts of *Man'yōshū* are very close stylistically to those of the *Wakanrōeishū* or "Collection of Han and Yamato Cantillations."

25 "Shinsen man'yōshū," in *Shinpen kokka taikan dainikan: shisenshuhen kashū*, ed. Shinpen kokka taikan henshū iinka (Tokyo: Kadokawa shoten, 1984), 184, poem 408. I use the modern characters from the standard edition. Since this poem resembles a waka that appears in *Kokinwakashū* (6:337), which is translated below, I have made the English translations as compatible as possible.

26 Amagasaki Akira, *Nihon no retorikku* (Tokyo: Chikuma shobō, 1988), 139.

27 Jean-François Billeter, in *The Chinese Art of Writing* (New York: Rizzoli, 1990), recounts the origins of the term *grass style*: "The Chinese call it *ts'ao-shu*, 'draft writing,' or literally 'straw writing,' because at first it was used for ephemeral purposes like articles of straw" (77–78).

28 Walter Benjamin, "On the Mimetic Faculty," in *Reflections*, ed. Peter Demetz (New York: Schocken Books, 1986), 333, 336.

29 Michael Taussig, "Physiognomic Aspects of Visual Worlds," in *Visualizing Theory: Selected Essays from V.A.R.*, ed. Lucien Taylor (New York: Routledge, 1994).

30 *Eiga monogatari*, 2 vols., ed. Matsumura Hiroji and Yamanaka Yutaka, Nihon koten bungaku taikei 76 (Tokyo: Iwanami shoten, 1965), 2:104–5. Komatsu mentions these screens in *Kana*, 77, as does Mitani Kuniaki in *Genji monogatari no sukeito* (Tokyo: Yūseidō, 1992), 40–41.

Three. Composition and Competition

1 Suzuki endorses Akiyama's scenario in his account of waka and kana (*Kodaiwakashiron*, 402–3). Akiyama seems to have devoted himself to establishing the Japaneseness of the *Kokin* aesthetic. Since he equates the boundary of waka expression with the phonetic transcription of Japanese speech, this does not take much of a leap. In "Kokinshū wa naze kihansei o mochieta ka," *Kokubungaku* 29:14 (November 1984), 39–45, he sketches some of the major concerns of his research (namely, the equation of kana inscription, waka expression, and Japanese speech and sensibility). His promotion of Japaneseness shows its symptoms to best effect in "Nihon teki miishiki no mondai: Kokinshū o megutte," in *Nihon bungaku kōza 2: bungakushi no shomondai* (Tokyo: Chikuma shobō, 1987), in which his excursion to the sakura or Japanese cherries of Washington D.C. (presented by the Japanese emperor) provide the impetus for a long incursion into the sources and substance of Japaneseness (along with the emperor).

2 Poems that separate the *hen* and *tsukuri* of characters appear in China as early as the late Han. Tanaka Kazuo enumerates a number of texts that include sections on "distancing and joining" (*rigō*) characters. "Kokinwakashū to Chūgokubungaku," in *Issatsu no kōza Kokinwakashū*, ed. Issatsu no kōza henshūbu, Nihon koten bungaku 4 (Tokyo: Yūseidō, 1987), 486–87.

3 *Wakanrōeishū*, ed. Oosone Shōsuke and Horiuchi Hideaki, Shinchō Nihon koten shūsei 61 (Tokyo: Shinchōsha, 1983), 89. The poem cited is number 224 by Ono no Takamura.

4 Suzuki Hideo gives a detailed account of how the standard waka sentiment "autumn is sad" derives from kanshi poetics (*Kodaiwakashiron*, 345) and discusses the role of *Shinsen man'yōshū* in this derivation (355).

5 Tsurayuki, "Kanajo," in *Kokinwakashū*, ed. Ozawa Masao, Nihon koten bungaku tenshū 7 (Tokyo: Shōgakukan, 1971), 58.

6 The transcription is partially adapted from *Idatebon Kokinwakashū: Fujiwara Teika hitsu*, 82, and the interpretation of kana and mana follows from it as well.

7 Ludwig Wittgenstein, *Philosophical Investigations*, 3d. ed., trans. G. E. M. Anscombe (London: Basil Blackwell & Mott, 1958), iixi, 193.

8   *Kokinwakashū* (10:439), 203; *Idatebon Kokin wakashū*, 133.

9   Helen C. McCullough, *Brocade by Night: "Kokin wakashū" and the Court Style in Japanese Classical Poetry* (Stanford: Stanford University Press, 1985), 478–81.

10 See Roy Andrew Miller's review of her study, "No Time for Literature," *Journal of the American Oriental Society* 107:4 (October-December 1987), 745–60.

11 Tokieda Motoki, *Kokugogakugenron* (Tokyo: Iwanami shoten, 1941). My account derives primarily from his final section entitled "Kokugomiron" (On the aesthetics of Japanese language), 502–50.

12 See "Toshiyori zuino," in *Karonshū*, ed. Hashimoto Mio, Ariyoshi Tamotsu, and Fujihira Haruo, Nihon koten bungaku zenshū 50 (Tokyo: Shōgakkan, 1975), 55.

13 The first line is a transcription of the version given in *Idatebon Kokinwakashū*, 130. It employs kana fairly similar to modern hiragana, with the exception that *ma* is derived from the character *man* (myriad) rather than *matsu* (end). Otherwise, one Chinese character is used, for *hito*. There are, of course, no voice marks like *do* or *gi*.

14 See the "moth brow mountain" poem by Li Po, cited in Tanizaki Jun'ichirō, "Ren'ai oyobi shikijō," *Tanizaki Jun'ichirō zenshū*, 28 vols. (Tokyo: Chūōkōronsha, 1966–1968), 22:244.

15 Amagasaki, *Nihon no retorikku*, 139–41.

16 Yoshino Tatsunori, in "Kakekotoba ron: seisei suru imi no dainamizumu," *Kodai bungaku* 31 (February 1992), 57–67, challenges the thesis put forth by Akiyama in the seminal work *Ōchō no bungaku kūkan* (Tokyo: Tōkyō daigaku shuppankai, 1984) in which Akiyama claims that kana inscription stabilizes *Kokin* expression and brings forth the use of pivotwords and kinwords (57–59).

17 Yoshino, "Kakekotobaron," 66.

18 Joshua S. Mostow, "Painted Poems, Forgotten Words: Poem-Pictures and Classical Japanese Literature," *Monumenta Nipponica* 47:3 (autumn 1992), 323–46. Komatsu uses a couple of the same examples in his account of kana and Japanese writing. Komatsu, *Kana*, 128–29.

19 Fujiwara Kintō, "Shinsen zuinō," in *Karonshū nōgakuronshū: Nihon koten bungaku taikei* 65, ed. Hisamatsu Sen'ichi and Nishio Minoru (Tokyo: Iwanami shoten, 1981), 27–28.

20 Yoshimoto, *Shokikayōron*, (Tokyo: Chūōseihan, 1977), 15–16, 426.

21 Tetsuo Najita and H. D. Harootunian discuss the shifts in how Yoshimoto Takaaki (or Ryūmei) articulated China in his discussions of Japan, calling attention to the historical moment and the political climate of his discovery of Chinese as a practical, contemporary language, in "Japanese Revolt Against the West: Political and Cultural Criticism in the Twentieth Century," in *Cambridge History of Japan*, vol. 6, ed. Peter Duus (Cambridge and New York: Cambridge University Press, 1988). See also Lawrence Olson's overview of Yoshimoto's career, "Intellectuals and 'The People'; on Yoshimoto Takaaki," *Journal of Japanese Studies* 4:2 (summer 1978), 327–57.

22 This account of awase draws primarily from the studies of Hagitani Boku, who has dominated the postwar compilation and study of poetry contests. His introduction (*kaisetsu*) to the volume of poetry contests gives an overview of the structure and history of contests. *Utaawaseshū*, ed. Hagitani Boku, Nihon koten taikei 74 (Tokyo: Iwanami, 1965). Setsuko Ito, in the introduction to her translation of various contests, *An Anthology of Traditional Japanese Poetry Competitions: Uta-awase 913–1815* (Bochum: Brockmeyer, 1991), closely fol-

lows Hagitani. In addition, Hagitani has himself published a detailed study of Heian poetry contests, *Heianchō utaawase gaisetsu* (Tokyo: Yamanouchi, 1969). See also Minegishi Tadaaki, *Utaawase no kenkyū* (Sanseidō, 1955).

23 The contest, entitled "Shōtai gannen aki teijiwin wominahesi ahase," appears in *Heianchō utaawase taisei: zōho shintei*, vol. 1, ed. Hagitani Boku (Kyoto: Dōhōsha, 1995), 99–111. The poem is number 24, anonymous.

24 Yoshimoto, *Shokikayōron*, 422–28. Yoshimoto borrows a theme with a long history—the idea that the Fujiwara regency was formed on the basis of Chinese culture—but he tries to avoid the idea of the negative valuation (as in Saigo's notion of degeneracy). He shows that waka betray a profound doubleness in their amalgamation of Yamato and Han.

25 Hagitani, "Kaisetsu," in *Utaawaseshū*, 7–47.

26 *Heianchō utaawase taisei: zōho shintei*, 1:101.

27 It is significant that the waka poem, which is so intimately involved with exchanges of wealth and the establishment of hierarchy, is not itself marked hierarchically; that is, the language of waka does not use honorifics or humilifics, as speakers at the Heian court purportedly did. We would have to think about what we mean by "daily speech" in the context of waka.

Four. Toward a History of Styles

1 Hirayama, *Eien no sho: Kūkai hen*, 26.

2 Komatsu Shigemi, in "Nihon shodō no ogonki," writes of the interpenetration of styles of sutra decoration and the calligraphic styles of scrolls presented at poem contests in the late Heian. In *Heian Kamakura no sho: sampitsu sanseki*, Nihon geijutsu zenshū 8 (Tokyo: Gakken, 1980).

3 We have seen that Suzuki, in *Kodaiwakashiron* (395), opposes kana culture to kanji culture. It is interesting that a scholar like Nakazawa Shin'ichi, for all his claims to poststructuralist and deconstructive modes of analysis, evokes the same distinction in his chapter on writing in *Ikonsofia* (Tokyo: Heibonsha, 1988). This is also true of his Deleuze-inspired chapter on early Japan in *Akutōteki shikō* (Tokyo: Heibonsha, 1988).

4 Christopher Seeley, *A History of Writing in Japan* (Leiden: E. J. Brill, 1991), 53.

5 Ibid., 76.

6 H. D. Harootunian, *Things Seen and Unseen: Discourse and Ideology in Tokugawa Nativism* (Chicago: University of Chicago Press, 1988), 44.

7 The dates for Wang Hsi-chih vary considerably. Billeter uses 321–79. It is also important to know that his calligraphy circulated in copies (or rather simulacra, as there was no logic of supplementarity in the act of copying), which Lothar Ledderose discusses in "Chinese Calligraphy: Its Aesthetic Dimension and Social Function," *Orientations* (October 1986), 35–60.

8 Emori Kenji reminds us that the term "three brushes" (*sampitsu*) was first mentioned in 1678. Although the three calligraphers are grouped together in the twelfth-century *Gōdanshō*, the framework of "three brushes, three precedents" derives from Edo Japan. *Ji to sho no rekishi* (Tokyo: Kinyōsha, 1968), 54.

9 Sometimes the "three precedents" are styled the three masters, intelligences, or wise

men (三賢). Haruna Yoshishige, "Heian jidai no shoron," in *Sho no Nihonshi* 2: *Heian*, ed. Tsuchida Naoshige (Tokyo: Heibonsha, 1975), 66. Shimatani Hiroyuki, in "Sanseki," in *Heian Kamakura no sho: sampitsu sanseki*, ed. Komatsu Shigemi, discusses the origins of the term *sanseki* (153).

10 Ayamura Kan'en, *Nihon no shodō* (Tokyo: Kawara shoten, 1966), 42–43.

11 Ibid., 43.

12 Tono Haruyuki, *Sho no kodaishi* (Tokyo: Iwanami Shoten, 1994), 3; 7. See Joan Piggot, "Mokkan: Wooden Documents from the Nara Period," *Monumenta Nipponica* 45:4 (1990), for information on the excavation and distribution of mokkan.

13 Emori Kenji, *Ji to sho no rekishi*, 46.

14 Lothar Ledderose, "Some Taoist Elements in the Calligraphy of the Six Dynasties," *T'oung Pao* 70 (1984), 246, 278.

15 Emori Kenji, *Ji to sho no rekishi*, 44.

16 There are any number of accounts of Kūkai and Fūshinjō. For a brief overview, see Emori Kenji, *Ji to sho no rekishi*, 58. See also the extensive plates of Kūkai calligraphy in *Shodō zenshū*. In this instance I consulted a reprint: Kūkai, *Fūshinjō, Genshoku hōchō sen* 11 (Tokyo: Nigensha, 1986).

17 Horie Tomohiko, "Heianjidai no shofū: sho no nagare 2," in *Sho no Nihonshi* 2: *Heian*, ed. Tsuchida Naoshige (Tokyo: Heibonsha, 1975), 37.

18 Ibid., 46.

19 Ibid., 47–49. Horie here refers to *wayō* as *jōdaiyō* (style of the ancient era) in order to establish it as the oldest stage in the Japanese aesthetic.

20 Yukinari, the grandson of Fujiwara no Koretada (924–972), was related to the powerful Fujiwara regents. Shimatani Hiroyuki gives an account of Yukinari in "Sanseki," in *Sampitsu sanseki*, 158–59.

21 Emori Kenji, *Ji to sho no rekishi*, 98–99.

22 Komatsu Shigemi, "Nihon shodō no ōgonki," in *Heian Kamakura no sho: sampitsu sanseki*, 137. See Billeter's description of the "current script" (*gyōsho*) with respect to attack, development, and endings of elements, in *Chinese Art of Writing*, 77.

23 Ayamura, *Nihon no shodō*, 92.

24 Shimatani, "Sanseki," 157. This Sung validation of Sukemasa is ironic, because the examples of Sukemasa's calligraphy in this volume are far more cursive than Yukinari's; although they are not in the grass style, they are more suggestive of kana than the Yukinari examples.

25 Emori Kenji, *Ji to sho rekishi*, reminds us that *karayō*, often translated as "Chinese styles," began with Eisai's importation of the architectural styles of the southern Sung. With respect to calligraphy, among monks of the Kamakura and Muromachi periods, *karayō* signals Sung styles; in the Edo period, it refers largely to Ming styles (100–1).

26 Kuboki Shōichi, "Kana: hassei to tenkai," in *Heian Kamakura no sho: sampitsu sanseki*, ed. Komatsu, 161. In *Kodaiwakashiron* (401), Suzuki also refers to kanji as ideographs (*hyōimoji*) and to kana as phonographs (*hyōonmoji*).

27 Shimatani, "Sanseki," 160.

28 John Carpenter, in "Authority and Conformity in Twelfth-Century Japanese Court Calligraphy," *Transactions of the Conference of Orientalists in Japan* 39 (1994), also discusses the

sources and the logic of tilting the brush and the resulting thickness and heaviness of the Hosshōji-ryū style compared to the Sesonji-ryū (72–73).

29 Helena Art, in "Heian jūni seki no ryōshi sōshoku ni okeru kingin hakuchirasi," *Kobijutsu* 83 (July 1987), 44–63, discusses the increase in elaboration of papers in the late Heian and early Kamakura periods.

30 Carpenter, "Authority and Conformity in Twelfth-Century Japanese Court Calligraphy," 60–80.

31 In fact, the work discussed in the next chapter, *Ashide shita-e Wakanrōeishū*, which comes from Fujiwara no Koreyuki in the Sesonji lineage, could be cited as an example of Hosshōji styles. Carpenter, "Authority and Conformity," 78.

32 Komatsu, "Nihon shodō no ōgonki," 139. The first fifty-odd plates of volume 14 of *Shodō zenshū* are devoted to the *Honganjibon sanjūrokunin kashū*. Art, in "Heian jūni seki no ryōshi sōshoku ni okeru kingin hakuchirasi," gives a thorough description of the papers used in this collection (45–46), comparing and contrasting them with those in *Gen'eibon Kokinwa-kashū* and other works (47).

Five. Heian Calligraphy

1 Gilles Deleuze and Félix Guattari, *A Thousand Plateaus*, trans. Brian Massumi (Minneapolis: University of Minnesota Press, 1987), 474–77.

2 Emori Kenji delineates three kinds of paper and the related paper formats in *Ji to sho no rekishi*, 92–94.

3 Thomas Keirstead does this most succinctly in his review of Michele Marra's *The Aesthetics of Discontent*, in *Journal of Japanese Studies* 51:3 (August 1992), 675–76.

4 Carole Cavanaugh, in "Text and Textile: Unweaving the Female Subject in Heian Writing" *positions* 4:3 (Winter 1996), 595–636, looks at many of the ways in which textiles inform early Japanese poetry and tales, with an eye to what authority their production might imply for court women.

5 Mostow, "Painted Poems, Forgotten Words," 338–39.

6 Murasaki Shikibu, *Genji monogatari*, 6 vols., ed. Abe Akio, Akiyama Ken, and Imai Gene (Tokyo: Shōgakukan, 1972), 3:412–13. See also Murasaki Shikibu, *The Tale of Genji*, trans. Edward Seidensticker (New York: Alfred A. Knopf, 1977), 519.

7 Naoki Sakai, *Voices of the Past*, 116. Neuropsychologists who study the development of perceptual integration arrive at an analogous "center of indeterminacy" (to borrow Deleuze's phrase). See Emily W. Bushnell, "The Ontogeny of Intermodal Relations: Vision and Touch in Infancy," in *Intersensory Perception and Sensory Integration*, ed. Richard D. Walk and Herbert L. Pick (New York: Plenum Press, 1981), 6.

8 John Hay, "The Human Body as a Microcosmic Source of Macrocosmic Values in Calligraphy," in *Theories of Art in China*, ed. Susan Bush and Christian Murck (Princeton: Princeton University Press, 1983), 75, 78.

9 This account draws primarily on two accounts of the *Shuo wen ch'ieh tzu*: those of David Kuo-wei Wang and Jean-François Billeter. See David Kuo-wei Wang, Definitions and Classifications of the Six Scripts According to Hsu Shen and Leading Ch'ing Scholars (Ph.D. dissertation, Georgetown University, 1979), 1–10; Billeter, *Chinese Art of Writing*, 16–20.

10 Billeter, *Chinese Art of Writing*, 20.

11 See Thomas Lamarre, "Diagram, Inscription, Sensation," in *Deleuze, Guattari, and the Philosophy of Expression*, special issue *Canadian Review of Comparative Literature* 24:3 (September 1997): 676, note 4, for a discussion that differentiates this notion of mimicry (via Deleuze and Benjamin) from pictography and from the ideas of Pound and Fenellosa.

12 Mireille Buydans, in *Sahara: L'Esthétique de Gilles Deleuze* (Paris: Librairie Philosophique J. Vrin, 1990), 9, gives a provisional definition of form that combines several approaches: form can be defined as a contour (an ideal or real link) that effects the characterization of an ensemble (of ideas, materials, or procedures) and imparts an individuated consistency.

13 These examples are from Komatsu, *Kana*, 36–37. Seeley uses similar examples and gives a number of others in *A History of Japanese Writing*, 49–53.

14 Paul Saenger, *Space between Words: The Origins of Silent Reading* (Stanford: Stanford University Press, 1997), 11.

15 *Shoryōshū* is a collection of statements made by Kūkai compiled by a disciple after his death. *Saiyōshū* is based on the teachings of Fujiwara no Norinaga (1109–1180), as imparted to Fujiwara no Koretsune (d. 1227) in the late twelfth century. *Jubokushō* was written in 1352 by Son'en (1298–1356) for Emperor Go-Kōgon (reigned 1352–1371) of the Northern court. Gary DeCoker translates and introduces these two works in "Secret Teachings in Medieval Calligraphy: *Jubokushō* and *Saiyōshū*," *Monumenta Nipponica* 43:2 (summer 1988), 197–228; 43:3 (fall 1988), 261–78.

16 This dictum is attributed to Kūkai by a disciple. My account of the *Shōryōshū* is gleaned from the discussions of Ayamura (see especially 104, 125) and Haruna Yoshihige (especially 64) as well as Hirayama.

17 Murasaki Shikibu, *Genji monogatari* 2:377–78. In this instance, I have deliberately geared my translation toward a presentation of movements rather than states. The counsellor is Tō no Chūjō, the prince is Hotaru. See also Seidensticker's translation: Murasaki Shikibu, *The Tale of Genji*, 314–15.

18 Murasaki Shikibu, *Genji monogatari*, 2:379; see also Murasaki, *The Tale of Genji*, 315.

19 Suzuki, *Kodaiwakashiron*, 395.

20 *Utsuho monogatari*, 3 vols., ed. Kōno Tama, Nihon bungaku taikei 10–12 (Tokyo: Iwanami shoten, 1962), 3: 101–2. Komatsu discusses this example (68), as do Seeley (77–78) and Kuboki (164).

21 Kuboki, "Kana: Hassei to tenkai," 164.

22 As Nomura Tadao indicates, the shift to the concubinage system (with the emergence of the politics of the inner palace) occurs around the time of the shift from Heijō-kyō to Heian-kyō and the attempt to revitalize the *ritsuryō* system. *Kōkyō to nyokan* (Tokyo: Kyōikusha, 1978).

23 The question of why there were so many female sovereigns (six women in eight reigns) in Nara Japan occupies Umehara Takeshi in *Ama to Tennō: Nihon to wa nani ka* (Tokyo: Asahi shimbunsha, 1991). The book is of interest for two reasons: first, because Umehara reviews in detail the polity of Nara Japan and the role of women; second, because he is so interested in establishing essential differences between Japan and China on this basis. The deviations of early Japan from the *ritsuryō* model of Sui and T'ang China dominate

his analysis, and he signals important differences. But this form of comparison, fundamentally static in its recourse to political codes, omits certain aspects that might suggest a more dynamic interplay between shamanka and Buddhist nuns and emperors; namely, the interpenetration of early T'ang governance with the formation of religious Taoism, in which female hierarchy and authority played an integral role. The gesture of distinguishing Japan and China on the basis of Japan's women is one that merits attention from feminist interpretations and other constructions of the archaic state. It is not surprising, then, that inscription in kana plays an important role in the final instance: the phantom of the mother tongue underlies the association of women with the Japaneseness of early institutions.

24 Mitani Kuniaki, in his analyses of Heian tales (*monogatari*), frequently alludes to the conjunction of seeing and knowing. At the outset of his article on picture scrolls, he gives a brief overview of the simultaneity of certain perceptual modes in early Japanese literature (89–91): "Monogatari bungaku no 'shisen': miru koto no kinki aruiwa 'katari' no kyōen," in *Monogatari no kenkyū dainishū: tokushū shisen* (Tokyo: Shinjidaisha, 1988), 89–108.

25 Emori Itsuo interprets Heian marriage customs through the accounts in Heian tales, with an emphasis on *Utsuho monogatari*: *Monogatari ni miru kokken to josei: "Utsuho monogatari" sono hoka* (Tokyo: Nihon editaasukuuru shuppanbu, 1990). He raises precisely this question about the rank and authority conferred on noble women through the possession of property, showing how many scholars have tended to see the relation of women and property in terms of women's independence and authority. He points out that the relationship between noble women and property was nonetheless beset with difficulties. In effect, in anthropological terms, we would need to differentiate clearly among matriarchal, matrilocal, and matrilineal modes of mediation. See also Peter Nickerson, "The Meaning of Matrilocality: Kinship, Property, and Politics in Mid-Heian," *Monumenta Nipponica* 48:4 (winter 1993), 429–67; and Wakita Haruo, "Marriage and Property in Premodern Japan From the Perspective of Women's History," *Journal of Japanese Studies* 10:1 (1984), 77–87.

26 Suzuki, in his chapter "Onna uta no honsei" in *Kodaiwakashiron*, discusses the feminine poem in terms of its expression. Feminine poems, which are not just poems by women but poems written in a manner characteristic of women, entail a particular kind of response to other poems, a response that includes exaggeration, rejection, and criticism of certain kinds of declarations (42–55).

27 Billeter, *Chinese Art of Writing*, 78–79.

28 Yoshiaki Shimizu and John M. Rosenfield, *Masters of Japanese Calligraphy: Eighth to Nineteenth Century* (New York: Asia Society Galleries and Japan House Gallery, 1984), 47.

Six. The Multisensible Figure: Ashide shita-e Wakanrōeishō

1 The *Ashide shita-e Wakanrōeishō* is also known as the *Eiryakubon Wakanrōeishū*. When I originally chose a section for analysis, I selected the passage that appears in Komatsu's *Kana*, 129. Because this is a black-and-white fragment, I refer the reader to reproductions of other portions of this manuscript. See, for example, *Shodō zenshū*, 18, plates 1–2 and notes (158–59). Another example appears in Komatsu, "Nihon shodō no ōgonki," in *Sampitsu sanseki*, 140, plate 4. Ultimately, however, the best edition is the full reproduction of both

scrolls: Fujiwara Koreyuki, *Ashide shitae Wakanrōeishō*, ed., with explication by, Komatsu Shigemi, Nihon meiseki sōkan 48–49 (Tokyo: Nigensha, 1980). This edition furnished the final point of reference for this account.

2   Kuboki Shōichi, in "Kana no hassei," in *Sampitsu sanseki*, lists 41 exemplars of *Kokinwaka-shū*, 27 of *Wakanrōeishū*, and 11 of the *Man'yōshū* in his enumeration of Heian manuscripts (168). See also Komatsu Shigemi's overview of manuscripts of *Wakanrōeishū*, in which he considers reed-hand under-picture editions in particular. "Ashide shitae bon Wakanrōei-shō," in *Kohitsugaku danshō* (Tokyo: Kōdansha, 1986), 455–60.

3   Eta Harich-Schneider, *Rōei: The Medieval Court Songs of Japan* (Tokyo: Sophia University Press, 1965), 1.

4   Ibid., 16.

5   Billeter, *Chinese Art of Writing*, 89–96.

6   Robert Garfias, *Music of a Thousand Autumns: The Tōgaku Style of Japanese Court Music* (Berkeley, Los Angeles and London: University of California Press, 1975), 169.

7   Komatsu Shigemi, in "Nihon shodō no ōgonki," lists the ten descendants of Yukinari who established themselves in the Sesonji lineage (139–140). The eighth descendant of Yukinari, Fujiwara no Yukiyoshi (1179–1251), seems to be the one who most securely fastened this name to the family lineage. Komatsu cites the passage from Prince Son'en's *Jubokushō* about Yukiyoshi and mentions Koreyuki's *Yakaku teikinshō* and Yukiyoshi's *Yakaku shosatsushō*.

8   Michel Foucault, *This Is Not a Pipe*, trans. James Harkness (Berkeley: University of California, 1983), 32–33.

9   Ibid., 21. In particular, Foucault challenges the logic of the proper name: "the proper name, in this particular context, is merely an artifice: it gives us a finger to point with, in other words, to pass surreptitiously from the space where one speaks to the space where one looks; in other words, to fold one over the other as though they were equivalents." Foucault, *The Order of Things: An Archaeology of the Human Sciences* (New York: Vintage Books, 1970), 9.

10   Foucault, *This Is Not a Pipe*, 22.

11   Ivan Morris, *The World of the Shining Prince: Court Life in Ancient Japan* (New York: Penguin Books, 1964), 169–70. As Morris indicates, the festival of the first day of the rat (with its pine saplings) was combined with the festival of new herbs. Dictionaries of classical Japanese terms give additional details under the heading *ne no hi* (day of the rat).

12   Horie Tomohiko, in "Heian jidai no shofū," remarks that it is our contemporary feeling that the layers of colors and under-pictures hamper the beauty of kana; as he indicates, the Heian aesthetic disturbs our expectations (44).

13   The transcription and translation of this sequence of poems is based on *Wakanrōeishū*, ed. Oosone Shosuke and Horiuchi Hideaki, Shinchō Nihon koten shūsei 61 (Tokyo: Shinchō-sha, 1983), 20–23.

14   Michel Butor, cited in Jean-François Lyotard, *Discours, figure* (Paris: Editions Klinksieck, 1971), 369.

15   In his study of the emergence of certain kinds of discourse on language in eighteenth-century Japan, Sakai, in *Voices of the Past*, looks at the nonverbal dimension of performance in puppet theater scripts, showing the development of the framing effect in the perfor-

mance of Chikamatsu's plays (156–63). These effects are, in many ways, decidedly modern methods (and in some respects modernist). In any event, it is important to note that such modes of framing emerged in sites other than Western Europe, though it took a particular form of social desire to institutionalize them.

16 With respect to the frame, Jacques Derrida, in "Parergon," discusses the problematic of the frame in Kant's aesthetics in *Truth in Painting* (Chicago: University of Chicago Press, 1987), 32–84. D. N. Rodowick, in "Impure Mimesis, or the Ends of the Aesthetic," gives an excellent discussion of some of the questions Derrida brings to the discourse on the frame. In *Deconstruction and the Spatial Arts*, eds. Peter Brunette and David Willis (Cambridge: Cambridge University Press, 1993), 97–117. Also useful is David Carroll's discussion in *Paraesthetics: Foucault, Lyotard, Derrida* (New York: Methuen, 1987).

17 Mark Morris, "Waka and Form, Waka and History," *Harvard Journal of Asiatic Studies* 46:2, 551–610.

18 "This example does resemble the structure of many classic *waka*, but is nothing strange to Western literature," writes poet Kenneth Rexroth with respect to the poetic technique of "superposition" that Pound derived in part from his encounter with the forms of Japanese poetry and Chinese characters. "The Influence of Classical Japanese Poetry on Modern American Poetry," in *Studies on Japanese Culture* 1 (November 1973), 375. Whatever else may be said about the accuracy of Pound's translations from Chinese and Japanese, his poetics marks an important encounter of modernist poets with nonmodern and nonwestern forms. In the wake of Pound, it was possible to envisage, as Rexroth does, a tentative overlap of Western literature and the classic waka.

19 Pound, cited in Andrew Welsh, *Roots of Lyric: Primitive Poetry and Modern Poetics* (Princeton: Princeton University Press, 1978), 69.

20 Tokieda Motoki, *Kokugogakugenron* (Tokyo: Iwanami shoten, 1941), 527–50. Again, I refer primarily to his account of aesthetic expression by way of pivotwords.

21 Deleuze and Guattari's characterization of Chinese writing and empire—"la ligne englobante chinoise, supra-phénoménale"—is rather too broad (the problem being in part the way in which China is evoked somewhat monolithically and ahistorically). Yet their description does shed light on the ways in which overcoding attends inscription with the advent of the T'ang empire. Deleuze and Guattari, *A Thousand Plateaus*, 497; *Mille Plateaux* (Paris: Edition de Minuit, 1980), 620–21.

22 In "Association and Progression: Principles of Integration in Anthologies and Sequences of Japanese Court Poetry," trans. Robert H. Brower and Earl Miner, *Harvard Journal of Asiatic Studies* 21 (1958): 67–127, Konishi Jin'ichi calls attention to the principles that link poems within the scrolls of *Kokinwakashū* and the *Shinkokinwakashū* (ca. 1201). The seasonal scrolls follow the chronology of seasons (spring, summer, fall, winter); within the first scroll on spring, for instance, poems begin with the tentative first day of spring, with snow and plum flowers, with snow falling and ice melting, with new herbs, etc. Clearly, these "narratives" are nonlinear and, in a sense, nonnarrative.

23 Since some are ancient Chinese characters that cannot be produced using any software, I therefore refer the reader to the poem in the Shinchō edition used here.

24 Two chapters from Deleuze's *Francis Bacon: La logique de sensation* (Paris, 1981) have appeared in English translation, in *The Deleuze Reader*, ed. Constantin V. Boundas (New York:

Columbia University Press, 1993). See page 192 for a translation of the relevant passage. A fuller discussion of this topic appears in Lamarre, "Diagram, Inscription, Sensation."

Seven. Two Prefaces, Two Modes of Appearance

1 Masuda Teruo, "Manajo," in *Issatsu no kōza: Kokinwakashū*, 64.

2 Matsuda Takeo, in *Kokinshū no kōzō ni kansuru kenkyū* (Tokyo: Kazama shobō, 1965), discusses the two prefaces, comparing and contrasting their structures in terms of thematic topology. Certain of his conclusions have become commonplace: the kana preface seems rather organic and animated in contrast to the regulated verse of the mana preface; the kana preface alternates its discussions of waka substance and history, while the mana preface treats these separately, and so on. Matsuda also points out the important commonalities: the esteem for the good (high ages) versus the devaluation of new.

3 Ozawa Masao, one of the scholars who played an important role in bringing the mana preface and Chinese poetics to the forefront of Heian studies (see Ceadel below), concludes one of his short essays with the problematic of "old diction" (that is, "old songs" or "old words") in order to claim that the "old diction" of *Kokinwakashū* comprises Chinese as well as Japanese rhetoric. "*Kokinshū ni okeru kanshibun no juyō*," in *Kokinwakashū*, ed. Nihon bungaku kenkyū shiryō kankōkai (Tokyo: Yūseidō, 1976), 195–203.

4 E. B. Ceadel, "The Two Prefaces of the *Kokinshū*," *Asia Major: A British Journal of Far Eastern Studies* 4 (1959): 40–51. Masuda Teruo, in "Manajo," poses the two theories about the primacy of one preface over the other (64–65) but, like Fujii Jōwa in "Kanajo" (*Issatsu no kōza: Kokinwakashū*, 55–63), he is unable to establish that one was compiled before the other. Fujii concludes that they are as two yet not as one. In short, their differences are not generic or systemic. Most of the other scholars cited (Suzuki, Yoshimoto, Saigo, Okada, Akiyama, etc.) who deal with the prefaces opt for the kana preface, simply on the basis of its subsequent importance.

5 Ceadel, "The Two Prefaces of the *Kokinshū*," 49.

6 John Timothy Wixted, "The *Kokinshū* Prefaces: Another Perspective," *Harvard Journal of Asiatic Studies* 43:1 (1983): 215–38.

7 Gibbs, "M. H. Abrams' Four Artistic Coordinates," 678; cited in ibid., 222.

8 Kang-I Sun Chang, in "Chinese 'Lyric Criticism' in the Six Dynasties," in *Theories of Art in China*, ed. Susan Bush and Christian Murck (Princeton: Princeton University Press, 1983), discusses a number of conceptions of poetry of interest to the study of Heian poetics, not least of which is the relation of poetic efficacy to the Tao.

9 Wixted, "The *Kokinshū* Prefaces," 238.

10 Bruce Batten, "Provincial Administration in Early Japan: From *Ritsuryō kokka* to *Ochō kokka*," *Harvard Journal of Asiatic Studies* 53:1 (June 1993), 103–5.

11 Ibid., 111–14. See also Joan Piggot, "*Mokkan*: Wooden Documents from the Nara Period," *Monumenta Nipponica* 45:4 (1990), in which she gives details on the extent of usage of ritsuryo tax documents throughout the archipelago.

12 Batten, "Provincial Administration in Early Japan," 134.

13 The distinction is a common one among Japanese scholars; naturally, the opposition takes on any number of different inflections. Naitō Akira, in "Hare to ke," in *Issatsu no*

kōza, 666–70, treats the opposition as something like a public/private distinction or a formal/informal distinction, which is not uncommon. Bower and Miner, though they do not use these terms, attempt to distinguish public/private from formal/informal in the space of waka (*Japanese Court Poetry*, 18). The legacy of ethnography (*minzokugaku*) relates hare and ke to issues of kingship and courtship; see Gotō Shōko's brief overview of Origuchi and the rhetoric of *irogonomi* (related to ke, the houses of passion) in "Irogonomi to Yamatouta" in *Uta, Utagokota, Utamakura: Kokubungaku* 34:13 (November 1989), 41–47. Suzuki also discusses hare and ke in some detail in *Kodaiwakashiron*, 367–75; he associates ke with an oral line of transmission that preserves a sense of poetic efficacy and magical incantation and links *Kokinwakashū* with the *Man'yōshū* via the ke lineage (81–86). All translations of passages in the kana and mana prefaces are mine. The page numbers refer to the Shōgakkan edition.

14 Batten gives an overview of the politics of clans (uji) with respect to the formation of the ritsuryō court in the seventh century in "Foreign Threat and Domestic Reform: The Emergence of the Ritsuryō State," *Monumenta Nipponica* 41:2 (1986), 200–5.

15 Amino Yoshihiko, *Umi to rettō no chūsei*, 23.

16 Suzuki, *Kodaiwakashiron*, 394.

17 Naitō Akira, "Hare to ke," 666–67.

18 Suzuki, *Kodaiwakashiron*, 397–98.

19 Yoshimochi, "Manajo," 419–20.

20 Tsurayuki, "Kanajo," 54.

21 Yoshimochi, "Manajo," 416.

22 Tsurayuki, "Kanajo," 55.

23 Philip Harries discusses house collections in terms of the emergence of "personal collections" (that is, *shikashū*): "Personal Poetry Collections," *Monumenta Nipponica* 35:3 (1980), 305–7.

24 Soper and Paine, *Art and Architecture of Japan*, 341.

25 Thomas Keirstead, "Gardens and Estates: Medievality and Space," *positions* 1:2 (fall 1993).

26 Hagitani Boku recounts some of the practices followed at poem contests; it would seem that a "clean copy" (*seisho*) of the poem would be prepared for recitation by a recitator. This may seem like a minor detail, but it serves to remind us that speaking need not necessarily come prior to writing; and even in cases when it did, its temporal priority does not establish its social priority. "Kodaihen kaisetsu," in *Utaawaseshū*, 16.

27 Tsurayuki, *Tosa nikki*, ed. Matsumura Seiichi, Kimura Masanori, and Imuta Tsunehisa, Nihon koten bungaku zenshū 9 (Tokyo: Iwanami, 1973), 46, 58, 47, 64, 50.

28 Maurice Blanchot, *The Infinite Conversation*, trans. Susan Hanson (Minneapolis: University of Minnesota Press, 1993), 25–32.

Eight. Tsurayuki's Song Machine

1 Tsurayuki, "Kanajo," 54.

2 Ibid., 49.

3 Ibid.

4 Some aspects of this argument are inspired by Bruno Latour's *We Have Never Been Modern*

(Cambridge: Harvard University Press, 1993), as well as by Georges Canguilhem's comments in "Machine and Organism" in *Zone 6: Incorporations* (New York: Urzoné, 1992). These approaches help to break down some of the organicist assumptions about archaic song.

5 Rodd and Henkenius, "Kanajo: The Japanese Preface by Ki no Tsurayuki," in *Kokinshū*, 35.

6 Tsurayuki, "Kanajo," 57.

7 Ibid.

8 Ibid., 58.

9 Ibid., 58.

10 This is an overview of Amino Yoshihiko's argument in *Nihon chūsei no hinōgyōmin to tennō* (Iwanami shoten, 1984). He adds to this discussion in his study of Emperor Godaigo's attempt to extend imperial power to strange peoples who moved outside the court, in *Igyō no ōken* (Tokyo: Heibonsha, 1986). Nakazawa Shin'ichi, in *Akutō teki shikō* (Tokyo: Heibonsha, 1988), provides a useful overview of Amino's account of emperorship in his first chapter on a bohemian theory of history.

11 Tsurayuki, "Kanajo," 58–59.

12 Konishi, "The Genesis of the *Kokinshū* Style," trans. Helen C. McCullough, *Harvard Journal of Asiatic Studies* 38:1 (1971), 71; see also Igawa Hiroko, "Mitate," 681.

13 Konishi, "Genesis," 118.

14 Ibid., 168.

15 Konishi, "Genesis," 165.

16 Morris, *World of the Shining Prince*, 12–13; Konishi, "Genesis," 170.

17 Igawa, "Mitate," 681.

18 Mostow, "Painted Poems, Forgotten Words," 328.

19 Hagitani, "Kaisetsu," *Utaawaseshū*, 23.

20 Tsurayuki, "Kanajo," 50.

21 Hyōdō Hiromi, in *Oken to monogatari* (Tokyo: Seikyūsha, 1989), gives an overview of various uses of the term *yomu* (181–83). One usage is especially germane here: to count figures or numbers; to count the moon and sun. This usage relates yomu directly to cosmology (in the form of *tembun*, that is, celestial pattern or design). Yomu is to read, recite, count the heavens.

22 Ts'ang Chieh, *Shu tuan*, cited in Billeter, *Chinese Art of Writing*, 189.

23 Tsurayuki, "Kanajo," 49, 50.

24 Mark Morris, in "Waka and Form, Waka and History," mentions that the term *waka*, when it appears in *Man'yōshū*, is often glossed as "poem in response," which suggests to him that there is nothing native about the category and that it came to mean something different by the time of *Kokinwakashū*. (598).

25 Clifton W. Royston, "*Utaawase* Judgments as Poetry Criticism," *Journal of Asian Studies* 34:1 (November 1974), 107.

26 *Shodō zenshū*, vol. 12 (Nihon 3, Heian 2), plate 9. Because the calligraphy is merely attributed to Tsurayuki, it is difficult to make any hard and fast statements about Tsurayuki's own hand. In fact, most attributions from the early-Heian period are difficult to associate with any one individual.

27 Masaoka Shiki, "Futatabi utayomi o atafuru sho," in *Shiki zenshū*, 23 vols., ed. Masaoka

Chūzaburō (Tokyo: Kōdansha, 1974), 7:23. Implicit in Shiki's positive evaluation of certain *Man'yōshū* poems was a sense of their pictorial objectivity, a quality he also admired in Buson's haiku and haiga and a quality he imparted to his own notions of *shasei*. In some instances, Shiki explicitly aligns the *Man'yōshū* with Buson ("Man'yōshū o yomu," *Shiki zenshū*, 7:313–4); but because he is interested in producing poetry rather than deriving a unified theory, he often qualifies or transforms his comments on the *Man'yōshū* and pictorial objectivity in other writings. In accounts of the *Kokinshū* versus the *Man'yōshū* it has become almost de rigeur to mention Shiki's observations in some register, for they are the locus classicus of questions about subjectivity, objectivity, visualization, or rationalism in early poetry. Shiota Ryōhei, in "Koten to Meiji igo no bungaku," *Nihon bungakushi* 14 (1959), 17–20, outlines the connections made between the Meiji notion of *shasei* (sketching nature) and revisions of *Man'yōshū*.

28 Yoshimoto Takaaki, *Shoki kayō ron* (Tokyo: Chūōseihan, 1977). 470–73.

29 Tsurayuki, "Kanajo," 56.

30 "*Eccentric*: In ancient astronomy the word denotes a circle round which a body revolves, but whose center is displaced from the visible center of motion. . . . In engineering an eccentric is a disk mounted out of center on a shaft, to give reciprocating movement to a lever; it is an agent much used in steam engines and other mechanisms. It is fixed with a key or screw onto the crankshaft and moves the valve rod to and fro to control the flow of steam and the exhaust" (abridged from the *Encyclopedia Britannica*).

WORKS CONSULTED

Abraham, Nicholas. *L'Écorce et le noyau*. Paris: Flammarion, 1978.

Ahmad Aijaz. *In Theory: Classes, Nations, Literature*. London: Verso, 1992.

Akiyama Ken. "*Kokinshū* wa naze kihansei o mochieta ka." *Kokubungaku* 29:14 (November 1984), 39–45.

Akiyama Ken. "Nihonteki bi ishiki no mondai: *Kokinshū* wo megutte." In *Nihon bungaku kōza 2: bungakushi no shomondai*. Tokyo: Daishūkan shoten, 1987.

Akiyama Ken. *Ōchō no bungaku kūkan*. Tokyo: Tokyo daigaku shuppankai, 1984.

Amagasaki Akira. *Nihon no retorikku*, Tokyo: Chikuma shobō, 1988.

Amino Yoshihiko. *Igyō no ōken*. Tokyo: Heibonsha, 1986.

Amino Yoshihiko. *Nihon chūsei no hinōgyōmin to tennō*. Tokyo: Iwanami shoten, 1984.

Amino Yoshihiko. *Nihon shakai no tennōsei*. Iwanami bukkretto 108. Tokyo: Iwanami shoten, 1988.

Amino Yoshihiko. *Umi to rettō no chūsei*. Tokyo: Nihon editaasukuuru, 1992.

Anderson, Benedict. *Imagined Communities: Reflections on the Origin and Spread of Nationalism*. London: Verso, 1983.

Art, Helena. "Heian jūni seki no ryōshi sōshoku ni okeru kingin hakuchirasi." *Kobijutsu* 83 (July 1983): 44–63.

Asada Akira, Jacques Derrida, and Karatani Kōjin. "Chōshōhi shakai to chishikijin no yakuwa-kuri." *Asahi jaanaru*. (25 January 1989), 170–73.

Ayamura Tan'en. *Nihon no shodō*. Tokyo: Kawara shoten, 1966.

Bakhtin, Mikhail. *The Dialogic Imagination: Four Essays by M. M. Bakhtin*. Austin: University of Texas Press, 1981.

Batten, Bruce. "Foreign Threat and Domestic Reform: The Emergence of the Ritsuryō State." *Monumenta Nipponica* 41:2 (1986), 200–5.

Batten, Bruce. "Provincial Administration in Early Japan: From Ritsuryō kokka to Ōchō kokka." *Harvard Journal of Asiatic Studies* 53:1 (June 1993), 103–34.

Benjamin, Walter. "On the Mimetic Faculty." In *Reflections*, ed. Peter Demetz. New York: Schocken Books, 1986.

Bernal, Martin. *Black Athena: The Afroasiatic Roots of the Classical Tradition*. New Brunswick: Rutgers University Press, 1987.

Billeter, Jean-François. *The Chinese Art of Writing*. New York: Rizzoli International, 1990.

Blanchot, Maurice. *The Infinite Conversation*. Trans. Susan Hanson. Minneapolis: University of Minnesota Press, 1993.

Borgen, Robert. *Sugawara no Michizane and the Early Heian Court*. Cambridge: Harvard University Press, 1986.

Bowring, Richard. "The Female Hand in Heian Japan." In *The Female Autograph*. Ed. Donna Stanton. Chicago: University of Chicago Press, 1984.

Brown, Delmer M., ed. *The Cambridge History of Japan*, vol. 1, *Ancient Japan*. Cambridge: Cambridge University Press, 1993.

Brower, Robert H., and Earl Miner. *Japanese Court Poetry*. Stanford: Stanford University Press, 1961.

Buck-Morss, Susan. *The Dialectics of Seeing: Walter Benjamin and the Arcades Project*. Cambridge: MIT Press, 1989.

Bushnell, Emily W. "The Ontogeny of Intermodal Relations: Vision and Touch in Infancy." In *Intersensory Perception and Sensory Integration*, ed. Richard D. Walk and Herbert L. Pick. New York: Plenum Press, 1981.

Buydens, Mireille. *Sahara: L'Esthétique de Gilles Deleuze*. Paris: Librairie Philosophique J. Vrin, 1990.

Canguilhem, Georges. "Machine and Organism." In *Zone 6: Incorporations*. New York: Urzone, 1992.

Carroll, David. *Paraesthetics: Foucault, Lyotard, Derrida*. New York: Methuen, 1987.

Carpenter, John. "Authority and Conformity in Twelfth-Century Calligraphy." *Transactions of the International Conference of Orientalists in Japan* 39 (1994): 60–80.

Cavanaugh, Carole. "Text and Textile: Unweaving the Female Subject in Heian Writing." *positions* 4:3 (winter 1996), 595–636.

Ceadel, E. B. "The Two prefaces of the *Kokinshū*." *Asia Major: A British Journal of Far Eastern Studies* 4 (1959), 40–51.

Chaves, Jonathan. "The Legacy of Ts'ang Chieh: The Written Word as Magic." *Oriental Art* 23:2 (1977), 200–15.

Chino Kaori. "Nihon no e wo yomu: tan'itsu kotei shiten wo megutte." In *Monogatari kenkyū dainishū: tokushū shisen*. Tokyo: Shinjidaisha, 1988.

Chang, Kang-I Sun, "Chinese 'Lyric Criticism' in the Six Dynasties." In *Theories of Art in China*. Ed. Susan Bush and Christian Murck. Princeton: Princeton University Press, 1983.

Chen Sheng Bao. "Chinese Borrowings from the Japanese Language." *Journal of Asian Studies Newsletter* 15:5–6 (1988), 19–23.

Chu Hsi. *Further Reflections on Things at Hand: A Reader*. Translation and commentary by Allen Wittenborn. Lanham, N.Y.: University Press of America, 1991.

Claudel, Paul. *Cent Phrases pour éventail*. Edited with commentary by Michel Truffet. Centre de recherches Jacques-Petit, vol. 42. Paris: Les Belles Lettres, 1985.

Crary, Jonathan. *Techniques of the Observer: On Vision and Modernity in the Nineteenth Century*. Cambridge: MIT Press, 1991.

Dean, Kenneth, and Brian Massumi. *First and Last Emperors: The Absolute State and the Body of the Emperor*. New York: Automedia, 1992.

DeCoker, Gary. "Secret Teachings in Medieval Calligraphy: *Jubokushō* and *Saiyōshō*." *Monumenta Nipponica* 43:2 (summer 1988), 197–228; 43:3 (fall 1988), 261–78.

Deleuze, Gilles. *The Deleuze Reader.* Ed. Constantin V. Boundas. New York: Columbia University Press, 1993.

Deleuze, Gilles. *Difference and Repetition.* Trans. Paul Patton. New York: Columbia University Press, 1994.

Deleuze, Gilles. *Francis Bacon: La Logique de la sensation.* Paris: Editions de la différence, 1981.

Deleuze, Gilles, and Félix Guattari. *A Thousand Plateaus.* Trans. Brian Massumi. Minneapolis: University of Minnesota Press, 1987.

Deon, Donald, Mark Hudson, and Tessa Morris-Suzuki. *Multicultural Japan: Palaeolithic to Postmodern.* Cambridge: Cambridge University Press, 1996.

Derrida, Jacques. *Of Grammatology.* Trans. Gayatri Chakravorty Spivak. Baltimore: Johns Hopkins Press, 1974.

Derrida, Jacques. *Truth in Painting.* Chicago: University of Chicago Press, 1987.

Ebersole, Gary L. *Ritual Poetry and the Politics of Death in Early Japan.* Princeton: Princeton University Press, 1989.

Eagleton, Terry. *Literary Theory: An Introduction.* Minneapolis: University of Minnesota Press, 1983.

Eagleton, Terry. "Nationalism: Irony and Commitment." In *Nationalism, Colonialism and Literature.* Minneapolis: University of Minnesota Press, 1990.

Eiga monogatari, 2 vols. Ed. Matsumura Hiroji and Yamanaka Yutaka. Nihon koten bungaku taikei 75–76. Tokyo: Iwanami shoten, 1965.

Emori Itsuo. *Monogatari ni miru kekkon to josei: "Utsuho monogatari" sono hoka.* Tokyo: Nihon editaasukuuru shuppanbu, 1990.

Emori Kenji. *Ji to sho no rekishi.* Tokyo: Kinyōsha, 1968.

Etiemble. *L'Europe chinoise,* 2 vols. Paris: Editions Gallimard, 1988.

Fenollosa, Ernest. *The Chinese Written Character as a Medium for Poetry.* New York: Arrow Editions, 1936.

Foucault, Michel, *The Order of Things: An Archaeology of the Human Sciences.* New York: Random House, 1970.

Foucault, Michel. *This Is Not a Pipe.* Trans. James Harkness. Berkeley: University of California Press, 1983.

Fujii Jōwa. "Kanajo." In *Issatsu no kōza: Kokinwakashū.* Ed. Issatsu no kōza henshūbu. Nihon no koten bungaku 4. Tokyo: Yūseidō, 1987.

Fujiwara Katsumi. "Ochō bungaku wa naze kanshibun no seiei ni hajimaru no ka." *Kokubungaku* 29:14 (November 1984), 18–24.

Fujiwara Koreyuki. *Ashide shita-e Wakanrōeishō,* 2 vols. Ed., with explications by, Komatsu Shigemi. Nihon meiseki sōkan genshoku hōchō sen 48–49. Tokyo: Nigensha, 1980.

Fukunaga Mitsuji. *Dōkyō to Nihon bunka.* Tokyo: Bunjin shoin, 1982.

Furuhashi Nobuyoshi. "Kokinshū no bungakushi: oto no jusei kara." *Bungaku* 53:12 (1985), 40–52.

Garfias, Robert. *Music of a Thousand Autumns; The Tōgaku Style of Japanese Court Music.* Berkeley: University of California Press, 1975.

Gotō Shōko. "Irogonomi to Yamato uta." *Kokubungaku: kaishaku to kyōzai no kenkyū* 34:13 (November 1989), 41–47.

Green, André. *Le Discours vivant: La Conception psychanalytique de l'affect*. Paris: Presses Universitaires de France, 1977.

Guattari, Félix. *Chaosmose*. Paris: Galilée, 1992.

Hagitani Boku. *Heianchō utaawase kaisetsu*. Tokyo: Yamanouchi, 1969.

Hardt, Michael. *Gilles Deleuze: An Apprenticeship in Philosophy*. Minneapolis: University of Minnesota Press, 1993.

Harich-Schneider, Eta. *Rōei: The Medieval Court Songs of Japan*. Tokyo: Sophia University Press, 1965.

Harootunian, H. D. "Cultural Politics in Tokugawa Japan." In *Undercurrents of the Floating World: Censorship of Japanese Prints*. New York: Asia Society Galleries, 1991.

Harootunian, H. D. "Disciplining Native Knowledge and Producing Place: Yanagita Kunio, Origuchi Shinobu, Takata Yasuma." In *Culture and Identity: Japanese Intellectuals During the Interwar Years*. Ed. J. Thomas Rimer. Princeton: Princeton University Press, 1990.

Harootunian, H. D. *Things Seen and Unseen: Discourse and Ideology in Tokugawa Nativism*. Chicago: University of Chicago Press, 1988.

Haruna Yoshishige. "Heian jidai no shoron." In *Sho no Nihonshi 2: Heian*. Ed. Tsuchida Naoshige. Tokyo: Heibonsha, 1975.

Harries, Philip T. "Personal Poetry Collections." *Monumenta Nipponica* 35:3 (1980), 299–317.

Hay, John. "The Human Body as a Microcosmic Source of Macrocosmic Values in Calligraphy." In *Theories of Art in China*. Ed. Susan Bush and Christian Murck. Princeton: Princeton University Press, 1983.

Heianchō utaawase taisei. Ed. Hagitani Boku. Kyoto: Dōhōsha, 1995.

Hegel, G. F. *Philosophy of History*. Colonial Press, 1899, reprinted New York: Dores Publications, 1956.

Heidegger, Martin. *On the Way to Language*. Trans. Peter D. Hertz. New York: Harper and Row, 1971.

Hérail, Francine. *La Cour du Japon à l'époque de Heian aux Xe et XIe siècles*. Paris: Hachette, 1995.

Hirayama Mitsuki. *Eien no sho: Kūkai hen*. Tokyo: Yūhōdō, 1969.

Hobsbawm, E. J. "Mass Producing Traditions." In *The Invention of Tradition*. Cambridge: Cambridge University Press, 1983.

Hobsbawm, E. J. *Nations and Nationalism Since 1780: Programme, Myth, and Reality*. Cambridge: Cambridge University Press, 1990.

Hong Wontaek. *Paekche of Korea and the Origins of Japan*. Seoul: Kudara International, 1994.

Horie Tomohiko, "Heian jidai no shofū: sho no nagare 2." In *Sho no Nihonshi 2: Heian*. Ed. Tsuchida Naoshige. Tokyo: Heibonsha, 1975.

Hyōdō Hiromi. *Oken to monogatari*. Tokyo: Seikyūsha, 1989.

Hyōdō Hiromi. "Waka hyōgen to seido." *Nihon bungaku* 32:2 (February 1985), 54–68.

Ikeda On. *Tō to Nihon. Kodai wo kangaeru shirizu*. Tokyo: Yoshikawa Kōbun kan, 1992.

Issatsu no kōza henshūbu, eds. *Issatsu no kōza Kokinwakashū*. Nihon no koten bungaku 4. Tokyo: Yūseidō, 1987.

Itō Haku. "Manyōjin to kotodama." In *Man'yōshū kōza 3: Gengo to hyōgen*. Ed. Hisamatsu Sen'ichi. Tokyo: Yūseidō, 1973.

Ito, Setsuko. *An Anthology of Traditional Japanese Poetry Competitions: Uta-awase 913–1815*. Bochum: Brockmeyer. 1991.

Izutsu Toshihiko and Itzutsu Toyo. *The Theory of Beauty in the Classical Aesthetics of Japan*. The Hague: Martinus Nijhoff, 1981.

Jay, Martin. *Downcast Eyes: The Denigration of Vision in Twentieth-Century French Thought*. Berkeley: University of California Press, 1993.

Kaneko Shūichi. "Sui tō kōtai to higashi ajia." In *Tō to Nihon*. Ed. Ikeda On. Tokyo: Yoshikawa Kōbun kan, 1992.

Karaki Junzō. *Nihon no kokoro no rekishi*, 2 vols. Tokyo: Chikuma shobō, 1976.

Karatani Kōjin. *Kindai nihon bungaku no kigen*. Tokyo: Chikuma shobō, 1980.

Karatani Kōjin. "One Spirit, Two Nineteenth Centuries." In *Postmodernism and Japan*. Ed. H. D. Harootunian and Masao Miyoshi. Durham: Duke University Press, 1989.

Karatani Kōjin. *Origins of Modern Japanese Literature*. Trans. and ed. Brett de Bary. Durham: Duke University Press, 1993.

Karonshū, ed. Hashimoto Mio, Ariyoshi Tamotsu, and Fujihira Haruo. Nihon Koten bungaku zenshū 50. Tokyo: Shōgakkan, 1975.

Karonshū nōgakuronshū. Ed. Hisamatsu Sen'ichi and Nishio Minoru. Nihon koten bungaku taikei 65. Tokyo: Iwanami shoten, 1961.

Keirstead, Thomas. "Gardens and Estates: Medievality and Space." *positions* 1:2 (fall 1993).

Keirstead, Thomas. "Review: Marra, *The Aesthetics of Discontent*." *Journal of Japanese Studies* 51:3 (August 1992), 675–76.

Kenner, Hugh. *The Pound Era*. Berkeley: University of California Press, 1971.

Kim Hyun Koo. "A Study of Korea-Japan Relations in Ancient Times: Centering on the Taika Reforms and the Formation of Cooperation among Silla, Japan, and Tang China." *Korea Journal* (October 1989), 18–27.

Kitayama Shigeo. *Nihon no rekishi 4: Heian-kyō*. Tokyo: Chūōkōronsha, 1973.

Kitayama Shigeo. *Ochō seiji shiron*. Tokyo: Iwanami shoten, 1970.

Kojima Noriyuki. *Kokinshū izen: shi to waka no kōryū*. Hanawa sensho 81. Tokyo: Hanawa shobō, 1976.

"Kokinrokujō." In *Shinpen kokka taikan dainikan: shisenshūhen kashū*. Ed. Shinpen kokka taikan henshū iinkai. Tokyo: Kadokawa shoten, 1984.

Kokinwakashū. Ed. Ozawa Masao. Nihon koten bungaku zenshū 7. Tokyo: Shōgakkan, 1971.

Kokinwakashū, 3rd. ed. Ed. Saeki Umetomo. Nihon koten bungaku taikei. Tokyo: Iwanami, 1961.

Kokinwakashū. *Idatebon Kokinwakashū: Fujiwara Teika hitsu*. Ed. Kusogami Noboru. Tokyo: Kasama shoinkan, 1972.

Kokinwakashū. *Kokinwakashū hyōshaku*, 3 vols. Ed. Kubota Utsubo. Tokyo: Tōkyōdō, 1985.

Kokinwakashū. *Kokinshū: A Collection of Japanese Poetry Ancient and Modern*. Trans. Laurel Rasplica Rodd with Mary Catherine Henkenius. Princeton: Princeton University Press, 1984.

Kokinwakashū. *Kokin wakashū: The First Imperial Anthology of Japanese Poetry*, Trans. Helen C. McCullough. Stanford: Stanford University Press, 1985.

Komachiya Teruhiko. "Chokusenshū jo no wakashi ishiki." In *Nihon bungakushi o yomu 2: kodai goki*. Tokyo: Yūseidō, 1991.

Komachiya Teruhiko. "Kokinrokujō o yomu: ōchō kago no tsuikyū." *Kokubungaku: kaishaku to kyōza no kenkyū* 34:13 (November 1989), 94–99.

Komatsu Shigemi. "Ashide shitae bon Wakanrōeishō." In *Kohitsugaku danshō*. Tokyo: Kodansha, 1986.

Komatsu Shigemi. *Kana.* Iwanami shinsho 679. Tokyo: Iwanami shoten, 1968.

Komatsu Shigemi. "Nihon shodō no ōgonki." In *Heian Kamakura no sho: sampitsu sanseki.* Ed. Komatsu Shigemi. Nihon geijutsu zenshū 8. Tokyo: Gakken, 1980.

Kondō Nobuyoshi. "Makurakotoba to wa nani ka." *Kokubungaku kaishaku to kanshō* (February 1969), 113–18.

Konishi Jin'ichi. "Association and Progression: Principles of Integration in Anthologies and Sequences of Japanese Court Poetry." Trans. Robert H. Brower and Earl Miner. *Harvard Journal of Asiatic Studies* 21 (1958), 67–127.

Konishi Jin'ichi. "The Genesis of the *Kokinshū* Style." Trans. Helen C. McCullough. *Harvard Journal of Asiatic Studies* 38:1 (1971), 61–170.

Konishi Jin'ichi. *A History of Japanese Literature*, vol. 2, *The Early Middle Ages*. Princeton: Princeton University Press, 1986.

Kuboki Shōichi. "Kana: hassei to tenkai." In *Heian Kamakura no sho: sampitsu sanseki.* Ed. Komatsu Shigemi. Nihon geijutsu zenshū 8. Tokyo: Gakken, 1980.

Kūkai. *Fushinjō.* Nihon meiseki sōkan genshoku hōchō sen 11. Tokyo: Nigensha, 1986.

Kūkai Kōbōdaishi. "Sangō shiiki," ed. Yamato Chikyō. In *Kōbōdaishi Kūkai zenshū*, vol. 6. Tokyo: Chikuma shobō, 1984.

Kūkai Kōbōdaishi. *Kūkai: Major Works.* Trans. Yoshita S. Hakeda. New York: Columbia University Press, 1972.

Lamarre, Thomas. "Diagram, Inscription, Sensation," *Canadian Review of Comparative Literature* special edition: *Deleuze, Guattari, and the Philosophy of Expression* 23:4 (September 1997).

Lamarre, Thomas. "History, Science and Culture in the Late Meiji Period: Mori Rintarō's Experiments." In *New Directions in Meiji Japan.* Ed. Helen Hardacre. Leiden: E. J. Brill, 1997.

Latour, Bruno. *We Have Never Been Modern.* Trans. Catherine Porter. Cambridge: Harvard University Press, 1993.

Ledderose, Lothar. "Some Taoist Elements in the Calligraphy of the Six Dynasties." *T'oung Pao* 70 (1984), 246–78.

Ledderose, Lothar. "Chinese Calligraphy: Its Aesthetic Dimension and Social Function." *Orientations* (October 1986), 35–50.

Leibnitz, G. W. *New Essays on Human Understanding.* Trans. and ed. Peter Remnant and Jonathan Bennett. Cambridge: Cambridge University Press, 1981.

Lyotard, Jean-François. *Discours, figure.* Paris: Editions Klincksieck, 1971.

Mani, Lata, and Ruth Frankenburg. "The Challenge of Orientalism." *Economy and Society* 14:2 (May 1985), 174–92.

Man'yōshū, 4 vols. Ed. Kojima Noriyuki, Kinoshita Masatoshi, and Satake Akihiro. Nihon koten bungaku zenshū 2–5. Tokyo: Shōgakkan, 1971.

Marra, Michele. *The Aesthetics of Discontent: Politics and Reclusion in Medieval Japanese Literature.* Honolulu: University of Hawai'i Press, 1991.

Masada Shigeo. "Tennōsei to waka: chokusenshū wo megutte." *Kokubungaku: kaishaku to kyōzai no kenkyū* 34:13 (November 1989), 54–60.

Masaoka Shiki. *Shiki zenshū,* 23 vols. Ed. Masaoka Chūzaburō. Tokyo: Kodansha, 1974.

Massumi, Brian. *A User's Guide to Capitalism and Schizophrenia: Deviations from Deleuze and Guattari*. Cambridge: MIT Press, 1992.

Matsuda Takeo. *Kokinshū no kōzō ni kansuru kenkyū*. Tokyo: Kazama Shobō, 1965.

McCullough, Helen C. *Brocade by Night: Kokin wakashū and the Court Style in Japanese Classical Poetry*. Stanford: Stanford University Press, 1985.

Miller, Roy Andrew. *The Japanese Language*. Chicago: University of Chicago Press, 1967.

Miller, Roy Andrew. "No Time For Literature." *Journal of the American Oriental Society* 107:4 (October–December, 1987), 745–60.

Minegishi Yoshiaki. *Utaawase no kenkyū*. Tokyo: Sanseidō, 1954.

Mitani Kuniaki. "Monogatari bungaku no 'shisen:' miru koto no kinki aruiwa 'katari' no kyōen." In *Monogatari kenkyū dainishū: tokushū shisen*. Tokyo: Shinjidaisha, 1988.

Mitani Kuniaki. *Genji monogatari no shitsukeito*. Tokyo: Yūseidō, 1992.

Momokawa Takahito. *Uchi naru Norinaga*. Tokyo: Tōkyō daigaku shuppankai, 1987.

Mori Ōgai. *Ōgai zenshū*, 3rd ed., 38 Vols. Ed. Kinoshita Mokutarō et al. Tokyo: Iwanami shoten, 1971–1981.

Morris, Ivan. *The World of the Shining Prince: Court Life in Ancient Japan*. New York: Knopf, 1964; Peregrine Books, 1985.

Morris, Mark. "Waka and Form, Waka and History." *Harvard Journal of Asiatic Studies* 46 (1986), 551–610.

Mostow, Joshua. "Painted Poems, Forgotten Words: Poem-Pictures and Classical Japanese Literature." *Monumenta Nipponica* 47:3 (1992), 323–46.

Mowitt, John. *Text: The Genealogy of an Antidisciplinary Object*. Durham: Duke University Press, 1992.

Murasaki Shikibu. *Genji monogatari*, 6 vols. Ed. Abe Akio, Akiyama Ken, and Imai Gen'e. Nihon koten bungaku zenshū 12–17. Tokyo: Shogakkan, 1972.

Murasaki Shikibu. *The Tale of Genji*. Trans. Edward G. Seidensticker. New York: Alfred A. Knopf, 1977.

Naito Akira. "Hare to ke." In *Issatsu no kōza: Kokinwakashū*. Ed. Issatsu no kōza henshūbu. Nihon no koten bungaku 4 (Tokyo: Yūseidō, 1987), 666–70.

Najita Tetsuo and H. D. Harootunian. "Japanese Revolt Against the West: Political and Cultural Criticism in the Twentieth Century." In *Cambridge History of Japan*, vol. 6. Ed. Peter Duus. Cambridge: Cambridge University Press, 1988.

Nakazawa Shin'ichi. *Akutōteki shikō*. Tokyo: Heibonsha, 1988.

Nakazawa Shin'ichi. *Ikonsofia*. Tokyo: Kawake, 1989.

Nomura Tadao. *Kōkyō no nyokan*. Rekishi shinsho 11. Tokyo: Kyōikusha, 1978.

Okada, Richard H. *Figures of Resistance: Language, Poetry, and Narrating in "The Tale of Genji" and Other Mid-Heian Texts*. Durham: Duke University Press, 1991.

Olson, Lawrence. "Intellectuals and 'The People' on Yoshimoto Takaaki." *Journal of Japanese Studies* 4:2 (summer 1978), 327–57.

Ong, Walter. *Orality and Literacy: Technologizing the Word*. New York: Methuen, 1982.

Oosone Shōsuke. "Shijin Sugawara no Michizane wa naze ippō de kajin datta no ka." *Kokubungaku* 29:14 (November 1984), 25–31.

Orikuchi Shinobu. "Jushi." In *Nihon bungakushi nooto*. Tokyo: Chūōkōronsha, 1954, 1–10.

Orikuchi Shinobu. "Nihon bungaku no hassei: daisankō." In *Orikuchi Shinbu zenshū*. Ed. Oriku-chi Hakushi kinen kodai kenkyūsho. Tokyo: Chūōkōronsha, 1965.

Ozawa Masao. "*Kokinshū* ni okeru kanshibun no juyō." In *Kokinwakashū*. Ed. Nihon bungaku-kenkyū shiryō kankōkai. Tokyo: Yūseidō, 1976, 195–203.

Ozawa Masao. *Kokinshū no sekai*. Tokyo: Hanawa shobō, 1961.

Paine, Robert Treat, and Alexander Soper. *The Art and Architecture of Japan*, 3rd. ed. New Haven: Yale University Press, 1981.

Park Hyongshik. *Nihongo no ruutsu wa kodai chōsongo datta*. Tokyo: HBJ shuppankyoku, 1991.

Pekarik, Andrew J. *The Thirty-Six Immortal Women Poets: A Poetry Album with Illustrations by Chōbunsai Eishi*. New York: George Braziller, 1991.

Piggot, Joan. "*Mokkan*: Wooden Documents from the Nara Period." *Monumenta Nipponica* 45:4 (1990), 449–70.

Pincus, Leslie. *Authenticating Culture: Kuki Shūzō and the Rise of National Aesthetics*. Berkeley: University of California Press, 1996.

Pound, Ezra. *Gaudier-Brzeska: A Memoir*. New York: New Directions, 1960.

Quian, Zhaoming. *Orientalism and Modernism: The Legacy of China in Pound and Williams*. Durham: Duke University Press, 1995.

Rexroth, Kenneth. "The Influence of Classical Japanese Poetry on Modern American Poetry." *Studies on Japanese Culture* 1 (November 1973), 374–92.

Riddel, Joseph. "Decentering the Image: The 'Project of American' Poetics?" In *Textual Strategies: Perspectives in Poststructuralist Criticism*. Ed. Josué V. Harari. Ithaca: Cornell University Press, 1979.

Rodowick, D. N. "Impure Mimesis, or the Ends of the Aesthetic." In *Deconstruction and the Spatial Arts*. Eds. Peter Brunette and David Willis. Cambridge: Cambridge University Press, 1993.

Royston, Cliff. "*Utaawase* Judgments as Poetry Criticism." *Journal of Asian Studies* 34:1 (November 1974).

Saenger, Paul. *Space between Words: The Origins of Silent Reading*. Stanford: Stanford University Press, 1997.

Saigo Nobutsuna. *Nihon kodai bungakushi*. Tokyo: Iwanami, 1951.

Sakai Naoki. "Joron: Nashonariti to bo(koku)go no seiji." In *Nashonariti no dakkōhiku*. Ed. Brett de Bary, Iyotani Toshio, and Sakai Naoki. Tokyo: Kashiwa shobō, 1996.

Sakai, Naoki. "Modernity and Its Critique: The Problem of Universalism and Particularism." In *Postmodernism and Japan*. Ed. Masao Miyoshi and H. D. Harootunian. Durham: Duke University Press, 1989.

Sakai, Naoki. *Voices of the Past: The Status of Language in Eighteenth-Century Discourse*. Ithaca: Cornell University Press, 1991.

Seely, Christopher. *A History of Writing in Japan*. Leiden: E. J. Brill, 1991.

Shimatani Hiroyuki. "Sanseki: Ono no Michikaze, Fujiwara no Sukemasa, Fujiwara no Yuki-nari." In *Heian Kamakura no sho: sampitsu sanseki*. Ed. Komatsu Shigemi. Nihon geijutsu zenshū 8. Tokyo: Gakken, 1980.

"Shinsen man'yōshū." In *Shinpen kokka taikan dainikan: shisenshūhen kashū*. Ed. Shinpen kokka taikan henshū iinka. Tokyo: Kadokawa shoten, 1984.

Shiota Ryōhei. "Koten to Meiji igo no bungaku." *Nihon bungakushi* 14 (1959), 3–39.

Shirane, Haruo. *The Bridge of Dreams: A Poetics of "The Tale of Genji."* Stanford: Stanford University Press, 1987.

Shodō zenshū. 3rd ed. 28 vols. Tokyo: Heibonsha, 1969.

Sissaouri, Vladislav. *Cosmos, magie et politique: La Musique ancienne de la Chine et du Japon.* Paris: Editions de la maison des sciences de l'homme, 1992.

Song Ki-Ho. "Several Questions in Studies of the History of Palhae." *Korea Journal* (June 1990), 4–20.

Stevens, Wallace. *The Collected Poems of Wallace Stevens.* New York: Random House, 1990.

Sugimoto Masayoshi and David L. Swain. *Science and Culture in Traditional Japan A.D. 600–1854.* Cambridge: MIT Press, 1978.

Suzuki Hideo. *Kodaiwakashiron.* Tokyo: Tōkyō daigaku shuppankai, 1990.

Tanizaki Jun'ichirō. *Tanizaki Jun'ichirō zenshū,* 28 vols. Tokyo: Chūōkōronsha, 1966–68.

Tono Haruyuki. *Sho no kodaishi.* Tokyo: Iwanami shoten, 1994.

Tsurada Naoshige. *Nihon no rekishi 5: ōchō no kizoku.* Tokyo: Chūōkōronsha, 1973.

Tsurayuki, Ki no. *Tosa nikki.* Ed. Matsumura Seiichi, Kimura Masanori, and Imuta Tsunehisa. Nihon bungaku zenshū 9. Tokyo: Iwanami, 1973.

Twine, Nanette. "The Genbunitchi Movement: Its Origins, Development and Conclusion." *Monumenta Nipponica* 33:3 (1979), 333–56.

Umehara Takeshi. *Ama to tennō: Nihon to wa nani ka.* Tokyo: Asahi shimbunsha, 1991.

Unger, J. Marshall. "The Etymology of the Japanese Word /kana/." *Papers in Japanese Linguistics* 7 (1980), 173–84.

Unger, J. Marshall. "The Very Idea: The Notion of Ideogram in China and Japan." *Monumenta Nipponica* 45:4 (1990), 391–411.

Unger, Steven. *Scandal and Aftereffect: Blanchot and France since 1930.* Minneapolis: University of Minnesota Press, 1994.

Utaawaseshū. Ed. Hagitani Boku and Taniyama Shigeru. Nihon koten bungaku taikei 74. Tokyo: Iwanami shoten, 1965.

Utsuho monogatari. Ed. Kōno Tama, 3 vols. Nihon bungaku taikei 10–12. Tokyo: Iwanami shoten, 1962.

Wada Atsumu, "Shinhakken no moji shiryō: sono kakkitekina yakuwari." In *Kotoba to moji.* Ed. Kishi Toshio. Nihon no kodai 14. Tokyo: Chūōkōronsha, 1983.

Wakanrōeishū. Ed. Oosone Shosuke and Horiuchi Hideaki. Shinchō Nihon koten shūsei 61. Tokyo: Shinchōsha, 1983.

Wakita Haruko. "Marriage and Property in Premodern Japan from the Perspective of Women's History." *Journal of Japanese Studies* 10:1 (1984), 77–87.

Wang, David Kuo-Wei. *Definitions and Classifications of the Six Scripts According to Hsu Shen (ca. A.D. 58–147) and Leading Ch'ing Scholars.* Georgetown University, Ph.D. dissertation, 1979.

Welsh, Andrew. *Roots of Lyric: Primitive Poetry and Modern Poetics.* Princeton: Princeton University Press, 1978.

Wittgenstein, Ludwig. *Philosophical Investigations,* 3rd. ed. Trans. G. E. M. Anscombe. New York, Macmillan, 1953.

Wixted, John Timothy. "The *Kokinshū* Prefaces: Another Perspective." *Harvard Journal of Asiatic Studies* 43:1 (1983), 215–38.

Yoda Tomiko. Inscribing Divisions: Gender, Discourse, and Subject in Heian Vernacular Narrative. Stanford University, Ph.D. dissertation, 1996.

Yoshiaki Shimizu and John M. Rosenfield. *Masters of Japanese Calligraphy: Eighth to Nineteenth Century*. New York: Asia Society Galleries, 1984.

Yoshino Tatsunori. "Kakekotoba ron: seisei suru imi no dainamizumu." *Kodai bungaku* 31 (February 1992), 57–67.

Yoshimoto Takaaki. *Shokikayōron*. Tokyo: Chūōseihan, 1977.

Yu Hak-ku. "Early Historical Relations between Korea and Japan: Some Methodological Issues." *Korea Journal* (June 1990), 45–48.

Žižek, Slavoj. *Looking Awry: An Introduction to Jacques Lacan Through Popular Culture*. Cambridge: MIT Press, 1991.

FIGURES

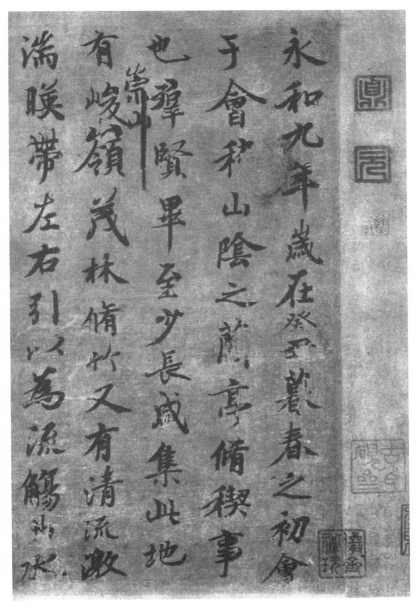

FIGURE I   The opening of *Lan t 'ing hsu* (*Ranteijo*) by Wang Hsi-chih,
copied by Chu Sung-liang (353).

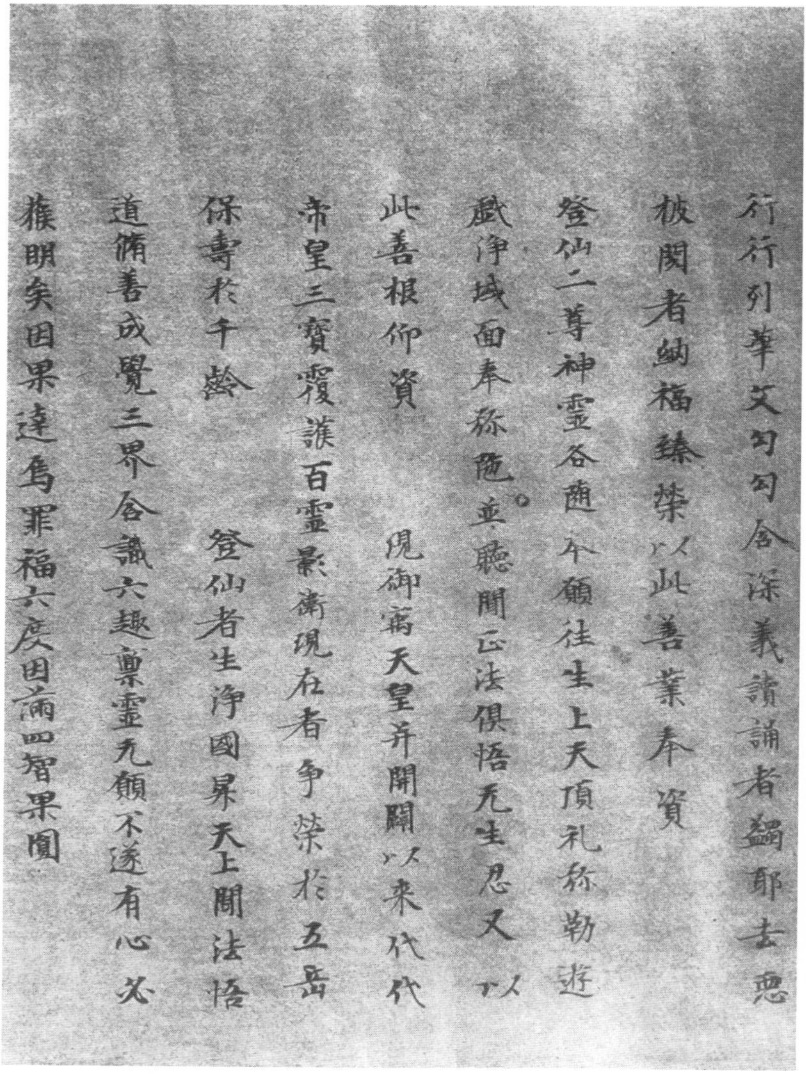

行行列苹文句含深義讀誦者翻邪去惡

披閱者紬福臻以此善業奉資

登仙二尊神靈各遇本願往生上天頂礼稱勒遊

戲淨域面奉隨並聽聞正法俱悟无生忍又以

此善根仰資　現御宇天皇并開闢以來代代

帝皇三寶覆護百靈影衛現在者爭榮於五岳

保壽於千齡　登仙者生淨國昇天上聞法悟

道備善成覺三界含識六趣稟靈无願不遂有心之

獲明矣因果達鳥罪福六度因滿四智果圓

FIGURE 2　A copy of the Prajñā-pāramitā sutra, requested by emperor Shōmu in the fifth year of Kinki (728). Tokyo: Nezu bijutsukan.

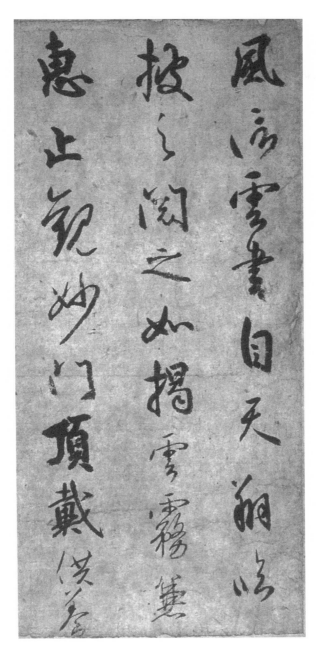

FIGURE 3   The opening of Kūkai's Fūshinjō (812).
Kyoto: Kyōōgokokuji.

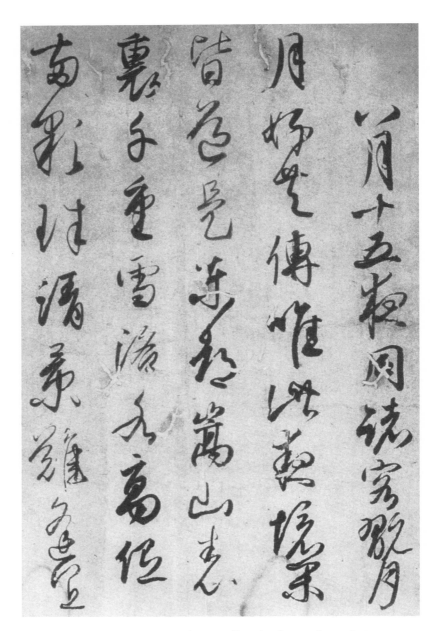

FIGURE 4   Fujiwara no Yukinari's calligraphy of "Poems by Po Chu-I"
(*Pai le-tien shih chuan*) (1018). Takamatsu Miyake.

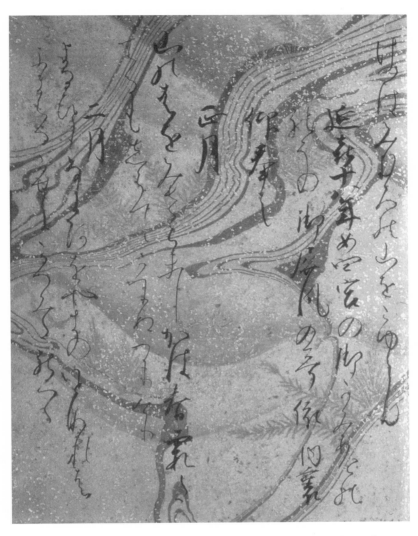

FIGURE 5   The "Tsurayuki Collection" from the Nishi-Honganji edition of
"The Collection of Thirty Six Poets" (*Sanjūrokuninshū* c. 1112), generally
attributed to Fujiwara no Sadasane, fourth in the Sesonji lineage from Fujiwara
no Yukinari. Nishi-Honganji temple.

FIGURE 6   The "Ise Collection" in the Ishiyama-gire from
"The Collection of Thirty Six Poets" (*Sanjūrokuninshū* c. 1112).

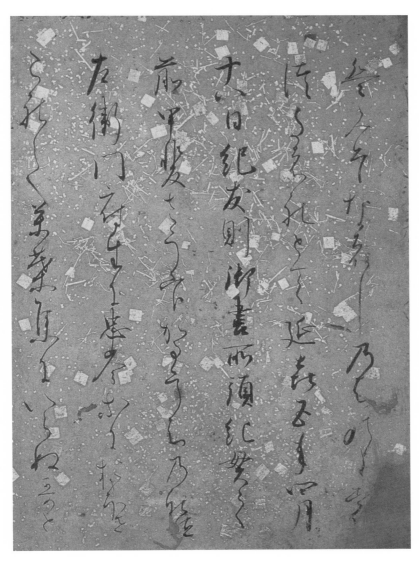

FIGURE 7　The opening of Tsurayuki's Kana preface from the earliest extant copy of *Kokinwakashū* (the Gen'ei edition, 1120), sometimes attributed to Fujiwara no Sadasane.

FIGURE 8   Poems near the end of second book of spring poems
from the earliest extant copy of *Kokinwakashū* (the Gen'ei edition, 1120).

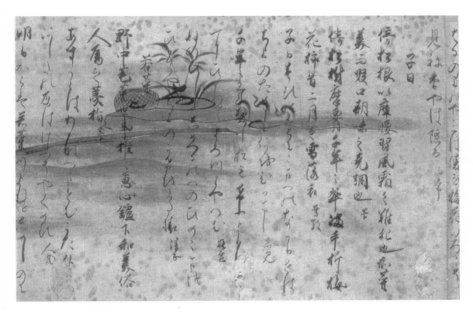

FIGURE 9   Sequence of poems on the first days of the new year from Fujiwara no
Koreyuki's *Ashide shita-e Wakanrōeishō* (1160). Although Koreyuki belongs to the
Sesonji lineage, the style of brushwork recalls the Hosshōji styles.

INDEX

Abyss, 138, 165

Acrostic, 60–61, 63, 69–70, 95, 100, 167; coherence of names or characters in, 54, 62; examples, 51, 53, 55–56, 57, 69; figural qualities, 50–51; proximity to Chinese poetics, 52–54. *See also* Rebus

Aesthetic (s), 5–6, 8–9, 60–61, 63, 67, 79, 81, 83–84, 136; of Chinese character, 9, 52; ethico-aesthetic, 92; judgment, 106–107, 124, 154, 159; microaesthetic, 50, 119, 123, 137; as normative order, 165–166; of papers, 93–94; of patchwork, 95–97; politico-aesthetic, 74, 160; symbolist, 127–128; and women's production, 111–113

Affect, 51, 106, 134

Akiyama Ken, 36, 52, 63–64, 136, 193 n.1

Alexandrine, 126

Alphabet, 19, 78

Amagasaki Akira, 44, 63

American (or Allied) Occupation of Japan, 3, 8, 34–35

Amino Yoshihiko, 30, 149, 169–170

Anderson, Benedict, 1–2, 4, 5, 18, 22, 47, 108, 174

Anexact layers, 183

Apollonaire, Guillaume, 121

Ariake no wakare, 113

Ariwara no Motokata, 186

Ariwara no Narihira, 50–51, 167, 171

Ashide. See Calligraphy: reed hand

Ashide Shitae Wakarōeishō: calligraphic styles,

131, 136; choreography, or layers of expression, 124, 138, 182; description, 116; difference from modern representation, 122–123; and double capture, 121–122; examples from, 125, 131–132, 134, 136–137; historical context, 119. *See also Wakanrōeishū*

Assembled character, 15–16, 17, 53, 82

Awase. See Contests

Ayamura Tan'en, 79, 87

Bacon, Francis, 138

Bakufu, 74, 90

Barthes, Roland, 66

Benjamin, Walter, 46

Billeter, Jean-François, 99–100, 118–119

Blanchot, Maurice, 158–159

Body proper, 118

Broken verse. *See* Acrostic

Buddhism, 28, 39, 78, 87, 90, 123; and calligraphic styles, 77, 94–95

Bunkashūreishū, 14, 149

Bunsho keikoku, 27–28

Butor, Michel, 127

Calendrics. *See* Cosmology

Calibration, 180, 187–188

Calligraphy, 153, 158; as bearer of order, 96, 114, 160; between seeing and reading, 97–98, 116; brushwork orientation, 97–98; calligram, 121–123, 127; *chirashi gaki*, 114; and compilation, 182, 184–185,

Calligraphy (*continued*)
187–188; difference from typography, 126–127; as discipline, 104–105; Heian characteristics of, 114–115; histories of, 77, 79–81; instruction and transmission of, 91–92, 109; intelligibility, 39–40; kana, 45, 85–87; kana versus mana, 26, 106; mad cursive, 114; neuter style, 109; phenomenological dimension, 98–99, 118–119, 138; poetic gesture, 131; proportion versus motion, 102–103, 133; reed hand, 66–67, 97–98, 100, 109, 116, 137; regulation of forms in, 87–88, 104–105, 112; rhythms of, 43–44, 126, 132; shift to Wang-centered styles, 81, 83–85; *tempyō* style, 81; treatises on, 98–99, 101–103. *See also* Center of motion; Chinese characters; Current style; Grass style; Inscription; Stiff style; Wa-style

Cantillation, 116; description, 117–118
Ceadel, E. B., 144–145
Center of motion, 102–103, 110, 130; of characters in series, 132–133, 180; of poems, 175–177
Ceremonies and ritual observances, 9–10, 48, 85, 87, 94, 104–105, 131, 149–150, 154
Chamberlain, Basil, 173
Chang-an, 30, 84
Chang Huai-kuan, 179
China, 46–47, 81, 83, 85, 87–88, 144–145, 147, 172–173, 174, 185; Japanese opposition to/or absorption of, 3, 5, 9, 15, 31–33; Middle Kingdom, 55, 82; in nativism, 31, 89–90. *See also* Han; Six Dynasties; Sui Dynasty; Sung Dynasty; T'ang Dynasty
Chinese characters: calligraphic simplification, 27, 45; coordinate center versus dynamic center, 102–103, 110, 133; cosmological forces in, 52, 54, 59, 78, 179; diacritic marks, 39; as ideographs, 65–66, 79, 88, 100; internal coherence of, 54, 59, 97–98; in *Man'yōshū*, 24–25, 179; modern elimination of figurality, 20–21, 158; mutations of, 116, 121; origins of, 101, 179; as phono- or logographic, 43; in Pound, 130, 179; as rebus, 47; rhythms of, 43, 125–126; smoothing of, 114; visual and vocal interplay in, 99–100, 115, 156; writ-

ing not written, 180. *See also* Calligraphy; Inscription; *Mana*; Stiff style
Chinese language, 25, 29, 39, 49, 82, 108, 142, 258. *See also* Classical Chinese
Chinese poetics (Han poetry), 14, 22, 32, 41–42, 52, 55, 86, 111, 117–118, 128, 142, 145, 158, 160, 167; examples, 53–55, 125–126, 137; poetic theory, 145–147. *See also* China; *Sandaishū*
Chōka, 182
Choreography, 123–125, 138
Chung Hung, 145
Cinema, 44, 46
Classical Chinese, 24–25, 39, 84, 129, 142, 144
Classical community, 1–2, 10, 37, 47, 87, 174
Classical Japanese language, 4, 14, 20–22, 24, 39, 61, 129, 142, 158, 178. *See also* Phonography; Transcription
Compilation, art of, 96, 112, 124, 126, 135; analogy with calligraphy, 182–185, 187–188; of *Kokin* scrolls, 180–182; of waka, 182–183
Concentric model (of resonance), 132–133, 135, 160
Confucianism, 7, 27, 34, 89, 95, 124, 163
Constellation of signs (constellar forces), 59, 68, 69, 74
Contests, 7, 55–56, 60, 86, 94, 114, 119, 124, 176; inscription and recitation of poems, 156; as permanent provocation or agonism, 73, 144, 151, 154; politics of, 71–74, 91, 106–107, 154–155; rise of, 68; structure of, 70–71
Cosmology, 10, 62, 73, 115, 138, 160, 185; configurations, patterns, and movements, 44, 120, 126, 144, 157, 159, 162–163, 167, 172, 174, 176; cosmological imagination of community, 9–10, 68, 108; cosmological language, 4; definition, 9; forces in poetry and characters, 51, 54, 58, 100–101, 104; and mimicry, 46, 101; and productive transactions at court, 113, 146; spontaneous emergence of order, 163–164; terrestrial and celestial phenomena, 58, 135, 163, 172, 178–179. *See also* Directional forces and taboos; Diurnal cycles

Counting, 181; and *omohu*, 164; and poetic composition, 162–163, 178–179. *See also* Waka: syllabic count and rhythm
Current (running or semi-cursive) style (*gyōsho*), 42, 84–85, 109, 131. *See also* Calligraphy; Grass style; Stiff style

Dark Ages of native styles, 15, 32
Decolonialism. *See* Empire
Deleuze, Gilles, 133
Derrida, Jacques, 80
Diacritic marks, 39
Differentiation/coordination: and mimicry, 46, 73; versus opposition/negation, 15, 42, 45, 71; and zone of indeterminacy, 49
Directional forces and taboos, 144, 168
Discipline, 4, 7, 104, 111, 118, 129, 156, 170
Discourse, 4, 8, 68, 121, 174, 184
Disjunctive synthesis, 97, 156, 182. *See also* Synthesis
Diurnal cycles, 151, 154, 156, 159–160
Double capture, 121–123, 126
Doubleness, 63–64; and *écriture*, 64–66
Doubling (regime of doubles), 48; as asymmetries, 183; and court organization, 73–74; and double court, 71–72
Dress, 29–30, 70, 110, 153, 167–168, 185

Écriture, 64–66
Edo. *See* Tokugawa
Eliot, T. S., 127
Emori Kenji, 83, 86–87
Emperor, 121–122, 134, 159, 175; agonist doubles, 73–74; awase, 153–154; emergence of regency, 71–72, 147, 154; nonagricultural peoples, 169–170; women sovereigns, 111, 198 n.23. *See also* Empire; Symbolic emperor
Empire: control of movement, 168–170; imperial line, 133–134; interimperial order, 174; Saigo Nobutsuna on T'ang empire, 33–35; Suzuki Hideo on T'ang empire, 26–40; T'ang empire and consolidation of styles, 84–85; Western imperialism, 37; Yamato imperial system, 83, 147, 160
Engo. *See* Kinword
Ethnolinguistic paradigm (or regime), 6–7,

63, 68, 72, 108, 110, 117, 136; ethnocentric identity, 142; problem of linguistic interpretation, 43, 51–52, 112, 129, 145–147; versus stylistic differential, 9, 115

Feminine hand, 37, 92, 104; association with kana, 107–109; cloistering of women, 111–113; and dynamic center, 110–111; and mother tongue discourse, 108
Feminine (or women's) poem, 65, 104, 111, 158, 160
Fenollosa, Ernest, 179
Figurality, 8, 40, 65–66, 68, 82, 115, 125, 136, 158, 160, 178, 185; as other than image versus text, 20; as prior to representation, 101, regulation of, 67; visuality of Chinese characters, 20–22, 43, 101, 137
Foucault, Michel, 146; on calligrams, 121–122; on separation of word and image, 120–121
Frame, 94, 120, 123, 126; difference of calligraphy from, 133, 184; imposition on waka, 128–129; and modernist raid on, 127–128, 130; and modern poetry, 126–127
Free verse, 127
Freud, Sigmund, 16–17
Fujiwara no Kintō: on character maladies, 67; as compiler of *Wakanrōeshū*, 117, 119–120, 124–125, 144
Fujiwara no Kiyosuke, 70
Fujiwara no Kiyotada, 136
Fujiwara no Koreyuki, 117, 119–120, 124–125, 130, 182
Fujiwara no Sukemasa, 81, 85–86, 87–88
Fujiwara no Tadamichi, 89
Fujiwara no Toshiyuki, 61
Fujiwara no Yukinari, 81, 85–86, 88, 119; description of calligraphy, 86–87
Fukuro no sōshi, 70
Funya no Yasuhide, 55–56, 60, 68, 167–168, 171
Fushimi, emperor, 88

Gembun itchi. *See* Unification of speech and writing
Genji monogatari. *See* Tale of Genji, the
Genji monogatari emaki, 91

Kamakura, 88, 90, 101–102, 148, 169, 183. See also *Bakufu*

Kana, 13, 41, 45, 110; associated with feminine hand, 107–109; calligraphic derivation, 26–27, 85, 109; calligraphic features of, 87; derivation of term, 26; as double of mana, 49, 52, 55, 68, 71, 106–107; and Indic phonetics, 21; as mode of appearance, 159–160; mutation into images, 116, 121, 136; myths about, 20–22, 78, 86; objectification of form, 63; and phonography, 19, 63–64, 88, 136, 156, 158; and prestige of mana, 27; regulation of forms, 87–88; and smooth space, 160; Suzuki Hideo on, 37–38. *See also* Akiyama Ken; Calligraphy; Feminine hand; Inscription; *Mana*

Kana preface (*kanajo*), 9–10, 187–188; association with unification of speech and writing, 155; Chinese models for, 145–147; as double of mana preface, 142–144; and generative forces, 161–163; and *hare* and *ke*, 159; on house poems versus imperial poems, 151–152; and movements of courtiers, 168–170; and normative self-cultivation, 163–164; theory of heart and word, 166–168

Kaneko Shūichi, 30

Kanshi. *See* Chinese poetics

Karaki Junzō, 8, 38–40, 129

Karatani Kōjin, 20

Katakana, 109

Ke. *See Hare* and *ke*

Keikokushū, 14, 149

Keirstead, Thomas, 155

Ki no Tomonori, 13, 47

Ki no Tsurayuki, 13, 51, 55, 61, 68; art of compiling scrolls, 180–182; art of compiling waka, 182–184; calligraphy of, 86, 142, 182; on cultivation of forces, 163–165; and emperor, 152, 175; and feminine styles, 111–113, 156; on heart and word, 166–168, 177; and kana preface, 9–10, 142, 145, 152–154, 157; as mechanic or calibrator, 185–188; poems, 57–59, 171–172, 175–176; on poetic count, 178; on poetry and generative patterns, 161–163, 176–177, 179; on poetry and regulation of

movements, 168–170; *Shinsenwakashū* preface, 144–145; "Tosa Journal," 156–157; and visual congruity, 171–172, 174–176. *See also Kokinwakashū*

Ki no Yoshimochi, 142, 145–146

Kinword, 60, 177, 191 n.7

Kōbōdaishi. *See* Kūkai

Kojiki, 2, 78

Kokinwakashū, 21, 111, 117, 129, 144, 147, 151, 155, 167, 172, 182, 184; and awase, 68; and Chinese influence, 32–33, 149–150; and diurnal oscillation, 159–160; examples, 47–48, 50–51, 55–56, 57–59, 61–62, 64–65, 66–67, 171–172, 175–176, 186; and *Man'yōshū*, 38, 41, 150, 158; native status of, 32; organization and compilation, 13–14, 180–182, 184–187, 190 n.1; as rational and mechanical, 54, 173, 185–187. *See also* Kana preface; Mana preface

Kōkō, emperor, 68, 72

Kokufū ankoku jidai. *See* Dark ages of native styles

Komatsu Shigemi, 86, 104; on maturation of wa-style, 89–90; on regulation of forms, 87–88; on Yukinari, 86–87

Konishi Jin'ichi, 8, 36, 145; on oblique style, 172–174; principles of associations and progression, 201 n.22

Korea, 21–23, 25, 29–30, 83, 174, 185

Kuboki Shōichi, 88, 109

Kugonin, 169

Kūkai, 27–29, 48, 81, 84–85, 101, 103

Kumiawasemoji. *See* Assembled character

Kyōtō. *See* Heian-kyō

Ledderrose, Lothar, 83–84

Lines: breaking poems into, 126–128; of calligraphy, 114, 132–134

Linguistic. *See* Ethnolinguistic paradigm

Logography, 19, 20; defined, 43

Love poems or scrolls, 59, 62, 64, 133, 151, 154, 177, 180–183

Lyric, 35, 146, 165, 185

Magritte, René, 122

Makurakotoba. *See* Pillow-word

Mana, 42, 52, 55, 106–107, 110, 144, 149; cosmological importance, 27; and histori-

Wa-style (*wayō*), 80, 87, 89, 113, 115; emer-
gence of, 81, 85–86
Wei Hung, 145
Wen Hsuan, 117, 145
Wittgenstein, Ludwig, 56
Wixted, John Timothy, 145–147
Wonnade. See Feminine hand
Wotokode. See Masculine hand
Writing. *See* Calligraphy; Ideography; In-
scription; Logography; Phonography;
Pictography; Typography
Wu, kingdom of, 79

Yakaku teikinshō, 119
Yamato, 13, 26, 44, 48, 53, 77, 80, 87, 131,
138, 142, 147; as Japanese, 3, 14, 108;
paired with Han and T'ang, 15, 29–30, 63,
92, 107, 110, 148
Yōrō Code, 147
Yoshimoto Taka'aki (Ryūmei), 8, 36, 67–68,
71, 136, 186–187
Yoshino Tatsunori, 64–66

Žižek, Slavoj, 17–18, 22–23

Thomas Lamarre is an
Associate Professor of East Asian Studies at McGill University.
Library of Congress Cataloging-in-Publication Data
LaMarre, Thomas.
Uncovering Heian Japan : an archaeology of sensation and inscription / Thomas LaMarre.
p. cm. — (Asia-Pacific)
Includes bibliographical references and indexes.
ISBN 0-8223-2482-2 (cloth : alk. paper) — ISBN 0-8223-2518-7 (pbk. : alk. paper)
1. Japan—Civilization—794–1185.   2. Arts, Japanese—Heian period, 794–1185.
I. Title.   II. Series.
DS822.L36 2000   895.6'11409—dc21   99-049889